SOCIAL WORK
with the
AGED
and their
FAMILIES

SOCIAL WORK
with the
AGED
and their
FAMILIES
Third Edition

Roberta R. Greene

AldineTransaction
A Division of Transaction Publishers
New Brunswick (U.S.A.) and London (U.K.)

Copyright © 2008 by Transaction Publishers, New Brunswick, New Jersey.

All rights reserved under International and Pan-American Copyright Conventions. No part of this book may be reproduced or transmitted in any form or by any means, electronic or mechanical, including photocopy, recording, or any information storage and retrieval system, without prior permission in writing from the publisher. All inquiries should be addressed to AldineTransaction, A Division of Transaction Publishers, Rutgers—The State University, 35 Berrue Circle, Piscataway, New Jersey 08854-8042. www.transactionpub.com

This book is printed on acid-free paper that meets the American National Standard for Permanence of Paper for Printed Library Materials.

Library of Congress Catalog Number: 2007047752
ISBN: 978-0-202-36182-6 (cloth); 978-0-202-36183-3 (paper)
Printed in the United States of America

Library of Congress Cataloging-in-Publication Data

Greene, Roberta R. (Roberta Rubin), 1940-
  Social work with the aged and their families / Roberta R. Greene.—3rd ed.
     p. cm.
  Includes bibliographical references and index.
  ISBN 978-0-202-36182-6 (alk. paper)
     1. Social work with older people—United States. 2. Older people—Family relationships—United States. 3. Family social work—United States. 4. Intergenerational relations—United States. I. Title.

HV1451.G74 2008
362.6—dc22   2007047752

In Reminiscence

Nancy Alison Greene

In Memory of Sadie Rubin—
My mother and Nancy's Grandmother,
Roberta R. Greene

She wore a stunning old locket around her graceful neck and had a fourteen-carat gold heart to go with it. When she spoke there was an unmistakable southern twang in her voice and she had all the southern hospitality to accompany it. She didn't live a charmed life but was willing to give you all-if that's what it took.

I was young and didn't understand when she told me, "Do this," "Try not to do that," and "It is for your own good." Now, I know, it was caring-caring about me and caring for me. Very few people take the time to do that for anyone, but she cared for everyone. She cared for you if you were the queen of England or a black person in the 1950s who needed a seat on the bus after a long day's work.

I remember nonsignificant things: who polished my nails first, taught me to click my tongue, and bought clothes at her favorite shop. Things only I should remember. When I got older she was my "Ann Landers" and I wrote her every few weeks. One week I got a package in the mail. It was the locket I admired. A few weeks later she died. Farewell, Grandma.

Contents

Preface

The major objective of this revised edition of *Social Work with the Aged and Their Families* is to further the social worker's capacity for direct practice with the aged, with their families, and with the societal agents with whom they interact. The book provides a model for implementing comprehensive assessments and social work interventions based on a clinical understanding of older adults within a family and social systems perspective.

The work is an outgrowth of the demand and need for geriatric services-a phenomenon that in large measure is a response to the increase in the number and proportion of aged individuals in the U.S. population. Continued social and demographic changes since the first edition of the book suggest that a sizable number of older adults and their families are likely to experience various forms of economic, social, and emotional distress. At the same time, there will be a limited number of social work personnel. To meet this demand, practitioners will need to make timely assessments and determine who is most in need of which services. In addition, schools of social work will experience an ever-increasing demand for education materials. This text introduces the Functional-Age Model of Intergenerational Therapy in hopes of making a contribution to this effort. As an intergenerational model, it provides the means of conducting a biopsyhosocial and spiritual assessment of an older adult as well as a systems assessment of his or her family.

The author would like to thank her family, friends, and colleagues for all their support while writing this book. A special memory of all my older clients was also most helpful.

Roberta R. Greene

1

Introduction

During the 1970s and the 1980s, theoreticians, researchers, and practitioners became increasingly interested in older adults and the aging process. Gerontologists drew from many related disciplines to better understand the biological, psychological, and social aspects of aging. As a result, there was a burgeoning of information related to the scientific and systematic study of aging known as *gerontology*.

During that same time period, geriatric social workers experimented with established social work theories in an attempt to find suitable techniques for working with their elderly clients. The need for specialized services gave birth to various services and programs. For example, meals-on-wheels and home health care services met specific physical needs of older adults. However, mental health services lagged far behind as practitioners struggled to adapt such specialties as family therapy to families of later years. The functional-age model of intergenerational treatment (FAM) presented here is an outgrowth of that demand.

The functional-age model of intergenerational treatment is an integrative theoretical framework for social workers interested in clinical social work practice with older adults and their families. Since its construction in 1986, the model has been augmented by more recent concepts related to successful aging (Rowe & Kahn, 1998), spirituality, (Canda, 1988, 1994; Hodge, 2001), and resiliency (Greene, 2002, 2007). These additions, together with the original assessment and intervention strategies, represent the major converging conceptual trends that constitute a model for twenty-first-century social work practice in the field of aging. This chapter describes the current context of current geriatric practice and describes the components of the functional-age model. It also discusses the model's theoretical underpinnings and conceptual linkages.

Social Work with the Aged and Their Families:
The Twenty-First Century

Social work practice in the field of aging needs to be understood within a contemporary cultural and historical context. An expanding knowledge base, changing technologies, and increasingly complex human and social concerns affect practice. As the numbers and proportion of elderly persons in the U. S. population increases, so, too, does the demand for geriatric services. Demographic changes have been so far reaching that the "emerging social, economic, and demographic realities have shaken the very foundations of existing paradigms regarding the elderly" (Scharlach & Kaye, 1997, p. xii). As a result of changes in the age composition within U. S. society and the associated political, economic, and social transformations, there is renewed interest in how people age and in how gerontologists view the aging process.

Demographic Patterns

Perhaps one of the most expected dramatic change in U. S. society during the twenty-first century will be the graying of American society (Rowe & Kahn, 1998). In 1900, people aged sixty-five years or older–3 million people–represented only 3 percent of the total population. In 2000, 35 million people were over the age of sixty-five. Among the older population, those eighty-five years of age and over showed the highest percentage increase (U. S. Census Bureau, 2001).

Family Structure

The increase in life expectancy will have numerous effects on the structure and function of U. S. society (Kiyak & Hooyman, 1999). Greater life expectancy will mean a dramatic growth in the number of three- and four-generation families (Cutler, 1997). Furthermore, gender and racial or ethnic gaps in life expectancy are anticipated to persist, with longevity being greater for women than for men, and whites living longer than nonwhites (U. S. Bureau of the Census, 2000). There will also be a greater variation in household and family composition, as well as kinship arrangements (Moen & Forest, 1995). As the numbers of frail elderly increase, so too will caregiving demands. Meeting these demands will be complicated by the continued participation of women in the workforce (Baltes, 1996; Fraenkel, 2003; Walsh, 1999).

Diversity among Older Adults

According to Walsh (2003), pathways through later life are increasingly varied, and family and social time frames are becoming more fluid (see table1.1). For example, theorists' views of the generative years of gay men and lesbians have expanded (Cohler, Hostetler & Boxer, 1998). Grandparents are increasingly raising grandchildren (Burnette, 1997). *Kinship care*, relatives who step into the role of parenting, always a family resource (Chan & Elder, 2000; Kolomer, 2000), is dramatically increasing (U. S. Census, 2000).

Table 1.1
Changing Demographics in the Twenty-First Century

The first half of the 21st century will witness a dramatic increase in the size and racial and ethnic composition of the over-65 population in the United States. Those changes will have profound implications for the scale and delivery of social services to the elderly population and for the education of geriatric social workers.

- As the baby boom generation—those born between 1946 and 1964—begin to celebrate their 65th birthdays in 2011, the over-65 population will surge. By 2030, an estimated 71.5 million people aged 65 years and older, almost twice the number in 2004, will live in the United States. That's 20 percent of the total population. Moreover, the 85 and over population is projected to increase from 4.6 million in 2002 to 9.6 million in 2030. In 2004, the latest year for which data were available, 36.3 million people aged 65 years or older represented 12.4 percent of the U.S. population, or about one in every eight Americans.
- Racial and ethnic groups, that is, all peoples other than the non-Hispanic white population, will account for nearly 90 percent of total growth in the U.S. population in the first half of the 21st century. Currently elders of racial and ethnic groups compose more than 16.1 percent of all older Americans (those aged 65 years or older). In the future, their numbers will increase dramatically. By 2030, members of racial and ethnic groups are projected to represent 26.4 percent of the older population.
- Between 1999 and 2030, the total population of adults 65 years and older in racial and ethnic groups is projected to increase by 217 percent, compared to 81 percent for the older white population. Reflecting continued immigration and larger family sizes, the Hispanic population will be the most rapidly increasing racial and ethnic group, growing by 322 percent, compared to 128 percent for black American elders, 301 percent for Asian American elders, and roughly 193 percent for American Indian and Alaska Natives.
- In 2003, older men were much more likely to be married than older women—71 percent of men compared to 41 percent of women. Almost half (43 percent) of all older women in 2003 were widows. More than four times as many widows (8.2 million) compared to widowers (2.0 million) resided in the United States in 2003. Divorced and separated (including married, but spouse absent) older people represented only 10.7 percent of all older people in 2003, but that percentage has increased from figures in 1980, when approximately 5.3 percent of the older population was divorced or separated, or married with a spouse absent.

- The proportion of individuals living alone increases with advanced age. Among women aged 75 years and older, about half (49.8 percent) lived alone. About 30.8 percent (10.5 million) of all noninstitutionalized older people lived alone (7.8 million women and 2.7 million men) in 2003. The proportion of adults living with their spouse decreases with age, especially for women. Only 28.7 percent of women at least 75 years old lived with a spouse.

- While a relatively small number (1.56 million) and percentage (4.5 percent) of the population that was at least 65 years old lived in nursing homes in 2000, the percentage increases dramatically with age, ranging from 1.1 percent for people aged 65–74 years to 4.7 percent for people aged 75–84 years and 18.2 percent for people aged 85 or more years. In addition, approximately 5 percent of elderly people lived in self-described senior housing of various types, many of which have supportive services available to their residents.

- About 3.6 million (10.2 percent) of elderly people in 2003 were below the poverty level. Another 2.3 million or 6.7 percent of elderly people were classified as "near-poor" (income between the poverty level and 125 percent of that level). One out of every 12 (8.8 percent) elderly white Americans was poor in 2003, compared to 23.7 percent of elderly black Americans, 14.3 percent of Asian Americans, and 19.5 percent of the elderly Hispanic population. Higher-than-average poverty rates for older people were found among those who lived in central cities (13.1 percent); outside metropolitan areas (that is, rural areas; 11.0 percent); and in the South (11.9 percent).

- Older women had a higher poverty rate (12.5 percent) than older men (7.3 percent) in 2003. Older people living alone were much more likely to be poor (18.6 percent) than were older people living with families (5.8 percent). The highest poverty rates (40.8 percent) were experienced by older Hispanic women who lived alone.

- For one-third of Americans older than age 65 years in 2002 social security benefits constituted 90 percent of their income. Other major sources of income as reported by the Social Security Administration for older people in 2002 were from assets (reported by 55 percent); private pensions (reported by 29 percent); government employee pensions (reported by 14 percent); and earnings (reported by 22 percent).

- Despite the overall increase in educational attainment among older Americans, substantial educational differences still exist among racial and ethnic groups. In 1998, about 72 percent of the non-Hispanic white population aged 65 years and older had finished high school, compared to 65 percent of the non-Hispanic Asian and Pacific Islander population, 44 percent of the non-Hispanic black older population, and 29 percent of the Hispanic older population. The educational level of the older population is increasing, however. Between 1970 and 2003, the percentage of older Americans who had completed high school rose from 28 percent to 71 percent. But the percentage who had completed high school varied considerably by race and ethnic origin in 2003: 76 percent of white Americans, 70 percent of Asians and Pacific Islanders, 52 percent of black Americans, and 36 percent of the Hispanic population.

- In 2004, 37.4 percent of noninstitutionalized older people assessed their heath as excellent or very good (compared to 65.8 percent for people aged 18–64 years). Little difference existed between the genders on this measure, but older black people (57.7 percent) and older Hispanic adults (60.1 percent) were less likely to rate their health as excellent or good than were older white people (76.9 percent).

- In 1997, more than half (54.5 percent) of the older population reported having at least one disability (physical or nonphysical) of some type. More than one-third (37.7 percent) reported at least one severe disability. Disability takes a much heavier toll on the very old. Almost three-fourths of those aged 80 or more years reported at least one disability. More than half of people aged 80 or more years had one or more severe disabilities, and more than a third of the population aged at least 80 years reported needing assistance as a result of disability.

- In 1999, more than 27.3 percent of community-resident Medicare beneficiaries older than age 65 years had difficulty performing one or more activities of daily living (ADLs). An additional 13.0 percent reported difficulties with instrumental activities of daily living (IADLs). (ADLs include bathing, dressing, eating, and getting around the house. IADLs include preparing meals, shopping, managing money, using the telephone, doing housework, and taking medication.) By contrast, 93.3 percent of institutionalized Medicare beneficiaries had difficulties with one or more ADLs and 76.3 percent of them had difficulty with three or more ADLS. Limitations on activities because of chronic conditions apparently increases with age: Among those aged 65–74 years old, 19.9 percent had difficulties with ADLs. In contrast, more than half (52.5 percent) of people 85 years and older had difficulties with ADLs.

- About 11 percent (3.7 million) of older Medicare enrollees received personal care from a paid or unpaid source in 1999. Almost all community-resident older people with chronic disabilities received either informal care (from family or friends) or formal care (from service provider agencies). More than 90 percent of all those older people with chronic disabilities received informal or formal care; and about two-thirds received only informal care. About 9 percent of that chronically disabled group received only formal services.

Sources:

U.S. Bureau of the Census. (2004, January). *Census internet release.*
http://www.census.gov/population/projections/nation/summary/np-t3-b.txt
Retrieved August 29, 2007.

U.S. Bureau of the Census. (2000). 65+ in the United States, in *Current Population Reports* (Special Studies, pp. 23–190); data for 2000 are from U.S. Bureau of the Census. (2000). 65+ in the United States. Washington, DC: Frank B. Hobbs with Bonnie L. Damon. http://www.census.gov/prod/1/pop/p23-190/p23-190.html
Retrieved August 29, 2007

U. S. Census Bureau (2001). Current Population Reports, "Americans with Disabilities, 1997" P70–73, February 2001.

http://www.census.gov/prod/2001pubs/p70-73.pdf
Retrieved August 28, 2007

U.S. Department of Health and Human Services Center for Disease Control and Prevention National Center for Statistics. *Vital and Health Statistics.*

http://.www.census.gov/prod/2006/p70-107.pdf
Retrieved August 28, 2007.

U. S. Census Bureau (2003). Current Population Survey, Annual Social and Economic Supplement, 2003

http://www//.google.com/search?sourceid=navclient&ie=UTF-
88rsi=GGLD,GGLD,2003-48,GGLD:en&q=current+population+survey+annual+soci
al+and+economic +supplement+2003
Retrieved August 28, 2007

U.S. Bureau of the Census. (2003, August). Income, poverty, and health insurance
coverage in the United States: 2003. In *Current Population Survey* (Annual Social and
Economic Suppl., (P60–226). Washington, DC: Carmen de Navas-Walt, Bernadette D.
Proctor, and Robert Mills.

http://www.census.gov/prod/2004pubs/p60/226.pdf
Retrieved August 28, 2007

Social Security Administration. (2003). *Fast facts and figures about social security.*:
Washington, DC: Author. http://www.gov/policy/docs/chartbooks/fast_facts/2000 Retrieved August 28, 2007

In addition, the population of older adults has become and will continue to become more ethnically diverse. There are significant income
and poverty differences between groups, with nonwhites experiencing
greater poverty (Robert & Ruel, 2006). Moreover, the number of the *baby
boomers*, those people born between 1946 and 1964, will dramatically
increase the numbers of adults aged sixty-five years or older between
2010 and 2030. Baby boomers tend to be better educated and have more
financial resources at retirement than previous generations of older adults
(Cutler, 1997; Hadley, 1998). Their potential resource base and life experiences may require a rethinking of work and retirement (Fahey, 1996;
Manchester, 1997; Rix, 1994).

Functional Well-Being

Although most persons aged sixty-five years or older are relatively
well-functioning individuals who will live into their seventies, a sizable
minority is likely to experience various forms of emotional, social, or
economic distress. Acute and disabling illnesses tend to rise sharply in
later years (Silverstone, 1996). Older adults continue to account for a
disproportionate use of health care services. For example, during the
1990s, older adults represented one-eighth of the U.S. population, but
accounted for more than one-third of health care expenditures; whereas
research continues to document health disparities between black and
white older adults (Robert & Ruel, 2006).

Given the sharp rise in chronic illnesses and the disproportionate use
of health care services, policymakers are fearful that by the year 2030
a growing number of elders that require health and social services will
outstrip delivery systems. Researchers (Zedlewski, Barnes, Burt, Mc-
Bride & Meyer, 1990) have predicted that the elderly population's need

for supportive services will far exceed the general increase in the elderly population. Participants in the 1995 and 2005 White House Conferences on Aging have called for coordination between health and mental health services to more effectively meet the needs of older adults (Gatz, 1995; http://www.whcoa.gov).

The increased numbers of older adults needing health and social services is a critical societal issue (Greene & Sullivan, 2004). However, many gerontologists have argued that one should not conclude that "the future population explosion of the elderly will result in an expanding number of stereotypically frail and dependent persons and place a serious burden on society" (U. S. Bureau of the Census, 1996, pp. 1/2-1/3). In addition to the growing concern about the dramatic increase in the population of persons aged sixty-five years or older, there is increased interest in augmenting the positive aspects of the life of older adults (Posner, 1995; Rowe & Kahn, 1998). For example, Kiyak and Hooyman (1999) have urged that researchers give more attention to how "families, employers, health and social service providers, and older adults themselves can enhance quality of life" (p. 56), and Riley (1994) has proposed that social institutions should consider providing more age-integrated opportunities for work, education, and leisure.

Successful Aging

The U. S. Bureau of the Census (1996) in its Current Population Reports examined the possible implications of the elderly population's changing characteristics. Findings suggested that, as scientific knowledge increases, there will be a reduction in the severity of illness and disability, leading to a possible reduction in health care demand. In addition, the past ten years of research funded by the MacArthur Foundation has revealed that scientists are increasingly identifying factors that contribute to a *successful aging process*, factors that maintain or enhance mental and physical functioning (Rowe & Kahn, 1998).

Successful aging, according to Rowe and Kahn, (1998), involves three major behaviors: (a) avoiding disease and disability, referring to a prevention orientation; (b) engaging with life, encompassing the need for social ties; and (c) maintaining high cognitive and physical function, including promoting and increasing self-efficacy (figure 1.1). Moreover, Crowther et al., have expanded the conceptualization of successful aging to include positive spirituality (figure 1.2).

Figure 1.1
Components of Successful Aging

Avoiding
disease

Successful
Aging

Engagement
with life

Maintaining high
cognitive and
physical function

Rowe, J. W.,& Kahn, R. L. (1998). Successful Aging. New York: Pantheon Book. (p. 39)

Prevention

Although most older adults who are seeking social work services are frail or have a chronic disease, Rowe and Kahn (1998) have cautioned against adopting the myth that "the horse is out of the barn." Practitioners need to be aware that interventions to prevent disease and disability in old age are possible at any age. Among the possible prevention strategies are exercise and physical activity, weight reduction, and cessation of smoking. "Even the oldest-old respond well to resistance training...the weakest nursing home residents...become stronger" (Rowe & Kahn, 1998, pp. 103-106).

Social workers of the twenty-first century will increasingly need to use mutual aid and prevention strategies such as health promotion, disease prevention, and self-health care programs (Greene, Kropf &

Figure 1.2
Revised Rowe and Kahn Model of Successful Aging

Minimize Risk
and Disability

Engage in   SUCCESSFUL   Maximize Physical
Active Life   AGING   and Mental Abilities

Maximize
Maximum
Spirituality

From Crowther, M. R., Parker, M, W., Achenbaum, W.A., Larimore, W. L., & Koenig, H. G. (2002). Rowe and Kahn's model of successful aging revisited: Positive spirituality- The forgotten factor. The Gerontologist, 42(5), 613-620.

Pugh, 1994; Kart & Engler, 1995; Greene, 2005). *Mutual aid* is a form of help that relies on family, friends, and support systems. *Prevention* encompasses a range of activities along a continuum of functional capacity–from the most capacity to the least capacity (Beaver & Miller, 1992; Greene, 1993; Greene, 1992). *Primary prevention* involves strategies that are needed when a person is facing severe challenges to his or her life function. *Secondary prevention* is an attempt to forestall the lessening of functional capacity. *Tertiary prevention* is designed for people who need to maintain or regain function. Prevention embodies "the social work principle of basing the level of care on the individual's functional capacity–from those who are most independent to those who are least independent" (Vourlekis & Greene, 1992, p. 15). Because a person's biopsychosocial and spiritual functioning strongly influences his or her ability to live independently, an evaluation of a client's competence to manage daily affairs is central to geriatric social work practice. As social workers assess a client's functional capacity (see chapters 3 through 5), they can mutually decide what services are needed, who should provide them, and in what settings such services are best delivered (Hooyman, Hooyman & Kethley, 1981; chapter 5).

Practice Model for Intergenerational Family Treatment:
Theoretical Background

In many respects, the roots of the functional-age model of intergenerational therapy parallel the historical development of social work and its dual mission to improve societal conditions and to enhance the social functioning among individuals, families, and groups. Throughout the profession's history, social workers have sought theoretical concepts to augment their knowledge base and interventive strategies. The development of timely interventions in social work with the aged and their families involves the further integration of the most current knowledge of human behavior and the adaptation of existing methods and techniques. The addition of new theoretical knowledge can result in an even wider range of treatment modalities that provide a broad foundation for today's practitioner. With each theoretical advance and expansion of the knowledge base comes information pertinent to professional social work, some of which is particularly suitable for practice with older adults and their families. The section below describes the theories and concepts that have influenced the functional-age model and are used throughout the text to guide assessment and intervention processes.

Casework Method

Early caseworkers used an approach that came to be called the *psychosocial treatment method*. The roots of the psychosocial treatment method may be traced to the Charity Organization Society movement and its concern with the alleviation of poverty (Garrett, 1950). During the early years, caseworkers supplied their clients with material services and tried to help them deal with economic, social, and health problems. Stressful social issues were of great concern, and interventions centered on making social changes and improving individual coping skills. The functional-age model incorporates this early interest in the practitioner's ability to obtain the specific resources needed by a client-family.

The works of Richmond (1917, 1922) best reflect social work's early interest in improving socioeconomic conditions through individual adjustment. She defined *casework* as "those processes which develop personality through adjustments consciously effected, individual by individual, between people and their environment" (Richmond, 1922, p. 98). The early definition of casework as a psychosocial method of intervention led to an interest in how clients' adjustment is affected by their cultural milieu and set the stage for including both personality issues and environmental factors in assessment. It also heightened the recognition of the need for an orderly and logical method for assembling information about these matters. As a result, a study-diagnosis treatment format emerged as a medium for clarifying client needs, and the aim of the practitioner became one of effecting change in the person, the environment, or both (Hamilton, 1951). The functional-age model adopted the psychosocial method of individualized assessment in determining social work interventions.

Psychodynamic Influence

Historically, social work method has maintained its concern with the individual and his or her environment; however, it has not always placed equal emphasis on both. During the 1930s, the Great Depression kept alive the need for direct environmental intervention. However, during the 1950s and 1960s, much of social work practice was based on the works of psychodynamic theorists such as Freud and Erikson (Hamilton, 1951; Hollis, 1977). Social workers who adopted the psychodynamic approach focused on a client's inner psychological issues; the social context in which they occurred was of less concern. Hallmarks of the psychodynamic approach were and still are the examination and explanation of the symbolic nature of symptoms, the uncovering of pertinent repressed materials, the expression of emotional conflicts, the reconstruction of and motivation to understand difficult early life events, the development of self-awareness, and use of the social worker-client relationship to foster growth (Greene, 1991/2008). Social workers studied an individual's current behaviors in light of that person's past experiences. Thus, history-taking, which came to be a central component in that social work treatment method, is also relevant in the functional-age model.

Psychoanalytic theory also became the primary resource for understanding human behavior and for diagnosing clients. Practitioners used the id-ego-superego triad as a means of examining personality structure and the ego's effectiveness in promoting well-being. This understanding provided a means of evaluating ego functioning and ego strengths and in selecting techniques for ego support (Anderson, Carter & Lowe, 1999; Perlman, 1957; Turner, 1988).

Using the psychoanalytic approach, practitioners worked with the client to achieve insight into his or her problem (assessment) to work toward the resolution or alleviation of the client's difficulties (treatment). The goal of treatment centered on helping clients *strengthen ego functioning*–the ability to master reality and to cope adaptively with the environment. Many practitioners were influenced by Freud's belief that older adults were poor candidates for clinical insight. However, geriatric social workers have effectively used select Freudian concepts such as ego strength and countertransference in their practice (Greene, 1989; Semel, 1996; see chapter 2).

Erikson's (1950) theoretical framework, with its emphasis on introspection, self-concept and adjustment to loss, gave new direction to clinical practice with the aged. Unlike Freud, Erikson's description of the eight stages of development, from birth until death, provided practitioners with psychiatry of the life cycle. According to Erikson, during the eighth stage of development, *integrity versus despair*, a person comes to terms with his or her life by naturally recalling early memories. This idea was the basis for life review therapy developed by Robert Butler (1969; see chapter 8). Practitioners may use this technique with the functional-age model as a tool to explore the lifelong strengths of a client's personality and to mobilize the resources of the environment needed to improve interpersonal functioning.

Role Theory

Throughout the 1940s and 1950s, the behavioral sciences supplied many useful ideas for social work practice. Some, such as role theory, added a whole new dimension to social work practice by providing a conceptual bridge between psychological and sociological processes (Ackerman, 1957). Using role theory as an assessment and treatment tool, social workers were better able to give further attention to the social and cultural influences on behavior. They also were able to address problems in interactional as well as intrapsychic terms.

As practitioners began to take a greater interest in the patterns of interaction in families, they found that role theory was an important vehicle for understanding the rights and obligations among family members. Inasmuch as role theory helps practitioners understand the continuous interplay between the person and his or her social experience, it is given major emphasis in the functional-age model. As explained in chapter 7, understanding the family as an interactional unit permits social workers to assess individual identity as expressed in the family group.

Role theory also allows practitioners to evaluate reciprocal or complementary family role behaviors (Ackerman, 1957; Perlman, 1968; Thompson, 1994). Role analysis not only provides an efficient means of understanding the individual and his or her family situation, but it can also lend itself to an appreciation of the biological aspects of role performance. Each role comprises a number of activities that include psychological, physical, social, and spiritual considerations, all of which contribute to satisfactory task performance. Because a biopsychosocial approach is useful to social work with the aged and their families, the role concept makes a substantial contribution to the functional-age model presented in this book.

Since the original development of the functional-age model, however, role theory has come under scrutiny (Thompson, 1994). With greater recognition that role theory addresses both individual and societal influences, theorists have called for a reexamination of role stereotypes. For example, Fraenkel (2003) drew increased attention to women's work and family roles, whereas Danis and Lockart (2004) questioned different criteria for evaluating anger displays in men and women. With the caveat that practitioners take care to address such diversity in role performance, practitioners may view role analysis as an effective vehicle for defining and clarifying many aspects of biopsychosocial and spiritual functioning.

Systems Theory

Systems theory, another theoretical approach used in the functional-age model, originally was an abstract model developed by a biologist, Bertalanffy (1968). Because of its inherently multidimensional and multidisciplinary nature, systems theory has had a major impact on social work thought. The value of the systems approach to social work has been best expressed by Berger and Federico (1982):

> Systems theory is helpful to the social worker in the struggle to incorporate information from multiple sources into a coherent whole. A systems approach is inherently multidisciplinary and calls upon the practitioner to draw from many social, behavioral, and biological disciplines rather than having an allegiance to any one discipline. Viewing the individual in interaction with environmental forces sharpens our focus for both assessment and intervention purposes and supports a process view of life consistent with professional purpose. (p. 40)

Social scientists use social systems theory primarily to examine the structure and organization of how people interact, particularly in families. Family treatment from this viewpoint assumes that each family is unique and has a discernible and understandable set of relationships and rules. Assessing family organizational properties and how members react to stress, developing more effective communication, and securing community resources are among the techniques that characterize this approach (Thompson, 1994; Walsh, 2003). Systems theory assumes that the human personality is in constant interplay with the surrounding environment, with each element–person and environment–adjusting to changes in the other. This person-environment construct is ideally suited to offer a framework in which social interaction can be understood without jeopardy to the work of individualization (Walsh, 2003).

Family Systems

Although family interviews have long been a part of clinical social work practice, it was not until the mid-1950s that family-centered treatment came to the fore. Social workers came to see that whenever one member of a family is in trouble, all are in trouble (Hartman, 1995). As a result, practitioners readily adopted family therapy, thus providing a greater opportunity to view the person as both an individual and as a family member. However, family treatment was not as popular among geriatric social workers until the mid-1980s (Greene, 1986/2000; Silverstone & Burack-Weiss, 1983). At that time, social workers increasingly refuted the belief that older people are abandoned by their families or left to be cared for in institutions (Brody, 1981).

Research consistently substantiated that families have complex, viable, and supportive exchange and caregiving patterns (Butler, Lewis & Sunderland, 1994). Therefore, practitioners need to understand that although families remain the primary source of elder care, many issues such as geographic proximity, employment, marital status, the presence of young children, emotional bonds, and family cohesiveness can affect family availability (Mimes, 1994, 1996).

Theorists who first focused on intergenerational family dynamics provided a strong theoretical basis for working with intergenerational families. They argued that there is a major connecting link between the generations based on loyalty, reciprocity, and indebtedness, which to some degree can be found in all families (Bowen, 1971; Boszormenyi-Nagy & Spark, 1973; Erikson, 1950). Boszormenyi-Nagy and Spark contended that each family has a unique system of exchange that must be explored in therapy; and Bowen stressed that people in each generation are healthier and more productive when viable emotional contact between generations is maintained.

The recognition of the family as a system and treatment unit of choice is central to thefunctional-age model. The model emphasizes the interdependence among family members as well as the dynamics of the family and societal change. It means that practitioners should evaluate and treat the family as an organizational structure that is a functioning whole within a societal context and suggests that systems theory is an integrating tool to accomplish this end.

Communication Theory

As therapists used several of the theoretical facets of role, system, and small group theories in their orientation to treatment, they also began to use communications theory to analyze casework as a helping process (Strean, 1971). They observed that *communication*, the transfer of information within and between systems, was closely related to family organization. This realization led to an interest in how practitioners could better address family issues by altering the forms of communication among its members. The therapist's task from this viewpoint is to explore interactional patterns and coach families about clearer modes of communication. (See chapter 8 for a discussion of how the functional-age model makes particular use of these concepts).

Because families come in various forms and social workers are increasingly serving a diversity of families, some theorists have questioned and modified the use of systems and communication theory in family treatment (Crawford, 1988; Hare-Mustin, 1990; Ho, 1987; Hoffman, 1992). The issue of what constitutes a functional or dysfunctional family is debatable. Hepworth, Rooney, and Larson (2002; Walsh, 2003) suggested that behavior considered acceptable or functional in one culture may be perceived by members of another culture as unacceptable, whereas Trepper (1987) argued for establishing universal standards for "normal" behavior. Clearly, the family systems approach to treatment is not as neutral as originally believed, and practitioners may be more effective helpers by paying attention to a family's culture, economic status, and ethnicity or race. They also must keep in mind the age, gender, and sexual orientation of family members (Greene, 1994).

Family Developmental Theory

Family developmental theory, another concept included in the functional-age model, is an outgrowth of family systems thinking; that is, understanding the interplay between individual and family development was a next logical step. Family developmentalists suggested that the family is more than a collection of individual life cycles. They contend that family member's life stages are intertwined, propelling family changes over time. Practitioners are concerned with the effects of a family's shifting membership, including births, marriages, or deaths; the changing status of the members in relationship to each another; and the challenges to a family's adaptational capacity at each stage (Carter & McGoldrick, 2005).

As theorists have increasingly understood that there are variant family forms, they have reviewed family developmental concepts. For example, theorists have proposed that family life cycles may vary according to cohabiting members in the household, patterns of childbearing, or the lifespan of parents. Consequently, when applying this concept in the functional-age model, practitioners need to consider that there is not just one family life cycle (Carter & McGoldrick, 2005; Tseng & Tsu, 1987). Rather, according to Walsh (2003), clinicians and theorists increasingly agree that definitions of family normality are social constructed.

Narrative Theory (Social Construction)

As family therapy evolved, postmodern theorists and practitioners began to question whether a systems view of treatment is as neutral as social workers once thought. Among the concepts they debated was the idea that the therapist is an expert or that a family system has an optimal or ideal level of functioning. Rather, postmodern theorists have argued that practitioners should consider a client to be the expert on his or her own story, "allow for the particular," and avoid sole reliance on universal truths or norms (Greene & Blundo, 1999, p. 91).

Just as there are differing views on the nature of family treatment, narrative theorists have varying views on the nature of development. They have defined *development* as an individual's smooth, continuous accumulation of skills and abilities at predictable stages over the life cycle. However, theorists are increasingly debating the idea that development is a universal, sequential, and fixed phenomenon (Bronfenbrenner, 1979). For example, theorists from the social construction and ecological schools of thought have argued that development is "culturally informed" and is a product of social interaction (Fleck-Henderson, 1993, p. 225). Others have proposed still another view of development, one adopted in this book: "Stages are not intended to meet strict theoretical standards. Instead, developmental psychologists use this enormously useful concept as a convenient way to describe major phases of life in a particular way" (Hoffman, Paris & Hall, 1994, p. 8). "We teach these various approaches partly for the tools they can provide the student in organizing information about a family" (Fleck-Henderson, 1993, p. 229).

Another feature of narrative therapies important to the functional age model is the reliance on clients' stories as a vehicle for learning about the context of their lives. According to Creswell (1998), a person's story can "uncover how life reflects cultural themes of the society, personal themes, institutional themes, and social histories" (p. 49). That is, personal stories are "nested within a set of larger stories or 'macro' narratives that reflect shared history, values, beliefs, expectations, myths" (Webster, 2002, p. 140), linking one's personal past and to collective historical events (Andersen, Reznik & Chen, 1997).

Ecological Perspective

During the 1980s and 1990s, social workers began to combine systems theory with the ecological perspective (Germain & Gitterman, 1996). The ecological perspective offers several useful concepts that social workers can now incorporated in the functional-age model. A major addition is that the ecological perspective suggests practitioners conduct a multi-level assessment that includes *microsystems*, small-scale systems, such as families and peer groups; *mesosystems*, the connections between two or more systems, such as family and health care systems; *exosystems*, connections between systems that do not directly involve the person, such as the social security and Medicare systems; and *macrosystems*, the overarching or large-scale systems, such as legal, political, economic, and value systems (Bronfenbrenner, 1979). The social worker examines all pertinent systems affecting the older adult's functional capacity including health care systems, religious institutions, and neighborhood networks. Through such a multisystem assessment, social workers can better learn what resources may strengthen the older adult and his or her family.

The ecological perspective also offers a multitheoretical approach that emphasizes person-environmental exchanges across the life course (Greene, 1991/2008). The *life course* concept does not subscribe to fixed, predetermined, or universal life tasks. Rather, it suggests that practitioners learn about each client as a member of his or her specific cohort, in a particular context, and with a unique personal history. The functional-age model has adopted the life course viewpoint as it modifies social workers' thinking about the life cycle because it gives practitioners more opportunity to explore such client diversity (Brown, 1995; Greene & Watkins, 1998).

Another related interest of ecological theorists adopted by the func-tional-age model is how people interact with others and with other social systems. Using the concept of *relatedness*, practitioners can assess how the older adult relates to others. Through such an understanding of how the older adult and his or her family are connected, social workers can assist in the choice of possible interventions across systems levels. This concept is particularly important for social workers who work in managed care or as case managers and need to access services to help persons with activities of daily living (Fillit, Hill, Picariello & Warburton, 1998; Raiff & Shore, 1993; Rose, 1992; Rothman, 1992; Vourlekis & Greene, 1992). In addition, the ecological perspective offers practitioners a positive view of change. It gives special attention to how people can achieve competence and can benefit from natural life experiences (Diehl, 1998; Willis, 1991, 1996a, 1996b). From the ecological perspective, social workers address *problems of living* (real-life concerns) and their solutions as complex phenomenon related to the totality of a client's life space (Germain, 1994). With this concept in mind, client assessment may involve a better understanding of how an older adult spends his or her day. Does the older adult have friends in the neighborhood, walk to the grocery store, or listen to music? Practitioners using this concept in the functional-age model can better promote health and continued growth (Germain & Gitterman, 1996).

Goodness of fit, another useful ecological concept adopted in the functional-age model, refers to the quality of match between person-environment over the life course. To the degree a social worker can address environmental barriers so that an older adult's surroundings become more supportive or a client is empowered to better secure resources, there is a better person-environment fit. To better understand the effects of goodness of fit, Lawton (1982) has suggested that practitioners examine *environmental press*, or the manner in which environmental forces affect individual needs (Lawton & Nahemow, 1973; see chapter 3).

For example, attendance at senior centers may be related to the distance of the center from an individual's home. Thus, distance is considered a negative environmental press that may reduce an older adult's participation in senior center activities, whereas a social worker who arranges for transportation alleviates distance as a negative effect (Lawton, 1982). Coulton (1981) has proposed another conception of how social workers may use the concept of goodness of fit in their practice. She suggested that the major role of social workers in hospital settings should be to assess the fit between the patient and the physical, spatial, psychosocial, behavioral, and economic aspects of health care and to act as an advocate to achieve a better match. Because the ecology of aging suggests that environments can either hinder or support competent functioning among older adults, it is a critical element in the functional-age model.

Strengths Perspective, a holistic view to assessment and intervention is clearly reflected in the functional-age model. However, current social work theorists are increasingly questioning a problem-saturated practice focus called for in the medical model and are emphasizing a strengths perspective (Saleebey, 2005). While strengths-based social work practice focuses on how clients react to stressful life situations, it gives greater attention to the political, social, and cultural context of practice (Borden, 1992; Weick & Saleebey, 1995). A *strengths perspective* generally assumes that clients have the inherent capability to transform their lives when they receive positive support (Saleebey, 2005). Social workers concerned with strengths-based practice are increasingly being challenged to respect a client's frame of reference and autonomy (De Jong & Miller, 1995). This is a particular concern for geriatric social workers who often see clients who may be frail or physically or mentally challenged.

Another concern in strengths-based practice pertinent to understanding older adult clients is how to reduce the asymmetry of power between client and social worker (Borden, 1992). Tice and Perkins (1996) have proposed that "a strengths perspective [with older adults] requires social workers to actively engage in relationships that position the clients as experts in their life situations" (p. 33). That is, practitioners establish a collaborative client-social worker relationship as they gather client information. They then choose interventions with the client-family. This viewpoint adopted by the functional-age model is congruent with feminist and social construction theory in that it recognizes that many social workers are eclectic in orientation (Greene & Blundo, 1999).

Resilience

Risk and resilience is another perspective that follows in the strength-based tradition. Resilience refers to a person's successful adaptation following an adverse event. A person's success in overcoming adversity is attributed to his or her natural healing capacity. Resilience is considered a dynamic phenomenon that depends on an individual's life context and is most important at life transitions (Masten, 1994). When assessing *resilience* among older adults, the practitioners examine their sense of continuity, competence, adaptability, and their inherent ability to bounce back across the life span (Greene & Cohen, 2005; Werner & Smith, 1992).

The assessment of *risk*, those factors or circumstances associated with problematic behaviors or situations, should always be made.

Cultural Competence

To use the functional-age model effectively, *cultural competence* is required. Social workers adopting the model need to shift their feelings, thoughts, and behaviors so that they are congruent with clients whose life contexts may be different from their own (Grant & Haynes, 1996; Green, 1995; Schlesinger & Devore, 1995). As U.S. society becomes more multicultural, social workers will increasingly need to serve diverse constituencies (De Jong & Miller, 1995; Giordano, 1992; Linsk, 1994; McDougall, 1993). For example, to be effective, social workers will need to communicate well across cultures, by (a) cultivating the ability to recognize and work with clients who may speak different languages; (b) using varying volumes of speech; (c) defining different meanings to touch; and (d) incorporating various attitudes about gestures, stance, and eye behaviors (Davidhizar & Giger-Newman, 1996; Yee & Weaver, 1994; table 1.1).

Use of the Functional-Age Model of Intergenerational Treatment

The functional-age model of intergenerational therapy has incorporated concepts from a number of different theories, adopting those that span the intrapsychic, interpersonal, developmental, and environmental dimensions (table 1.2; figure 1.3). The aim of the functional-age model is to provide practitioners with a comprehensive framework that will enable them to assess and treat the older adult within a familial and societal context.

The functional-age model of intergenerational family treatment is a systems approach practitioners can use wherever an older adult is part of the family constellation. The model is concerned with the older client's functional capacity–those skills that are instrumental in meeting environmental demands–and is designed to assist an older adult meet such environmental demands within a family context. That is, the functional-age model offers an approach for assessing the client system that is a composite of one particular member's biopsychosocial and spiritual functioning within a family and societal context. As an intergenerational model, it addresses the interdependence among family members and the dynamic nature of family structure and organization. In addition, it involves a mutual process in which the client and social worker process and

Table 1.2
The Functional-Age Model of Intergenerational Treatment: Model Elements

---

The Functional-Age Model (FAM) of Intergenerational Treatment is a conceptual framework for social work practice with older adults and their families. The model's interrelated components are grounded in professional values and ethics, and offer strategies to guide the social worker's assessment and intervention plan.

Foundation Elements

- Focus on client strengths and challenges in relation to their environments.
- Address the role of culture in the helping process.
- Call for culturally sensitive social work practice.
- Encompass behaviors in keeping with the NASW Code of Ethics.
- Attend to issues of social and economic justice

Functional-Age Elements

- Recognize the role of biological factors in client functioning.
- Examine client psychological well-being and adaptation.
- Explore client social relationships and support networks.
- Discuss client spirituality as a source of life satisfaction.
- Help determine client level of functionality and need for intervention.

Family Elements

- Address the family as a caregiving system.
- Explore the development of family care over time.
- Examine the role(s) that family members play in caregiving activities.
- Discuss how diverse family forms provide care.
- Help determine a family's caregiving capacity and need for intervention.

Family-Community-Societal Elements

- Consider the current cultural and historical milieu in which practice takes place.
- Explore the family's connection to larger social systems.
- Help determine the need for additional community/societal resources.

integrate information, thus allowing the family to understand behavioral patterns and to choose appropriate family-centered interventions.

Assessment of the Older Adult's Functional Age

Activities of Daily Living. Older adults are most likely brought to the attention of a social service agency because of factors that interfere with activities of daily living. It is not the particular diseases of old age but the effects of these conditions on mental and physical functioning that affect the older adult's performance of certain daily tasks. Subsequently, geriatricians need to focus on "a functional [or behavioral] approach as compared with the 'classical' disease-oriented approach in making decisions about treatment and the need for supportive care in older persons" (Ferrucci, Guralnik, Baroni, Tesi, Antonini & Marchionni, 1991, p. 52). The ideal method for achieving this goal is to call on a multidisciplinary assessment team (Gallo, Teichel & Andersen, 1995; Ryan, Cott & Robertson, 1997). However, such a team is a luxury few social workers have; consequently, geriatric practitioners must be knowledgeable in all the areas related to the client's functioning (see chapter 3).

Functional Age. The core of the functional-age model of intergenerational treatment is the older member's functional age. *Functional age* comprises four basic spheres related to adaptational capacity: the biological, psychological, sociocultural, and spiritual. The social, psychological, physical and spiritual aspects of a person's functional capacity are so intimately related that all demand attention to understand the presenting concerns, to ascertain the older adult's structure of life and daily living habits, and to arrive at an appropriate care plan (chapters 3 to 5).

- *Biological Age.* Geriatric social workers need to talk with clients about health-related issues such as the number and types of medication the older adult is currently taking, as well as the side effects of the medications, and must be cognizant of the ways in which various drugs affect mental functioning (Rowe & Kahn, 1998). Decrements in memory, cognition, judgment, and orientation, as well as changes in affect, may be related to these organic brain disorders. Symptoms may be brought about by multi-infarct (stroke), infection, thyroid deficiencies, tumors, malnutrition, and illnesses such as diabetes (see chapter 3).
- *Psychological Age.* Psychological age refers to how a person has adapted over time. In this regard, it is essential for social workers to take a complete history. Without it, social workers cannot fully understand the affective or emotional aspects of an elderly client's functioning. In addition, professionals will want to explore the client's potential for growth and change.

- *Social Age*. Although practitioners and others tend to see the aged population as one homogeneous group, there is a wide variation among them in their norms, values, and so forth, relative to ethnic, religious, and cultural milieus, communities, or groups. A client's position or role in a given social structure is an important variable to include in assessing and planning with and for the client. For instance, Western society generally values involvement in work and devalues leisure time (Longman, 1997; Sterns & Sterns, 1997).
- *Spiritual Age* may include a person's relationship with his or her faith/religious community and or an inner system of beliefs, discovering what contributes to a person's ability to transcend the immediate situation and find meaning in seemingly meaningless events (Canda & Besthorn, 2002; Canda & Smith, 2002; Crowther et al., 2002).

Geriatric social workers must develop expertise in the biological, psychological, sociocultural and spiritual aspects of aging, all of which influence the client's functional capacity. An understanding of these factors allows both the practitioner and client to come to a biopsychosocial and spiritual assessment or evaluation of the client's needs as part of a holistic individualized treatment plan.

Family Assessment

An intergenerational clinical social work approach, however, requires more than an understanding of the biopsychosocial and spiritual function of the older adult. It also demands active concern with and, whenever possible, participation by family members. All too often when a family reaches out for help for an older member in crisis, helping professionals may view the presenting problem as resting with the older relative, whom they then designated as "the identified patient." For example, a family typically comes to a social services agency with a specific complaint involving the older relative: "Our mother seems to forget so much lately…and she seems so confused…. We are all pretty shaken up about it." The specificity of such a complaint makes it far too easy to identify the mother as the client. This book presents a different conception of social work with the older adult in crisis. The author suggests that social workers reach out to the family and view the family group as the client system.

The picture of the intergenerational network as the client system is rather inclusive. It may involve the family of origin, a family of choice, or kin network. In the situation of the older mother who "needs help with her forgetfulness," the families of her children and grandchildren may all conceivably be involved. In this example, the social worker will need to explore the circumstances around the forgetfulness of the mother, as well as discover the meaning of this behavior within the family system.

During a crisis, the older adult becomes central to the event occurring within the family network; the social worker can expect that changes in the older person's functioning will affect other family members. By taking this theoretical position, the practitioner can come to understand the presenting concerns in family systems terms. The issue then becomes how the mother's forgetfulness affects all the family members. In an individualistic approach, the identified client–the older mother—is part of the family system, but on the periphery. The members of the family all point to the mother as "the problem." If the social worker does not redefine or reframe the problem in family terms, then the practitioner may treat the older person as an individual apart from the rest of the individuals in the system. In a systems approach, the mother is central to all family happenings, just as the axis is central to the spokes of a wheel. In these terms, the social worker helps the family to understand the crisis within a family context. In this way, the mother's forgetfulness is everybody's personal concern and the practitioner considers the family system to be the client. To underscore that practitioners should view all family members as the client, this book refers to the crisis-connected older member as the *pivotal client* rather than the *identified patient*.[1]

Most elderly clients come to the attention of an agency during a crisis. At that time, the practitioner should ask himself or herself, "Who is the client?" The family-centered practitioner understands that a crisis involves the entire family. Consequently, when determining assessment and treatment options, practitioners must consider both the elderly person's bio-psychosocial needs and the family's adapting and coping capacity. Social workers must be careful not to get caught up in the vulnerability of the older person, and unintentionally–in some cases, unnecessarily–become surrogate family members. Chapter 2 suggests ways of reaching out to families during the initial interview or intake process.

Thinking in intergenerational terms means that social workers have considered the family group as a caregiving resource. Family members are often available and can work with a therapist on behalf of the older person. A family member may be able to care for an older relative at home with the assistance of support services such as a homemaker, Meals-on-Wheels, or respite care. A family member also may act as a case manager by planning, arranging, or maintaining services for the elderly relative. In the process of working out these arrangements, the social worker not only is empowering, but becomes aware of the unique dynamics that characterize that client system. The practitioner can use this information to collaborate with the family in selecting appropriate interventive techniques.

The family, however, is more than a source of information or a caregiving resource. It is an important treatment unit. Geriatric social workers have a major responsibility for assessing and addressing family needs. They need to be professionally prepared to understand the complexity of biopsychosocial functioning of the aged person as well the effect it has on family functioning. As family therapists, they should be well equipped to understand intergenerational relationships and the structural changes brought about by a biopsychosocial or spiritual crisis in any one of the family members. A major obstacle to easing such a crisis, though, is often the family's lack of familiarity with the various aspects of the aging process and their reluctance to accept the functional changes in their older member. The family group seeking help is usually bewildered by the often sudden turn of events in their lives as a result of the physical, psychological, social, or spiritual changes. They often are confused and frustrated with their own inability to understand, accept, and deal with their concerns. Geriatric social workers can play a critical role in the resolution of these family difficulties. The functional-age model provides practitioners with a framework for using innovative assessment and treatment modalities for finding solutions in crises.

- *The Family as a Social System.* Because the family is distinguished by a high level of interdependence and interrelatedness, when competencies of the older member change practitioners should expect to see some degree of change throughout the family system. Moreover, when changes in the older adult's functional capacities reach crisis proportions, practitioners should anticipate noticeable changes in family functioning. Therefore, social workers must first understand the family unit as a social system. Of particular importance to the functional-age model is the concept that the family is more than just a summation of the individual lives of its members. As these individual members interact, they create an additional entity—the life of the family group. The perspective of the family as a system necessitates that practitioners assess the life of the group and treat the family as an organizational structure that is a functioning whole (see chapters 6 and 7).
- *The Family as a Set of Reciprocal Roles.* A role in the social structure carries with it expectations of behaviors that society defines. Translating the concept of role into family terms means that there is a division of labor within the family group and that each member is expected to behave in a somewhat prescribed pattern in a given situation. The

functional-age model of intergenerational therapy suggests that practitioners need to learn how role expectations help define interaction
among family members. Who is the family member usually called
on to care for his or her mother? Who is the "good child" and who
is the "bad"? Social workers who understand how these expectations
enter into family functioning and who do not take role performance
as inflexible are better equipped to help the client system in meeting
life transitions (Thompson, 1994).

- *The Family as a Developmental Unit.* Family functioning is not static;
  rather, it changes as a "result of significant changes in formal family
  organization and changes in the number, age and composition of the
  generations" (Eyde & Rich, 1983, p. 11). The dynamic nature of the
  family life cycle is an important element included in the functional-age
  model. Family developmental theory offers social workers a perspective on how each family member is influenced by and, in turn, shapes
  other members' development. The adoption of this perspective allows
  social workers to place the older person's developmental history in
  a unique family context (Walsh, 2003). In short, the use of the family developmental history permits social workers to understand the
  course of a particular family's life over time to assist with the current
  developmental issues. What other crises has the family faced? What
  and who has solved them?

Assessment of the Family as it Relates to Other Social Systems

The family is one of many systems affecting the older adult's life. The
functional-age model suggests that social workers examine the connection and influences among systems affecting the aged person and his or
her family. The final phase of a holistic assessment must consider how a
family obtains its physical and material needs from its environment. At
any time in a family's life, their internal resources may become overbur-
dened (Hartman & Laird, 1983). Using family-centered interviews and
an ecomap as a tool, the social worker needs to consider what resources
may support family functioning (see chapter 7). As can be seen in figure
1.3, these resources may come from friends, health care agencies, or
recreation facilities.

Perhaps what is most challenging about working with elderly clients
is their position in society and the accompanying sociopolitical implications (Scharlach & Kaye, 1997). Questions related to an older person's
access to public services and the aged person's general societal status
are of almost daily concern to social workers. The extent to which
practitioners engage in hearings, lobby for legislation, and participate in
conferences is an individual matter. However, it is important for social
worker and client alike to understand that the ability to meet the need

Figure 1.3
Functional-Age Model of Intergenerational Treatment

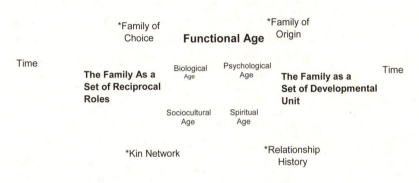

Societal Systems

Family System

*Family of
Choice   **Functional Age**   *Family of
Origin

Time   Time
Biological   Psychological
The Family As a   Age   Age   **The Family as a**
Set of Reciprocal   **Set of Developmental**
Roles   **Unit**

Sociocultural   Spiritual
Age   Age

*Kin Network   *Relationship
History

Modified by Eunkyung Kim

for services, the funding of those services, and the general availability of programs relates at least in part to the political process. One example is the increased number of states that have developed programs to provide financial assistance to supplement family care at home (Capitman & Yee, 1997; Keigher & Linsk, 1997). This advancement in policy came about through the joint lobbying efforts of social workers in direct practice, social planners, politicians, clients, and their families. This advocacy approach suggests that social workers must address both political and clinical aspects of a substantial number of the problems for which their clients are seeking services.

It is apparent that the functional-age model for intergenerational treatment offers a framework for assessment and treatment of the older adult within a family and societal context. It provides a tool for the simultaneous assessment of the older adult's biopsychosocial and spiritual functioning, the life of the family group, and the broader environment in which they live. The model offers practitioners a means for bridging the gap among an adequate understanding of the older person, a sufficient knowledge of the family as a unit, and the meaning of other system influences. This integrated assessment process suggests that social workers engage the family in selecting family-focused treatment modalities and advocate for societal change.

Older Adults Alone

Many elders who have families live alone and have special concerns. Although the model emphasizes working with the family, it also provide sufficient information and techniques for practice with the older adult whose family is unavailable. In addition, in a qualitative study in which the researchers interviewed elders who lived alone, Rubinstein, Kilbride, and Nagy (1992) learned that an older adult's subjective perception of his or her degree of frailty and choice was a key factor in that person's ability to live alone. They also found that there is a culture of living alone successfully, involving an older adult's (a) wish to manage his or her own affairs; (b) desire to keep a schedule; (c) need to connect or have social supports; (d) wish to pass the time; and (e) need to maintain a sense of self-identity. Practitioners should keep in mind that they may have to mobilize informal helping networks.

Families of Choice

Research on family caregiving has primarily focused on older adults within traditional nuclear family constellations, excluding the experiences of lesbian and gay men. Stereotypes of older lesbians and gays picture them as more depressed and lonely than their heterosexual counterparts (Dorfman et al., 1995). However, studies have shown that there is no significant difference between homosexuals and heterosexuals in terms of levels of depression or social supports in old age. Practitioners will have to explore where sources of support are derived: Lesbians and gay men are more likely to receive support from partners and friends called *families of choice*; while heterosexual females and males are more likely to receive support from their biological families referred to as *families of origin* (Quam, 2001). Once the sources of help have been identified, the functional-age model can be applied.

Note

1.   Thanks to Jirina Polivka for help in this conception.

References

Ackerman, N. (1957). An orientation to psychiatric research on the family. *Marriage and Family Living, 19*, 68-74.
Anderson, R. E., Carter, I., & Lowe, G. (1999). *Human behavior in the social environment: A social systems approach*. Hawthorne, NY: Aldine De Gruyter.

Andersen, S. M., Reznik, I., & Chen, S. (1997). The self in relation to others: Cognitive and motivational underpinnings. In J.G. Snodgrass & R.L. Thompson (Eds.), *The self across psychology: Self- recognition, self-awareness, and the self-concept* (pp. 233-275). New York: New York Academy of Science.

Baltes, M. M. (1996). *The many faces of dependency in old age.* New York: Cambridge University Press.

Berger, R., & Federico, R. (1982). *Human behavior: A social work perspective.* New York: Longman.

Bertalanffy, L. (1968). *General systems theory: Human relations.* New York: Brazillier.

Borden, W. (1992). Narrative perspectives in psychosocial intervention following adverse life events. *Social Work, 37,* 135-141.

Boszormenyi-Nagy, I., & Spark, G. (1973). *Invisible loyalties.* New York: Harper & Row.

Bowen, M. (1971). Aging: A symposium. *Georgetown Medical Bulletin, 30,* 4-27.

Brody, E. (1981). Women in the middle and family help to older people. *The Gerontologist, 21,* 471-480.

Bronfenbrenner, U. (1979).*The ecology of human development.* Cambridge, MA: Harvard University Press.

Brown, C. (1995). A feminist life span perspective on aging. In N. Van Den Bergh (Ed.), *Feminist practice in the 21st century* (pp. 330-354). Washington, DC: NASW Press.

Burnette, D. (1997). Grandparents raising grandchildren in the inner city. *Families in Society, 78,* 489-499

Butler, R. N., Lewis, M., & Sunderland, T. (1999). *Aging and mental health: Positive psychosocial and biomedical approaches.* Boston: Allyn & Bacon.

Canda, E. R. (1988). Conceptualizing spirituality for social work: Insights from diverse perspectives. *Social Thought, 14*(1), 30-46.

Canda, E. R. (1994). Does religion and spirituality have a significant place in the core HBSE curriculum. In M. Bloom & W. Klein (Eds.), *Controversial issues in human behavior in the social environment.* Boston: Allyn & Bacon.

Canda, E. & Besthorn, F. (2002). Revisioning environment: Deep ecology for education and teaching in social work. *Journal of Teaching in Social Work, 22* (1/2), 79-101.

Canda, E. & Smith, E. (2002) *Transpersonal perspectives on spirituality in social work.* New York: Haworth.

Capitman, J. A., & Yee, D. L. (1997). Should family members be paid to provide care to elderly persons? Yes. In A. E. Scharlach & L. W. Kaye (Eds.), *Controversial issues in aging* (pp. 148-159). Boston: Allyn & Bacon.

Carter, B., & McGoldrick, M. (Eds.) (2005). *The expanded family life cycle: Individual, family,and social perspectives.* Boston: Allyn & Bacon.

Chan, C. G., & Elder, G. H. (2000). Matrilineal advantage in grandchild-grandparent relations. *The Gerontologist, 40,* (2), 179-190.

Cohen, H. & Greene, R. R. (2005). Older adults who overcame oppression. *Families in Society, 87*(1), 1-8.

Cohen. H. L. & Murray, Y. (2006). Older lesbian and gay caregivers: Caring for families of choice and caring for families of origin. In R. R. Greene (Ed.), *Contemporary issues of care* (pp. 257-298). New York: Haworth.

Cohler, B. J., Hostetler, A., & Boxer, A. (1998). Generativity, social context, and lived experience: Narratives of gay men in middle adulthood. In D. McAdams & E. de St. Aubin (Eds.),

Generativity and adult development: Psychosocial perspectives on caring and contributions to the next generation. Washington, DC: American Psychological Association Press.

Corman, J. M., & Kingson, E. R. (1996). Trends, issues, perspectives and values for the aging of the baby boomers cohort. *The Gerontologist, 36*, 15-26.

Coulton, C. J. (1981). Person-environment fit as the focus of health care. *Social Work, 26*, 26-35.

Creswell, J. W. (1998). *Qualitative inquiry and research design: Choosing among five traditions.* Thousand Oaks, CA: Sage.

Crowther, M. R., Parker, M, W., Achenbaum, W.A., Larimore, W. L., & Koenig, H. G. (2002). Rowe and Kahn's model of successful aging revisited: Positive spirituality—The forgotten factor. *The Gerontologist, 42*(5), 613-620.

Cutler, N. E. (1997). The false alarms and blaring sirens of financial literacy: Middle-agers knowledge of retirement income, health finance, and long-term care. *Generations, 21*, 34-40.

Crawford, S. (1988). Cultural context as a factor in the expansion of therapeutic conversation with lesbian families. *Journal of Strategic and Systemic Therapies, 7*, 2-10.

Danis, F. S., Lockhart, L. L. (2004). *Breaking the silence in social work education.* Alexandria, VA: Council on Social Work Education.

Davidhizar, R., & Giger-Newman, J. (1996). Reflections on the minority elderly in healthcare. *Hospital Topics, 74*, 20-29.

De Jong, P., & Miller, S. D. (1995). How to interview for client strengths. *Social Work, 40*, 729-736.

Diehl, M. (1998). Everyday competence in later life: Current status and future directions. *The Gerontologist, 38*, 422-433.

Dorfman, R., Walters K., Burke P., Hardin, L., Karanik, T., Raphel, J., & Silverstein, E. (1995). Old, sad and alone: the myth of the aging homosexual. *Journal of Gerontological Social Work, 24*(1/2), 28-42.

Erikson, E. (1950). *Childhood and society,* (2nd ed.) New York: W. W. Norton.

Eyde, D. R., & Rich, J. (1983). *Psychological distress in aging: A family management model.* Rockville, MD: Aspen Publications.

Fahey, C. J. (1996). Social work education and the field of aging. *The Gerontologist, 36*, 36-41.

Ferrucci, L., Guralnik, J. M., Baroni, A., Tesi, G., Antonini, E., & Marchionni, N. (1991). Value of combined assessment of physical health and functional status in community-dwelling aged: A prospective study in Florence, Italy. *Journal of Gerontology: Medical Sciences, 46*, 52-56.

Fillit, H. M., Hill, J., Picariello, G., & Warburton, S. (1998). How the principles of geriatric assessment are shaping managed care. *Geriatrics, 53*, 76-84.

Fleck-Henderson, A. (1993). A constructivist approach to human behavior in the social environment. In J. Laird (Ed.) *Revisioning social work education: A social constructivist approach* (pp. 219-238). New York: Haworth.

Fraenkel, (2003). Contemporary two-parent families: Navigating work and family challenges. In F. Walsh (Ed.), *Normal family processes: Growing diversity and complexity* (pp. 61-95). New York: Guilford Press.

Galambos, C. Greene, R.R. (in press). A competency approach to curriculum building: A social work mission. *Journal of Gerontological Social Work, 48.*

Gallo, J. J., Reichel, W. Andersen, L. M. (1995). *Handbook of geriatric assessment* (2nd ed.). Gaithersburg, MD: Aspen.

Garrett, A. (1950). Historical survey of the evolution of casework. In C. Kasius, (Ed.), *Principles and techniques of casework* (pp. 393-411). New York: Family Service Association of America.

Gatz, M. (Ed.) (1995). *Emerging issues in mental health and aging.* Washington, DC: American Psychological Association.

Gergen, K. L. (1985b). The social constructionist movement in modern psychology. *American Psychologist, 40*(3), 266–275.

Germain, C. B. (1994). Human behavior in the social environment. In F. G. Reamer (Ed.), *The foundations of social work knowledge* (pp. 88-121). New York: Columbia University Press.

Germain, C. B., & Gitterman, A. (1996). *The life model of social work practice.* New York: Columbia University Press.

Giordano, J. (1992). Ethnicity and aging. *Journal of Gerontological Social Work, 18,* 23-39.

Grant, D., & Haynes, D. (1996). A developmental framework for cultural competence training with children. In P. L. Ewalt, E. M. Freeman, S. A. Kirk, & D. L. Poole (Eds.), *Multicultural issues in social work.* Washington, DC: NASW Press.

Green, J. (1995). *Cultural awareness in the human services.* Englewood Cliffs, NJ: Prentice Hall.

Greene, R. R. (1989). A life systems approach to understanding parent-child relationships in aging families. *Journal of Family Psychotherapy, 5,* 57-68.

Greene, R. R. (1992). Case management: An arena for social work practice. In B. Vourlekis & R. R. Greene (Eds.). *Social work case management* (pp. 11-25). Hawthorne, NY: Aldine de Gruyter.

Greene, R. R. (1993). Public information, prevention, and health promotion. In S. Finckel, C. Dye, A. Garcia, M. Gatz, R. Greene, D. P. Hay, M. Smyer, & M. L. Wykle. *Report of the interdisciplinary coordination group on mental health and the elderly.* Washington, DC: National Institute of Mental Health.

Greene, R. R. (1994). *Human behavior theory: A diversity framework.* Hawthorne, NY: Aldine De Gruyter.

Greene, R. R. (1991/2008). *Human behavior theory and social work practice.* Hawthorne, NY: Aldine De Gruyter.

Greene, R. R. (2008). *Human behavior theory and social work practice. New Brunswick, NJ: Aldine Transaction Press.*

Greene, R. R. (2002). *Resiliency theory: An integrated framework for practice, research, and policy.* Washington, DC: NASW Press.

Greene, R. R. (2005). Redefining social work for the new millennium: Setting a context. *Journal of Human Behavior and the Social Environment, 10*(4), 37-54.

Greene, R. R. (2007). *Social work practice: A risk and resilience perspective.* Monterey, CA: Brooks/Cole.

Greene, R. R., & Blundo, R. (1999). Post modern critique of systems theory in social work with the aged and their families. *Journal of Gerontological Social Work, 31,* 87-100.

Greene, R. R. & Cohen, H. (2005). Social Work with older adults and their families: Changing practice paradigms. *Families in Society, 86*(3), 367-373.

Greene, R. R., Kropf, N., & Pugh, K. L. (1994). Planning health education for older adults: The use of a health model and interview data. *Gerontology & Geriatric Education, 15.*

Greene, R. R., & Sullivan, W. P. (2004). Putting social work values into action: Use of the ecological perspective with older adults in the managed care arena. *Journal of Gerontological Social Work, 42*(3/4), 131–50.

Greene, R. R., & Watkins, M. (Eds.) (1998). *Serving diverse constituencies: Applying the ecological perspective.* Hawthorne, NY: Aldine De Gruyter.

Greene, R. R., & Sullivan, P. W. (2004). Putting social work values into action: Use of the ecological perspective with older adults in the managed care arena. *Journal of Gerontological Social Work, 42*(3/4), 131-150.

Hamilton, G. (1951). *Theory and Practice of Social Casework*. New York: Columbia University Press.

Hare-Mustin, R. T. (1990). Sex, lies, and headaches: The problem is power. In T. J. Goodrich (Ed.), *Women and power: Perspectives for family therapy* (pp. 61-83). New York: W. W. Norton.

Hareven, T. K. (1996). *Aging and generational relations over the life course: A historical and cross-cultural perspective*. New York: Aldine de Gruyter.

Hartman, A. (1995). Family therapy. In R. L. Edwards (Ed.-in-Chief), *Encyclopedia of social work* (vol. 2, 19th ed., pp. 983-991). Washington, DC: NASW Press.

Hartman, A., & Laird, J. (1983). *Family-centered social work practice*. New York: The Free Press.

Heilbrun, C. (1997). *The last gift of time: Life beyond 60*. New York: Dial Press.

Hepworth, D. H., Rooney, & Larsen, J. A. (2002). *Direct social work practice: Theory and skills*. Pacific Grove, CA: Thomson Wadsworth.

Ho, M. K. (1987). *Family therapy with ethnic minorities*. Newbury Park, CA: Sage.

Hodge, D. R. (2001). Spirituality assessment: A review of major qualitative methods and a new framework for assessing spirituality. *Social Work, 46*(3), 203-207.

Hoffman, L. (1992). A reflective stance for family therapy. In S. McNamee & K. J. Gergen (Eds.), *Therapy as social construction* (pp. 7-24). Newbury Park, CA: Sage.

Hoffman, L., Paris, S., & Hall, E. (1994). *Developmental psychology today*. New York: McGraw-Hill.

Hollis, F. (1977). Social casework: The psychosocial approach. In J. B. Turner, (Ed.-in-Chief), *The encyclopedia of social work* (vol. 2, 17th Issue, pp. 1300-1308). Washington, DC: NASW.

Institute for Health & Aging, University of California, San Francisco. (1996). *Chronic care in America: A 21st century challenge*. Princeton, NJ: Robert Wood Johnson Foundation.

Janchill, M. P. (1969). Systems concepts in casework theory and practice. *Social Casework, 15*,

Kart, C. S & Engler, C. A. (1995). Self-health care among the elderly. *Research on Aging, 17*, 434-458.

Keigher, S. M., & Linsk, N. L. (1997). Should family members be paid to provide care to elderly persons? Yes. In A. E. Scharlach, & L. W. Kaye (Eds.), *Controversial issues in aging* (pp. 148-159). Boston: Allyn & Bacon.

Kiyak, H. A. & Hooyman, N. (1999). Aging in the twenty-first century. *Hallyn International Journal of Aging, 1*, 56-66.

Kolomer, S., McCallion, P., & Janicki, M. P. (2002). *Journal of Gerontological Social Work, 37* (3/4), 45-62.

Lawton, P. M. (1982). Competence, environmental press, and adaptation of older people. In M. P.

Lawton, P. G. Windley & T. O. Byers (Eds.) *Aging and the environment: Theoretical approaches* (pp. 33-59). New York: Springer.

Lawton, M. P. & Nahemow, L. (1973). Ecology and the aging process. In C. Eisdorf, & M. P. Lawton (Eds.). *The psychology of adult development and aging* (pp. 619-674). Washington, DC: American Psychological Association.

Lifton, R. J. ([1993] 1999). *The protean self: Human resilience in an age of fragmentation*. Chicago: University of Chicago Press.

Linsk, N. L. (1994). HIV and the elderly. *Families in Society, 75*, 362-372.

Longman, P. (1997). Should there be an affirmative action policy for hiring older persons? No. In A. E. Scharlach, & L. W. Kaye (Eds.), *Controversial issues in aging* (pp. 34-44) Boston: Allyn & Bacon.

Manchester, J. (1997). Aging baby boomers and retirement: Who is at risk? *Generations, 21*, 19-22.

Masten, A. (1994). Resilience in individual development: Successful adaptation despite risk and adversity. In M. C. Wang & E. Gordon (Eds.), *Educational resilience in inner-city America: Challenges and prospects* (pp. 3–25). Hillsdale, NJ: Lawrence Erlbaum.

McDougall, G. J. (1993). Therapeutic issues with gay and lesbian elders. In T. L. Brink (Ed.), *The forgotten aged: Ethnic, psychiatric, and societal minorities* (pp. 45-57). New York: Haworth.

Mimes, C. (1994). Parental caregiving by adult women. *Research on Aging, 16*, 191-212.

Mimes, C. (1996). Factors influencing parental caregiving by adult women. *Research on Aging, 18*, 349-371

Moen, P., & Forest, K. B. (1995). Family policy for an aging society: Moving to the 21st century. *The Gerontologist, 35*, 825-830.

Pearlin, L. I., Aneshensel, C. S., Mullan, J. T., & Whitlach, C. J. (1996). Caregiving and its social support. In R. H. Binstock & L. George (Eds.), *Handbook of aging and the social sciences* (pp. 283-302). San Diego, CA: Academic Press.

Perlman, H. H. (1957). *Social Casework. A Problem-Solving Process*. Chicago: University of Chicago Press.

Perlman, H. H. (1968). *Persona: social role and personality*. Chicago: University of Chicago Press.

Posner, R. A. (1995). *Aging and old age*. Chicago: University of Chicago Press.

Quam, J. K. (2001). *Gay and lesbian aging. SEICUS Report, June/July 1993*. Retrieved April 4, 2003, from http://cyfc.umn.edu/seniors/resources/gayaging.html.

Raiff, N. R., & Shore, B. K. (1993). *Advanced case management*. Newbury Park: Sage.

Richmond, M. (1917). *Social diagnosis*. New York: Russell Sage Foundation.

Richmond, M. (1922). *What is social casework? An introductory description*. New York: Russell Sage Foundation.

Riley, M. W. (1994). Aging and society: Past, present, and future. *The Gerontologist, 34*, 436-446.

Rix, S. (1994). *Older workers: How do they measure up? An overview of age differences on employee costs and performances*. Washington, DC: AARP.

Robert, S. A. Ruel, E. (2006). Racial segregation and health disparities between black and white older adults. *The Journals of Gerontology Series B: Psychological Sciences and Social Sciences, 61*: S203-S211.

Rose, S. M. (1992). *Case management social work practice*. New York: Longman.

Rothman, J. (1992). *Guidelines for case management: Putting research to professional use*. Itasca, IL: F. E. Peacock.

Rowe, J. W., & Kahn, R. L. (1998). *Successful aging*. New York: Pantheon Books.

Rubinstein, R. L., Kilbride, J. C., & Nagy, S. (1992). *Elders living alone: Frailty and the perception of choice*. Hawthorne, NY: Aldine De Gruyter.

Rutter, M. (1989). Pathways from childhood to adult life. *Journal of Psychology and Psychiatry, 30*(3), 23–51.

Ryan, D. P., Cott, C., & Robertson, D. (1997). Conceptual tools for thinking about inter-team work in clinical gerontology. *Educational Gerontologist, 23*, 651-667.

Saleebey, D. (1993). Notes on interpreting the human condition: A constructed HBSE curriculum. In J. Laird (Ed.) *Revisioning social work education: A social constructivist approach* (pp. 197-218). New York: Haworth.

Saleebey, D. (2005). *The strengths perspective in social work practice* (4th ed.). Boston: Allyn & Bacon.

Scharlach, A. E., & Kaye, L. W. (Eds.) (1997). *Controversial issues in aging*. Boston: Allyn & Bacon.

Schlesinger, E. G., & Devore, W. (1995). Ethnic-sensitive practice. In R. L. Edwards (Ed.-in-Chief), *Encyclopedia of social work* (vol. 1, 19th ed., pp. 902-908). Washington, DC: NASW Press.

Seligman, M. E. P. (1990). *Learned optimism*. New York: Alfred A. Knopf.

Seligman, M. E. P. (2002). Positive psychology, positive prevention, and positive therapy. In C. R. Snyder & S. J. Lopez (Eds.), *Handbook of positive psychology* (pp. 3–7). New York: Oxford University Press.

Semel, V. G. (1996). Modern psychoanalytic treatment of the older patient. In S. Zarit & B. Knight (Eds.), *A guide to psychotherapy and aging: Effective clinical interventions in a life-stage context*, (pp. 101-120). Washington, DC: American Psychological Association.

Silverstone, B. (1996). Older people of tomorrow: A psychosocial profile. *The Gerontologist, 36*, 27-32.

Silverstone, B., & Burack-Weiss, A. (1983). *Social Work Practice with the frail elderly and their families*. Springfield, IL: Charles C Thomas.

Sterns, A. A., & Sterns, H. L. (1997). Should there be an affirmative action policy for hiring older persons? Yes. In A. E. Scharlach, & L. W. Kaye (Eds.), *Controversial issues in aging*. (pp. 34-44) Boston: Allyn & Bacon.

Strean, H.S. (1971). The application of role theory to social casework. In H. S. Strean (Ed), *Social casework theories in action*. Metuchen, NJ: Scarecrow Press.

Thompson, K. H. (1994). Role theory and social work practice. In R. R. Greene, *Human behavior: A diversity framework*. (pp. 93-114). Hawthorne, NY: Aldine De Gruyter.

Tice, C. J., & Perkins, K. (1996). *Mental health issues and aging: Building on the strengths of older persons*. Pacific Grove, CA: Brooks/Cole.

Trepper, T. (1987). Senior editors' comments. In W. S. Tseng, & J. Hsu (Eds.), *Culture and family problems and family therapy* (pp. xi-xii). New York: Haworth.

Tseng, W. S., & Hsu, J. (1987). *Culture and family problems and family therapy*. New York: Haworth.

Turner, F. J. (1988). Psychosocial therapy. In R. A. Dorfman (Ed.), *Paradigms of clinical social work*. (pp. 106-122). New York: Brunner Mazel.

U. S. Bureau of the Census. (1996). *Current populations report, 65+ in the United States*, special studies. , Washington, DC. U. S. Government Printing Office.

Vourlekis, B., & Greene, R. R. (Eds.) (1992). *Social work case management*. New York: Aldine De Gruyter.

Walsh, F. (1998). *Strengthening family resilience*. New York: Guilford Publications.

Walsh, F. (1999). Families in later life: Challenges and opportunities. In B. Carter, & M. McGoldrick Eds.), *The expanded family life cycle: Individual, family, and social perspectives*. (pp. 307-326). Boston: Allyn & Bacon.

Walsh, F. (2003). Changing families in a changing world: Reconstructing family normality. In F. Walsh (Ed.), *Normal family processes: Growing diversity and complexity* (pp. 3-26). New York: Guilford Press.

Webster, J. (2002). Reminiscence functions in adulthood: Age, race, and family dynamics correlates. In J. D. Webster & B. K. Haight (Eds.), *Critical advances in reminiscence work* (pp. 140-152). New York: Springer.

Weick, A., & Saleebey, D. (1995). Supporting family strengths: Orienting policy and practice toward the 21st century. *Families in Society, 76*, 141-149.

Werner, E., & Smith, R. (1992). *Overcoming the odds: High risk children from birth to adulthood*. Ithaca, NY: Cornell University Press.

Willis, S. L. (1991). Cognition and everyday competence. In K. W. Schaie (Ed.), *Annual review of gerontology and geriatrics* (Vol. 11, pp. 80-109). New York: Springer.

Willis, S. L. (1996a). Assessing everyday competence in the cognitively challenged elderly. In M. Smyer, K. Schaie, W. Kapp, & B. Marshall (Eds.). *Older adults' decision making and the law.* New York: Springer.

Willis, S. L. (1996b). Everyday cognitive competence in elderly persons: Conceptual issues and empirical findings. *The Gerontologist, 36*, 595-601.

Yee, B. W. K., & Weaver, G. D. (1994). Ethnic minorities and health promotion: Developing a "culturally competent" agenda. *Generations, 18*, 39-45.

Zedlewski, S. R., Barnes, R. O., Burt, M. R., McBride, T. D., & Meyer, J. A. (1990). *The needs of the elderly in the 21st century.* Washington, DC: Urban Institute.

2

Beginning the Helping Process: Special Issues

The interviews that initiate the therapeutic process set the tone of the helping relationship. During this critical phase, the social worker and client begin to create a mutual relationship, define concerns, become oriented to the treatment process, and determine whether the services required are within the purview of the agency's functions. That is, the client and practitioner discuss how the helping process can be beneficial. This is an interactional process in which the social worker and client family review difficulties and explore solutions to improve the client's everyday functioning.

Ageism

To provide services in the field of aging effectively, social workers need to become more aware of the negative stereotyping of older adults. The image of an old person as weak, infirm, feeble, helpless, and nonproductive has been so pervasive that Butler (1969) coined the term *ageism* to describe the prejudices and stereotypes that are applied to older people solely on the basis of their age. Ageism is a form of blatant prejudice and discrimination against the elderly. It is

> a process of systematic stereotyping of and discrimination against people because they are old, just as racism and sexism accomplish this with skin color and gender. Ageism allows the younger generations to see older people as different from themselves. Thus, they subtly cease to identify with their elders as human beings. (Butler, 1975, p. 12)

Prejudice toward older adults, which can be found to some degree in all of us, is a way of pigeonholing people and not seeing them as individuals. Ageism is similar to other forms of prejudice, such as sexism and racism, in that it pervades social institutions as well as individual belief systems. Partly because of ageism, discrimination in areas such as employment and health care delivery are widespread. Although misconceptions about the aging process have lessened in recent years, thinking in a negative manner about older adults continues to have damaging effects on service delivery. Unfortunately, ageism can interfere with the choices presented to older clients and whether clients think positively about themselves (Blum, 1991; Grant, 1994; Hummert, Shaner, Garstka & Henry, 1998).

Myths and Stereotypes

Myths and stereotypes of older adults reflect U. S. society's negative views of the aged and the aging process. Schneider and Kropf (1992) identified common stereotypes of old age that can serve as a check list for social workers who want to examine their own attitudes toward older adults (Table 2.1). Particularly important for our discussion are the myths and stereotypes that can interfere with the successful application of the functional-age intergenerational treatment model. To apply the model appropriately, the practitioner must avoid the tendency to accept unsubstantiated ideas about the aged. To this end, the following fallacies and facts are provided.

Countertransference

Freud (1920/1966) was among the first to focus on how the interpersonal experiences between patient and therapist affect therapy. Freud contended that for treatment to be effective, a patient's irrational feelings for the therapist—*transference*—and the therapist's inappropriate responses—*countertransference*—need to be examined. He believed that the curative nature of therapy itself stems from the analysis of the emotional exchange between patient and practitioner. Historically, countertransference was defined as the therapist's distorted reactions to the client. These distortions are based on the therapist's past parental relationships, rather than on the real attributes of the client. Irrational feelings toward the client may include anxiety, anger, defensiveness, and oversolicitousness.

The idea that all personal relationships are patterned after people's past relationships with significant others has been a dominant theme in psychiatric and social work literature. Over the past two decades, the concept of countertransference has remained useful and continues to be redefined to include additional interactional aspects of therapy (McInnis-Dittrich, 2002). For example, Muslin and Clark (1988) cautioned therapists to broadly consider their "civilian reactions" or nontherapeutic responses to the client (p. 58), whereas Lang (1974) viewed countertransference behaviors as disturbances in the communication process.

Table 2.1
Myths of Aging Checklist

Biological Myths

- Getting older means a life fraught with physical complaints and illness.
- Old people are not attractive people. They smell, have no teeth, can hardly see or hear, and are underweight.
- Old people should not exert themselves; they may have a heart attack or fall and break a bone.
- Old people sleep all the time.
- Sex ends at sixty. Older persons are asexual, have no interest in sex, and are unable to function as sexual beings.

Psychological Myths

- Most people are set in their ways and unable to change.
- Old age is a time of relative peace and tranquility when people can relax and enjoy the fruits of their labor after the stresses of life have passed.
- Old people are unresponsive to therapy.
- Senility is inevitable in old age.
- Older people cannot learn anything new. Intelligence declines with advancing age.
- Old people cannot solve day-to-day problems.

Social Myths

- Old people are dependent and need someone to take care of them. The elderly are dependent but socially isolated and neglected by their families.
- Older people inevitably withdraw from the mainstream of society as they grow older.
- The elderly neither can nor want to work. Old people are poor people.
- The elderly desire to be left alone and spend most of their time watching television.
- Most elderly are abused and neglected.
- Generation gaps lead to alienation of the elderly.
- Older people cannot learn anything new. Intelligence declines with advancing age.
- Old people cannot solve day-to-day problems.

Social Myths

- Old people are dependent and need someone to take care of them. The elderly are dependent but socially isolated and neglected by their families.
- Older people inevitably withdraw from the mainstream of society as they grow older.
- The elderly neither can nor want to work. Old people are poor people.
- The elderly desire to be left alone and spend most of their time watching television.
- Most elderly are abused and neglected.
- Generation gaps lead to alienation of the elderly.

Schneider & Kropf (1992, pp. 33-55).

Parsons (1951), a sociologist who contributed a classical view of societal structures, suggests still another view of countertransference. His viewpoint implies that the therapeutic relationship is a social system of complementary roles. Therefore, client and therapist bring preestablished attitudes, beliefs, and expectations of how each person should behave in the helping process. In addition, family therapists, such as White and Epson (1990), have cautioned that practitioners may bring negative societal attitudes involving gender, sexual orientation, age, ethnicity, and so forth to the client-therapist relationship. These biases can also distort the therapeutic conversation.

Death anxiety, while not strictly considered a countertransference phenomenon, can play an important role in practitioners' attitudes toward their older clients. *Death anxiety* is "an emotional reaction involving subjective feelings of unpleasant concern based on contemplation or anticipation of any of the several facets related to death (Hoelter, 1979, p. 996). Working with older adults often brings practitioners face-to-face with their own mortality. In this regard, Genevay (1990) reminded practitioners that "being professional is being human" (p. 36). She cautioned that there is no such phenomenon as professional perfection. Social workers may invest too much in "fixing clients" or find that a client's death mirrors something familiar in how a loved one died (p. 34).

As can be seen in the following example, these experiences with life struggles can be met with ambivalence, fear, denial, concern, anxiety, or acceptance:

Mrs. T., a social worker at a nursing home for many years, received a request to help plan for a living will with an alert resident and her husband (Mr. and Mrs. Q.). Mrs. T. felt she would have no difficulty with this request because her many years of experience had allowed her to develop a "comfortable philosophy about death with dignity." However, during several peer supervision group discussions she said "I am strongly against heroic measures such as forced feeding."

As the details of the situation emerged, Mrs. T. learned that Mrs. Q. had a tracheotomy, had a gastroscopy, and was constantly on oxygen. There was also a history of mental illness. The resident had required a round-the-clock companion for the last 2½ years. In discussions with Mr. T., her husband, the social worker found that "his questions could only be answered medically." Mrs. Q., who could speak only using a "special buzzing electrical device," had not been brought into the discussion. The husband felt that his wife's life should not be prolonged through hospitalization but was not sure he was "making the right decision." Mr. Q. sought out the social worker several times to ask questions about "the arrangements." "Will my wife be in pain?" "Will I have to give permission at the time of the medical emergency?" He was referred back to the physician for "correct information."

Mrs. T. said she had serious questions about her social worker role. Should she "impose her views about not keeping people alive under such untenable situations?"

The group supported her by suggesting that the social work role was to help Mr. Q explore the emotional component of this seemingly medical matter. Questions were also raised about why Mrs. Q. was not participating in the decision. The group concluded that intellectually Mr. Q. appeared to have realized that he did not want his wife rushed to the hospital if her present supports were not sufficient to sustain her. However, emotionally he was not prepared to face that eventuality. Once the social worker could sort out her own anxieties about imposing her views, she would be better prepared to help Mr. Q. examine his feelings. The social worker indicated that the peer group discussion had served as a catalyst to seek further supervision when needed.

Ethical Issues

Geriatric social workers often practice in settings in which ethical issues are likely to occur, such as the right to forego life-sustaining treatment (Moody, 1994; President's Commission for the study of ethical problems in medicine and biomedical and behavioral research, 1983). Such situations require ongoing discussion and may necessitate the use of ethical assessments tools (Corey, Corey & Callanan, 1993; Dolgoff, Loewenberg & Harrington, 2005; Figure 2.1).

For example, Elaine Congress (1999) developed a five-step model to help social workers resolve ethical dilemmas called ETHIC:

Examine relevant personal, societal, agency, client, and professional values.

Think about what ethical standard of the NASW *Code of Ethics* (NASW, 1996) applies to the situation, and consider relevant laws and case decisions.

Hypothesize about possible consequences of different decisions.

Identify who will benefit and who will be harmed in view of social work's commitment to the most vulnerable people.

Consult with one's supervisor and colleagues about the most ethical choice (pp. 31–33).

Supervision and Peer Support

Supervision can help practitioners better understand why they may have difficulty being effective with a particular client family and what they can do to promote a more professional response. It may also provide the opportunity to discuss ethical issues. Supervision as it has been traditionally practiced had its origins in the Charity Organization Society movement in the nineteenth century. During that time there was a concern that limited funds go to the neediest families. Financial aid was given only after a lengthy investigation, with the initial assessment conducted

Figure 2. 1.
Ethical Assessment Screen

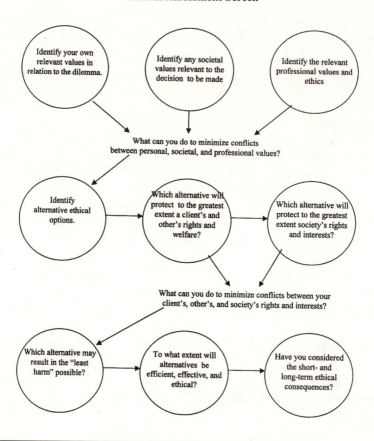

Source adapted from: Dolgoff, R., Loewenberg, F. M., & Harrington, D. (2005). Ethical decisions for social work practice (7th ed.). Belmont, CA: Brooks/Cole–Thomson Learning, p. 60.

by a paid employee of the Society. In addition to receiving financial assistance, families were visited by volunteers who offered personal support and "moral counseling." These "friendly visitors" discussed their cases with paid personnel who, in turn, discussed their disposition with district committees. As the first supervisory structure, this system provided a basis for decision making, gave continuity to the work of staff and volunteers, offered an administrative point of contact, and served as a channel of communication (Kadushin & Kadushin, 1997).

The supervisory conference has remained an important social work function (Fox, 1988). The intent of supervision is to help the social worker better accomplish his or her job within an agency framework. Most social workers become familiar with supervision as students in field practicum. The purpose of reviewing student work is to teach practice knowledge, skills, and techniques. Supervision generally continues in some form throughout the social worker's professional career and serves three major purposes: *Supervision* is (a) an administrative activity; (b) an educational process; and (c) a means of support. Other purposes are to assure that the mandate of the organization is properly carried out; to evaluate the work of supervisees, to guarantee the best quality service for agency clients; to support practitioner efforts, and to reduce practitioner stress and maximize job satisfaction or performance (Shulman, 1995). The supervisory process usually involves a structured learning situation that facilitates the development of the social worker's professional expertise through self-understanding, self-awareness, and emotional growth.

In agencies where supervision is minimal, similar functions can be achieved (or supplemented) through peer support. Such supervision provided by colleagues can help professionals prevent job-related stress and *burnout*, a syndrome of emotional exhaustion resulting from excessive demands being placed on the practitioner's energy, strength, and resources. Social workers should not be embarrassed to take sick leave or vacation time off to regain their sense of balance. Other means of dealing with situations in which the social worker is not an appropriate therapist include transferring the client to another social worker (Genevay & Katz, 1990).

The Functional Age Model at Intake

Intake has been defined as a process in which a request is made by or on behalf of a prospective client and a decision is made about the disposition of the application (Northen, 1995). During the intake process, the social worker and client explore the potential areas of work and the nature of the helping process (Shulman, 2005). While many agencies no longer use the term intake, the initial client interviews still focus on clarifying the purposes of social work interventions. Increasingly, social workers do not engage in a fact-finding exercise but concentrate on obtaining a dynamic picture of the client in interaction with others (see chapter 3). Social workers also clarify their role and indicate how and in what ways they may be helpful.

Although intake procedures with the aged and their families are in some respects similar to those used with other client groups, there are important differences. This chapter focuses on some of the special considerations related to the initial contacts with older adults and their families. It also provides specific suggestions for using the functional-age model of intergenerational treatment as a framework at this critical stage of intervention.

Formulating Questions at Intake

Practitioners and students alike are often puzzled by what questions to ask during the first interviews: Should I encourage the client to talk? Should I interrupt with a question? Is some information more relevant than other information? What do I need to know about the client to properly understand the problem? Questions such as these can be answered more easily if the social worker comes to the initial contact with an assessment and treatment practice framework.

Having an assessment and treatment orientation is one of the most critical aspects of the professional use of self and is first put into action at intake. Such a frame of reference provides the social worker with a theoretical foundation that, with mutual input from the client-family, shapes the direction of his or her therapeutic activity. Having such a model and a working knowledge of its assumptions offers those much needed guidelines about whom to include in the interview and how to conduct it. For example, the functional-age model suggests that if a family operates as a social system, then the practitioner must retain that mindset throughout the social work process. Questions at intake should be focused on learning how family members perceive their concerns, how members interact as a unit, and so on.

For example, in a situation in which a daughter requests Meals-on-Wheels for her father, both family members would be considered part of the client system. In some situations, other siblings or members of the daughter's family, perhaps even a close neighbor, would be included. The request would be explored from both the father's and daughter's perspective to better understand the presenting concern and its effects on the family. Social work goals would be mutually agreed upon, with the older person (as pivotal client) taking as active a role as possible.

With a theoretical practice model, the social worker has a guide to help with professional decisions: What questions can be asked? Who should be requested to attend an interview? What should be the location of the interview? The practitioner who believes in family-focused social work strives to promote the interdependence of the family group and seeks to reinforce reciprocity among its members. Therefore, the social worker's activities, interventions, and use of resources build on the strengths of the family group. The functional age practice model offers more than just a philosophical stance. It is a point of departure in helping a client find solutions for his or her problem.

Although maintaining an interview focus is the social worker's responsibility, it is the client family that provides the information about the problems of daily living. From the initial contact, the social worker perceives and uses client information differently, depending on his or her treatment orientation. From a systems point of view, a practitioner uses the theory to develop "hypotheses" about the nature of the concerns presented by the client system. The practitioner interprets the information gathered as it relates to both the problem(s) and the course of treatment. At the same time, the client amends the description of the situation as new information is presented and as circumstances change (Silverstone & Burack-Weiss, 1983). Practitioners who use narrative approaches may gain their information by listening to client stories (White & Epson, 1990). However, the client's feedback suggests what additional information must be gathered to complete the assessment in an integrated form (see chapters 3 to 5).

Assessment begins with the first intake interview, whether it takes place by phone or in person. At that time, the social worker needs to have a beginning idea of what it is he or she hopes to accomplish, what information he or she needs to obtain, and what plan for successive interviews he or she plans to put into action. For example, if there might be a need to see the family together or make a home visit. Parameters for this social work activity can be derived from the functional-age model. The model suggests that when there is an important change in an older adult's biopsychosocial and spiritual functioning, a family crisis is precipitated. Therefore, the crisis can best be resolved through family-focused assessment and treatment modalities. Consequently, the social worker must be prepared at intake to begin gathering and evaluating pertinent information about the older adult and the developmental and systems properties of the family.

The following situation illustrates how the functional-age model can serve as a framework for the practitioner at intake:

Mrs. G. called the intake worker of an Atlanta family service agency and requested a list of senior citizen apartments for her 85-year-old mother, Mrs. S., who lived in New York. The daughter sounded upset and indicated that she had just received a phone call from her mother's neighbor who said, "Mrs. S. is always wandering around 'lost.' You are her daughter. Why don't you come up here and get her!"

The social worker suggested that Mrs. G. might want to come into the agency to get the housing information and to discuss her concerns. The intake interview obtained the following information: Mrs. S., the oldest of ten children, was the only member of her extended family to migrate to the United States from Italy. She raised Mrs. G., an only child, "single-handedly," as she was widowed when Mrs. G. was only 3 years old. Mrs. G. described her mother as "fiercely independent and hard working," struggling as a laundress and taking in extra ironing to save for Mrs. G.'s college education. Having retired only 6 years ago, Mrs. S. still lived in the same apartment in the old neighborhood. There were several friends who "looked in" on her, and she knew most of the neighborhood shopkeepers.

Mrs. G. was very concerned about "what to do with her mother." She said that she visited her several times a year, and, within the next few weeks, was going to New York to bring her mother to Atlanta for her usual summer visit. She was thinking of "just packing up the apartment and bringing Mother to Atlanta permanently." The social worker suggested that Mrs. G. not "hurry things along" and offered to meet with them both before any action was taken. The social worker also explained some of the dynamics of uprooting an older person, especially if he or she had not participated in the decision. The possibility of establishing a more structured helping network in New York comprised of neighbors and friends was also suggested.

When Mrs. G. returned with her mother from New York, she called to request an appointment "only for herself." "You won't believe what my mother's apartment was like. Even worse than last time." Assuring Mrs. G. that "it would be okay to discuss this with her mother present," the social worker requested that Mrs. G. ask her mother to join them.

As they entered the office, Mrs. G. said, "Mother came with me today, but I doubt if it will do much good. She insists that she can only speak and understand Italian." Turning her head toward Mrs. S., the caseworker said she knew only a little Italian and raised her eyebrows as if to say, "What do we do now?" Mrs. S. replied, "That's all right, dear. I'll speak English for you." The social worker used that opportunity to ask Mrs. S. if she would be willing to explain what it was like to live in the "old neighborhood."

Mrs. S. went into detail about each of her neighbors, explaining how they had seen Mrs. G. grow up to be a college-educated woman with children of her own. Mrs. S. said that "there was no way she could imagine life without them; nor could she live in an area where she could not buy 'real' Italian vegetables and meats." How would she manage without St. Patrick's Cathedral?

With some prompting by the social worker, Mrs. G. said she felt she could not let her mother go back to her apartment in New York. "Mama, you've let it get so run-down! I would be worried about you." The social worker acknowledged their feelings and asked if there might be a resolution that would satisfy them both. She encouraged mother and daughter to discuss solutions with each other and make suggestions, describing programs such as homemaker services, community helping networks, and friendly visiting. She also stressed the importance of Mrs. S.'s receiving a medical examination.

Mrs. S. was persuaded to follow up and received a complete physical. The doctor concluded that Mrs. S. had not been receiving a proper diet and could benefit from a more structured meal plan. The social worker was given permission to talk with the physician and then met with the family twice more. Using the information she had collected about the family, the social worker was able to help them arrive at a plan:

Mrs. S. would return to New York where one of her Italian neighbors would "share" the cooking responsibilities with her. Mrs. S. also agreed to obtain homemaker services once every 2 weeks so that her "daughter would not worry."

Satisfactory and speedy resolution of this situation was possible because the social worker was able to use her listening and assessment skills to facilitate timely decision making. She initiated and maintained a family-centered approach and quickly moved to engage both mother and daughter in the decision-making process. The social worker's interview focus permitted her to redefine the daughter's concern in family terms. She also obtained a brief history about living in the old neighborhood to better understand how past events affected present day client-system functioning. Biological, sociocultural, psychological, and spiritual factors were all taken into account. The family established treatment goals with the pivotal client taking the lead and the social worker making suggestions.

Intake and assessment are not clearly delineated phases. Despite this fact, illustrated by the above family situation, there are questions that need to be answered as early as possible in the helping process: What was the precipitating event that brought the client(s) to the attention of the agency? How does the request for service reflect the family's concern? How can the precipitating event be understood from a cultural and family perspective? Who are the persons who constitute the client-family system and the support network?

As the interviews move into the assessment and treatment phases, the social worker should be able to organize and interpret this information with the family. The assessment needs to contain a description of the family viewpoint of presenting issues. Assessment also describes how the change(s) in the functional capacities of the older adult have altered the balance within the family system. In this way, interventions and services to help restore individual and family functioning can be introduced. Incorporating feedback from the client family is essential to the selection of effective interventions. That is, a central treatment goal is arriving at a family-focused biopsychosocial and spiritual assessment acceptable to the client.

Expectations Concerning the Helping Process

The intake interview begins before the participants meet. Before the social worker and client see each other for the first time, the social worker has a preestablished framework to guide the establishment of the therapeutic relationship; a client family brings expectations or preconceptions to the helping process. A client's decision to contact the agency is often the result of a series of complex, interrelated factors. The client family that comes to a social service agency already has some idea of what they want, "a conception of a better tomorrow" (Perlman, 1957, p. 33). They bring with them expectations concerning the nature of the agency and the role of the helping professional, and they often make concrete requests that reflect their thoughts about a solution to the problem. "Is my mother eligible for a day-care center with Spanish-speaking staff?" "Can you refer my father to a senior housing project in his old neighborhood?" "Can your agency provide my grandmother with a kosher Meals-on-Wheels program?"

Problems of living brought to social services agencies are complicated and multifaceted. At the same time, clients often describe their concerns in a specific manner that may reflect their general expectations for help and already-tried but failed solutions. That is, clients often presume that the practitioner will provide a specific service or help them make particular arrangements. When the social worker creates a distinction between requests for concrete versus therapeutic services, he or she establishes a false dichotomy. It is important for the social worker to look beyond the specific request to understand how a particular service is perceived by the client. If the social worker pays sufficient attention to the request and explores the full ramifications of the situation with the family, they can mutually decide if a request is appropriate. In most instances, geriatric social work involves a complex interweaving of what Richmond (1922) termed "direct counseling" and "indirect action."

The social work principle of "starting where the client is" suggests that the practitioner ask why a family has arrived at a particular solution for their relative. Including specific questions in early interviews can often provide needed information and, at the same time, lessen family concern. The following are examples of such questions asked of a mother and daughter who made a homemaker request:

(For the daughter who has initiated contact): What makes you feel your mother needs a homemaker? Have you tried other ways of helping her, such as other services? Can you tell me what she is not able to do now that she was able to do previously? How would a homemaker help you as her daughter? Does your mother know of your concern and thoughts about obtaining a homemaker?

(For the mother): Do you know that your daughter is concerned about how you are managing? How did you feel about your daughter calling us? How do you think you are managing here in your apartment? Are there any difficulties? Do you know about our agency and what we do? Are there ways you think the agency could help you?

The way a family tackles an issue reflects the nature of their inter-personal relationships and their developmental history. Before the client contacted the agency, these relationships may have been taxed by the task of caregiving over an extended period of time and by difficulties brought to the surface during the crisis situation. At intake, the practitioner may observe unresolved issues come to the fore. The social worker should listen carefully for clues to the nature of such family relationships as they affect the family's views of the agency, their expectations of the worker, and their potential for involvement in treatment: "My mother always has been demanding." "Dad and I never were really close." "My brother and I never have seen eye-to-eye about our mother." "You know, I really never liked my mother, nor she me. My sister is going to have to take care of her now."

Expectations about the social worker and the agency are also shaped by cultural norms. Membership in an ethnic or minority group (culture) can influence the client's perception of the issues and his or her outlook about treatment. Unfortunately, many programs and services for the elderly are primarily designed to meet the needs of the majority population and do not consider the heterogeneous nature of the older population (Green, 1995). When inappropriate or unacceptable services and programs are offered to minority elderly persons, such discrimination becomes an obstacle to treatment. The social worker can sometimes ameliorate such difficulties at intake by assessing and treating problems of living in culturally relevant terms.

The expectations that clients have about the agency and the helping process are usually best dealt with in a straightforward manner. Clients should be encouraged to express their concerns, doubts, and fears about treatment and agency services. This is not easily accomplished, as clients may be reluctant to share information, particularly if the social worker is seen as an authority figure. However, the social work process rests on the ability of the practitioner to hear the client's story and to demonstrate that she or he has sufficient interest and professional competence to help.

Although establishing of a helping relationship at intake is strongly influenced by the client's preconceived ideas about the treatment process, the social worker's professional skills, values, and attitudes are equally important. Practitioners' ideas and values about themselves as helping professionals are a product of their individual and professional socialization. These values set the stage for practice and affect the quality of social work intervention. For example, the belief in self-determination suggests that a client has the right to make his or her own decisions and choose among alternatives. Putting this into practice can present difficulties when there is lack of agreement between the values of the social worker and the perceptions of the client, as in the following situation:

> Mrs. C., an "eccentric" 88-year-old woman, lived alone in a two-bedroom house with an estimated 35 cats. She had been known for many years to the family service agency and the Department of Human Services. Periodically, these agencies would receive complaints from her neighbors about her "deplorable living conditions."
>
> Mrs. C. came to know one of the "young sweet social workers" whom she would allow, on occasion, to enter her home. While the social worker considered the house to be in "a most unsatisfactory condition" from her own viewpoint, she nonetheless observed that Mrs. C. was able to take care of her personal needs, including hygiene and meal management. Mrs. C. also indicated that she would resist any efforts to "make her go to one of those old age homes." Attempts by the neighbors to have Mrs. C. declared a "protective service case" were not followed through, as it became evident that Mrs. C. was capable of making her own decisions.
>
> This stance was severely tested one very cold winter, when neighbors learned that the heat had been turned off because Mrs. C. had forgotten to pay the bill. Once the bill was paid, the gas company refused to reenter the home to turn the heat back on unless the house was cleaned first. The social worker, who was concerned because of the below-freezing temperatures, made a home visit. She brought several blankets with her, knowing she might fail to convince Mrs. C. to stay at a hotel or shelter until the heat could be turned back on.
>
> At first, Mrs. C. refused to leave the house or even to allow a cleaning service to enter. However, the social worker was able to draw on her previous experiences and positive relationship with her client. She outlined the alternatives to Mrs. C. in an honest, direct fashion, making it clear that there "is no way I can just walk away and allow you to freeze. What should we do?" Mrs. C. decided to permit the cleaning crew in the next day but said she "would only pay for 3 hours of service." She thanked the social worker for the blankets, which she used that night.

Situations such as these test the caseworker's ability to walk that fine line between a client's right to self-determination and a decision that is not consistent with client safety and welfare. Far too often, in such situations there are no clear-cut right or wrong answers. Peer supervision and support can be critical in resolving such dilemmas about "what is best for the client."

Another potentially thorny intake issue involves the development of treatment goals and objectives. There is a growing body of literature indicating that the elderly respond positively to interventions that call on them to play an active role in decision making, often with the participation of family members (High, 1988). Most elderly clients, while frightened by illness or advancing frailty, prefer that the least restrictive measures be taken to assure their safety. Difficulties in the client-social worker relationship are more likely to occur when goals are not established mutually. If goals solely reflect the family's or the social worker's viewpoint, treatment can be adversely affected. The following example illustrates the need to establish mutual goals on a person-by-person basis:

Mrs. B. was brought to the attention of a family service agency by her son, who was concerned about her recently diagnosed "heart problem." Mrs. B. was vague about her condition but said it meant she could "no longer be on my own." Upon hearing her medical diagnosis, Mrs. B. gave up her apartment in Florida, where she had retired, and shipped all her belongings to her son's home.

Mrs. B. lived with her son for a short time, but problems with his wife, her daughter-in-law, led the son to contact the agency for "help in locating an apartment for my mother."

During the time that housing was being sought, there were reportedly many disagreements and difficulties between the son's mother and wife. The son, who called the agency daily, was sure everything would be okay as soon as "mother has a place of her own." Because Mrs. B. said she "only wanted to be out of my daughter-in-law's kitchen" the social worker assumed that Mrs. B. wanted to have her own apartment. The social worker proceeded to help Mrs. B. find "suitable housing."

In the next 2 years, Mrs. B. tried several different living arrangements, moving from her own private apartment to a shared duplex, and finally to sheltered housing that provided meals and a daytime nurse. Each move followed a series of "attacks" for which "no physical cause" could be found. Mrs. B. would call her son in the middle of the night, describing a "pounding of her heart." He would meet her in the hospital emergency room where the doctors would reassure Mrs. B. and her son that she had not suffered a heart attack. The son finally became desperate when the housing manager, troubled by the repeated appearance of rescue vehicles and personnel, asked Mrs. B. to move.

The social worker decided to have a family meeting to deal with the crisis. She encouraged everyone to openly express what they thought would best solve the problem. She herself admitted that she was "at a loss as to how Mrs. B. could continue in her own place." The son pointed out that he too "felt like a failure in trying to help preserve my mother's sense of independence." The social worker then asked Mrs. B. what she felt was the best solution based on her life's experience. "What were the happiest days of your life?" Mrs. B. said that one of her best memories was when she "had tuberculosis at the age of 12." She described how she was nursed back to health by her mother, who allowed her to "sit under a tree in summer and sip lemonade and eat cake." The social worker asked what the equivalent would be for Mrs. B. at age 75. She replied, "Sitting in the beautiful lobby of the [nursing] home."

Once the family and social worker were able to hear Mrs. B.'s story, they were prepared to help her in a way that was congruent with her needs. When she knew she would not be cared for in her son's home, she set her own alternative—moving to a community-sponsored nursing home, which she perceived as nurturing, safe, and secure. The social worker's strong preference for independent living biased the intake and assessment process. By listening more carefully to Mrs. B's story, the social worker realized that she had impeded earlier resolution of the problem by basing interventions on her own values rather than those of the client. This case illustrates that client values, expectations, and concerns can be understood only if practitioners first understand their own issues (in this case independence) in the helping relationship.

Beginning the Helping Process

Agencies serving the aged are usually approached in a variety of indirect processes rather than through direct contact by the older person (Silverstone & Burack-Weiss, 1983). Despite their growing number and their increased risk of mental disorder, the elderly are reluctant to seek help and continue to be underserved by mental health workers (Gatz, 1995). Many elderly people associate social work services with "the poor" or "those unable to cope with adversity." Practitioners should learn early in the helping process how the older adult came to the attention of the agency. The request for help may be initiated through a referral by another agency or program (nutrition site, golden age club or hospital), through calls by a concerned friend or relative, or through an outreach program of a community agency. In addition, the older client's initial contact with an agency may occur only after many unsuccessful attempts to handle a problem independently (Silverstone & Burack-Weiss, 1983).

There are no sure-fire lists of rules for intake (first) interviews. Nonetheless, the practitioner needs to keep in mind that one of its most crucial features is to achieve a consciously selected purpose (Cournoyer, 2000; Kadushin & Kadushin, 1997). Whatever form the request for service—whether by the older person or someone on his or her behalf—a practitioner's major goal during intake is to establish a working relationship with the older adult and, whenever possible, with the family. When a family member calls an agency about an older relative, the social worker needs to remember that the family is the client. Family-centered social work can best be achieved when the practitioner focuses intake questions on both the older adult's functional capacity and the family's adaptive response, as seen in the following example:

> An adult daughter called a social service agency to request "Meals-on-Wheels" for her recently widowed, 65-year-old father. During intake, the social worker kept in mind the relatively young age of the father, his cultural attitudes about his role, and the possible effects of loss on the family system. She explored the appropriateness of the request by inquiring about the father's ability to shop for himself, drive or walk to the grocery, and prepare meals.
>
> The social worker also inquired about the daughter's concerns. Did she take her father shopping or prepare his meals? How would she describe their relationship? How had the relationship changed following the death of her mother? The social worker also wanted to find out if the father knew of the daughter's call to the agency. The social worker's goal was to hold a joint interview, at which time she could further

explore the father's situation, observe the interaction between father and daughter, and explain the functions of the agency.

The social worker arranged to meet the daughter at the father's apartment to better assess his activities of daily living within the home environment. She learned that the father was agile and alert and was "keeping up" the apartment to his own satisfaction. He enjoyed shopping for groceries weekly with his daughter but seemed to call almost daily about a "forgotten item." He would keep the daughter on the phone for "long periods of time" about "small, unimportant matters."

As the social worker listened to the family, she wondered out loud if the father felt lonely and depressed following the death of his wife. Were his calls to the daughter about meal preparation an attempt to talk with her daily? Once the issue was reframed with the family, the social worker was better able to offer appropriate services, including grief counseling.

When an older person is referred to the agency by another family member or agency, social workers need to guard against designating the older adult as "a case." Rather, unless they learn otherwise, practitioners should assume that the older person is competent to understand the functions of the agency and to describe his or her own situation. While the social worker may wish to obtain additional information from other agencies after gaining permission from an older client, older adults are often best able to relate their own experiences. The following is an example of a woman referred to an adult assessment agency by the senior apartment's resident manager. The apartment manager described her as very confused and thought she needed a nursing home placement:

The resident manager of a senior citizens housing project, Mrs. T., called the intake service of an adult assessment agency. She requested help in "getting Mrs. L. out of the building, where she was a danger to herself and others," and into a nursing home facility. Mrs. T. said that Mrs. L. often sat in the lobby with a dazed look. That morning, Mrs. L. had left a pot on the stove too long and "had almost burned down the building." The manager stressed that Mrs. L. did not belong in a senior apartment "as she was no longer able to take care of herself."

The social worker indicated that she would need to talk with Mrs. L. before any plans could be made. She asked the apartment manager to inform Mrs. L. that the assessment agency had been contacted and that a social worker wanted to visit with her. The social worker followed up with a phone call to offer an appointment time and to assure Mrs. L. that she "wanted to hear her side of the story."

When the social worker arrived, Mrs. L. seemed somewhat confused and disoriented. However, when the social worker adjusted her interviewing pace to meet the client's needs, Mrs. L. was able to describe her situation. Mrs. L. indicated that she was a childless widow who had worked for the government for 40 years until her retirement. She had moved into the senior apartment building 5 years ago to be near her only relative, a niece, who had recently had cancer surgery. Mrs. L. "absolutely did not want to bother her niece with any problems." When the social worker asked what these problems might be, suggesting she might be able to help, Mrs. L. seemed relieved and anxious to talk. She said she had been very worried lately and wondered why she was always so tired. She explained that she usually read the paper daily, paid her own bills, and generally took care of her own affairs. For the last several months, she had noticed troubling changes. She fell asleep in the lobby, was thirsty, and had to urinate frequently. She repeated that she "did not want to trouble her niece."

The social worker who noted the changes in Mrs. L.'s physical as well as psychological functioning, suggested a medical examination. Mrs. L. was willing to make an appointment with her family physician if someone could provide transportation. The social worker arranged for a volunteer driver and encouraged Mrs. L. to talk with her niece about recent developments.

During the medical exam, lab tests indicated that Mrs. L. had diabetes, which quickly responded to a change in diet and proper medication. Mrs. L.'s mental functioning dramatically improved. At Mrs. L.'s request, the social worker then advocated with the resident manager for Mrs. L. to remain in the building.

In situations where the older person has been referred by the staff of another agency, it is important to respect the older person's right to privacy, confidentiality, and selection or rejection of service. In addition, not all family members may wish to be involved in planning for a relative; or the older person may refuse to involve his or her family. This, too, should be respected. Accustomed roles, old alliances, and communication patterns should be taken into account. Quick assessment of the nature of long-standing relationships can provide needed direction for the social worker in such circumstances. Inquiries about the client's expectations of the agency can also offer guidelines.

Interviewing Individuals and Families

The Social Work Interview

Practice experience suggests that geriatric social workers use a combination of interview styles. Some interviews, or parts of interviews, are more structured and purposive. Practitioners use their expertise of biopsychosocial and spiritual functioning to gather specific assessment facts and information. Other interviews are less structured and may follow the client's lead. In this instance, the social worker is listening to client stories. In each instance, there is an agreement about client meaning and assessment. All social work interview approaches, whether the theory base is psychoanalytic, Rogerian, behavioral, or so forth, use questions, summaries, transitions, reflection, and silences as techniques and are based on a client-social worker relationship. The general purpose of most social work interviews is to gather information or conduct a social study, to make an assessment or arrive at an understanding of the client, and to be therapeutic or effect change (see Cournoyer, 2000; Kadushin & Kadushin, 1997; Northen, 1995; Shulman, 2005).

Interviews with Families

The theoretical orientation in family systems therapy tends toward interviewing the whole family group. In practice, however, while some family therapists confine themselves exclusively to interviews with the entire family, others may work with one person, emphasizing a family focus, and still others may work with various combinations of selected family members. In social work with the aged and their families, the decision of who to include in the interviews has to be flexible. Sometimes the older person may have no immediate family; in other situations the family may be estranged or physically unavailable. There are also times when assessment considerations suggest working with the individual alone (maintaining the goal of understanding the elderly client within a family perspective).

Such seemingly procedural questions are often decided by the social worker's preference, or even bias, for or against family therapy. Clients rarely experience their problems as located within the total family. It is the therapist who communicates this orientation and helps each family member see "the concern" as a "family concern." By asking to meet with the whole family, the practitioner creates (a) the opportunity for members to communicate and listen to each other and (b) challenges the family's capacities for decision making and change (Walsh, 2006). However, the social worker first must be convinced of the value of this approach and impart it to the family. Some possible ways of accomplishing this are

"Please join us at our first meeting. We'd like your point of view. Your input will be valuable to the family."

"I'd like to hear from everyone in the family."

"In my experience, I have found it most helpful to hear from everyone. Can you meet with us at least one time to give us your ideas?"

There are many benefits to be gained from conducting a family group interview. Family interviews can help the social worker understand each family member in terms of his or her own personality, and in terms of his or her relationship to other family members. Family transactions and alignments among members can be observed in the "here and now." Family interviews can also assist the family in learning about their patterns of communication and interaction and can give them the chance to direct their energies to a combined resolution of the problem (Greene, 1989).

The practitioner puts a family focus into motion at intake, when the family is most mobilized to deal with the crisis at hand. If despite the social worker's efforts the family does not wish to participate, care should be taken to understand the older client's role in the family from that person's perspective (Walker, Pratt & Eddy, 1995). The impression should not be conveyed that older adults do not request counseling or other services for themselves. They do:

> Mrs. C. called a family service agency requesting an appointment to talk with a social worker. She explained that while her husband had died over 2 years ago, she recently felt very depressed and found herself "crying at the drop of a hat." Mrs. C. said that she had managed to get through the first few months after Mr. C.'s death by just functioning day to day. Gradually, she returned to her usual activities and routine but had recently found she did not want to go anywhere.
>
> Several family members had encouraged Mrs. C. to seek help. Her adult daughter, who lived locally, insisted that she had "to get out and do things" and could not understand why her mother continued to be so upset. When her son came to town on a business trip, he noticed her depression and suggested she go to a United Way Agency. Mrs. C.'s sister-in-law also came to visit and was concerned. During their conversations, Mrs. C. said she came to realize that she still did not believe her husband was dead. It was as if he "might still walk through the door." "When I spoke of my husband, I never said, 'Harold is dead' or 'My husband died.' But rather, 'My darling left me' or 'My sweetheart is gone.' These realizations, recalled at the initial interview, led Mrs. C. to seek counseling.
>
> Other pertinent information was elicited during the intake interviews: Mrs. C. was one of four siblings. Following her marriage to Mr. C., she moved away from her hometown. She was the only family member to do so, and her parents were very reluctant to see her go. Mrs. C. tried to get her parents to visit her, but they never did. Two years after Mrs. C. and her husband moved to the Midwest, Mrs. C.'s father died. She "confessed" to the social worker that she "still felt guilty about leaving home, and knew my father's health began to deteriorate soon after I left."
>
> Mrs. C.'s most pressing present concern was her relationship with her daughter, Joan. What Mrs. C. described as a "close, model mother-daughter relationship" had changed since Mr. C.'s death. Joan was "not very patient and was easily aggravated." While her son often talked about Mr. C. and how much he had loved his father, Joan had never discussed the loss. Mrs. C. was sure her daughter "was just not dealing with her father's death."

While Mrs. C. was seen for individual counseling, the social worker obtained a picture of her past and present relationships. This information provided both the therapist and client with an awareness of family patterns in dealing with death. This, in turn, led to an understanding of the dynamics of Mrs. C.'s depression and the selection of appropriate interventions. In effect, the social worker was able to conduct family-focused interviews without other family members being physically present.

For older adults who have no significant others, information regarding their family of origin is a vital part of the biopsychosocial assessment. The social worker should also obtain a history of relationships at work and in neighborhood settings. The older client who is truly an isolate is rare. When there are no naturally occurring relationships, practitioners can explore providing a friendly visitor or creating a neighborhood-family network.

Whether an interview be with an individual or a family group, there are some special considerations in interviewing frail or ill elderly clients. Geriatric social workers often find themselves in a variety of nontraditional interview settings with older adults who may have limiting, and sometimes multiple, impairments. This requires that the interviewer have special sensitivity, flexibility, and skill. Even in the most complex situations, it is usually possible for the therapist to elicit needed information from the older client in a manner that respects his or her dignity and in a manner that assures his or her participation in decision making and planning.

Forming a Professional Relationship

The professional relationship—the interactional and emotional bond between the client and the therapist (Perlman, 1957)—has been considered "the soul of social casework" (Biestek, 1957, p. 3). In fact, many treatment models, including the one presented in this text, suggest that the helping relationship is the basis for therapeutic growth and change (Rogers, 1957; White & Epson, 19). For example, Perlman (1957) said "the relationship was the enabling dynamic in the problem-solving method, and the "glue" of the social work process" (p. 33). She argued that it is only through a trusting relationship that the client knows that she is working with someone who is concerned about her welfare. Nowhere is this more true than in social work with older adults.

Empathy, Warmth, and Genuine Regard

Forty years of outcomes research suggests that the relationship is a principal element of therapy that accounts for client improvement. The research suggests that the helping process is a form of healing with Rogers's core ingredients necessary to *any* form of successful intervention (Asay & Lambert, 1999; Hubble, Duncan & Miller, 1999). Rogers (1957, 1967), the theorists most associated with relationship formation, asserted that a client's natural capacity for change can be mobilized through a caring helping relationship characterized by empathy, warmth, and genuineness.

Empathy, the ability or capacity of the social worker to deal sensitively and accurately with the client's feelings and experiences, enables the practitioner to enter into the client's world through his or her own imagination. *Nonpossessive warmth*, the practitioner's acceptance of the client as an individual, provides the client a nurturing but nonpatronizing and nondominating environment; whereas *genuineness*, the social worker's capacity to be open or real with the client, demonstrates a practitioner's willingness to acknowledge and address feelings about the client.

Contemporary theorists (O'Hanlon, 1993) continue to base their methods on Rogers's optimistic view of the therapeutic relationship. For example, O'Hanlon (1993) developed *possibility therapy*—a method by which the client is validated and valued, whereas Tice and Perkins (1996) proposed a strengths perspective in which the client is recognized as expert. They suggested that a practitioner can put the client in the position of expert by

- maintaining a positive and affirmative attitude toward the client;
- engaging in active listening related to concerns and possibilities;
- conducting client meetings in familiar environments;
- talking candidly about client behavior and activities;
- remaining nonjudgmental;
- expressing a willingness to assist; and
- initiating action according to client directions (p. 40).

While the concept of the therapist-client relationship has always been central to most social work methods, family therapists have emphasized different aspects of the relationship. Family therapists, who are primarily concerned with educating the family group about its dysfunctions and improving communication among family members, often see themselves as consultants, facilitators, or coaches. The efforts of the therapist are directed toward observing patterns of behavior and confronting members in the "here-and-now" to help the group deal with presenting concerns. The practitioner is careful not to "favor" or form a special relationship with one family member over another unless that is part of a planned therapeutic technique. The functional-age model of intergenerational family treatment model offers the social worker a number of such family therapy techniques (see chapter 8), and it also emphasizes the need for a caring, mutual client-social worker relationship.

References

Asay, T. P., & Lambert, M. J. (1999). The empirical case for the common factors in therapy: Quantitative findings. In M. A. Hubble, B. L. Duncan, & D. Miller (Eds.), *The heart & soul of change* (pp. 23–55). Washington, DC: APA Press.

Biestek, F. B. (1957). *The casework relationship.* Chicago: Loyola University.

Birren, J. E., & Sloane, R. B. (Eds.). (1969). *Handbook of mental health and aging.* Englewood Cliffs, NJ: Prentice Hall.

Blum, N. (1991). The management of stigma by Alzheimer family caregivers. *Journal of Contemporary Ethnography, 20,* 263-258.

Butler, R. N. (1963). The life review: An interpretation of reminiscence in the aged. *Psychiatry, 26,* 65-76.

Butler, R. N. (1968). Toward a psychiatry of the life cycle: Implications of sociologic and psychologic studies of the aging process for the psychotherapeutic situation. In A. Simon & L. Epstein (Eds.), *Aging in modern society* (pp. 233-248). Washington, DC: American Psychiatric Association.

Butler, R. N. (1969). Directions in psychiatric treatment of the elderly: Role of perspectives of the life cycle. *The Gerontologist, 9,* 134-138.

Butler, R. N. (1975). *Why survive? Being old in America.* New York: Harper & Row.

Carter, B., & McGoldrick, M. (Eds.). (2005). *The expanded family life cycle: Individual, family, and social perspectives.* Boston: Allyn & Bacon.

Congress, E. P. (1999). *Social work values and ethics.* Belmont, CA: Wadsworth.

Corey, G., Corey, M., & Callanan, P. (1993). *Issues and ethics in the helping professions* (4th ed.). Pacific Grove, CA: Brooks/Cole.

Cournoyer, B. (2000). *The social work skills workbook* (3rd ed.). Belmont, CA: Thompson Brooks/Cole.

Dolgoff, R., Loewenberg, F. M., & Harrington, D. (2005). *Ethical decisions for social work practice* (7th ed.). Belmont, CA: Brooks/Cole–Thomson Learning.

Fox, R. (1988). Relationship: The cornerstone of clinical supervision. *Social Casework, 70,* 146-152.

Freud, S. (1920/1966). *Introductory lectures on psychoanalysis.* New York: W. W. Norton.

Gatz, M. (Ed.). (1995). *Emerging issues in mental health and aging.* Washington, DC: American Psychological Association.

Genevay, B. (1990). Creating a more humane dying. In B. Genevay & R. S. Katz (Eds.), *Countertransference and older clients* (pp. 28-39). Newbury Park, CA: Sage.

Germain, C. B. (1994). Human behavior in the social environment. In F. G. Reamer (Ed.), *The foundations of social work knowledge* (pp. 88-121). New York: Columbia University Press.

Grant, L. D. (1994). Effects of ageism on individual and health care providers' response to healthy aging. *Health and Social Work, 21*(1), 9-16.

Green, J. (1995). *Cultural awareness in the human services.* Englewood Cliffs, NJ: Prentice-Hall.

Greene, R. R., & Blundo, R. (1999). Post modern critique of systems theory in social work with the aged and their families. *Journal of Gerontological Social Work, 31.*

Haraeven, T. K. (1996). *Aging and generational relations over the life course: A historical and cross-cultural perspective.* Hawthorne, NY: Aldine de Gruyter.

High, D. M. (1988). All in the family: Extended autonomy and expectations in surrogate health care decision making. *The Gerontologist, 28,* 46-51.

Hoelter, J. W. (1979). Multidimensional treatment of fear of death. *Journal of Consulting and Clinical Psychology, 47,* 996-999.

Hubble, M. A., Duncan, B. L., & Miller, S. (1999). *The heart & soul of change.* Washington, DC: APA Press.

Hummert, M. L., Shaner, J. L., Garstka, T. A., & Henry, C. (1998). Communication with older adults: The influence of age stereotypes, context, and communicator age. *Human Communication Research, 25,* 124-152.

Janoff-Bulman, R., & Berger, A. R. (2000). The other side of trauma: Towards a psychology of appreciation. In J. H. Harvey & E. D. Miller (Eds.), *Loss and trauma: General and close relationship perspectives* (pp. 29–44). Philadelphia: Brunner-Routledge.

Kadushin, A., & Kadushin, G. (1997). *The social work interview: A guide for human service professionals.* New York: Columbia University Press.

Lambert, M. J. (1992). Implications of outcome research for psychotherapy integration. In J. C. Norcross & M. R. Goldstein (Eds.), *Handbook of psychotherapy integration* (pp. 94–129). New York: Basic Books.

Langs, R. (1974). *The technique of psychoanalytic psychotherapy.* New York: Jason Aronson.

McInnis-Dittrich, K. (2002). *Social work with elders: A biopsychosocial approach.* Boston: Allyn & Bacon.

Moody, H. R. (1994). *Aging concepts and controversies.* Thousand Oaks, CA: Pine Forge Press.

Muslin, H., & Clarke, S. C. (1988). The inner world of the therapist of the elderly. *Clinical Gerontologist, 8,* 58-62.

Northen, H. (1995). *Clinical social work knowledge and skills.* New York: Columbia University Press.

O'Hanlon, W. H. (1993). Possibility therapy: From iatrogenic injury to iatrogenic healing. In S. Gilligan & R. Price (Eds.), *Therapeutic conversations* (pp. 3-21). New York: W. W. Norton.

Parsons, T. (1951). *The social system.* New York: Free Press.

Perlman, H. H. (1957). *Social casework: A problem-solving process.* Chicago: University of Chicago Press.

President's Commission for the Study of Ethical Problems in Medicine and Biomedical and Behavioral Research. (1983). *Deciding to forego life sustaining treatment.* Washington, DC: U. S. Government Printing Office.

Richmond, M. (1922). *What is social casework? An introductory description.* New York: Russell Sage Foundation.

Rogers, C. R. (1957). The necessary and sufficient condition of therapeutic personality change. *Journal of Consulting Psychology, 21,* 95-103.

Rogers, C. R. (1967). *The Therapeutic Relationship and Its Impact.* Madison: University of Wisconsin Press.

Rosen, H. (1996). Meaning-making narratives: Foundations for constructivist and social constructionist psychotherapies. In H. Rosen & K. T. Kuehlwein (Eds.), *Constructing realities: Meaning-making perspectives for psychotherapists* (pp. 3–51). San Francisco, CA: Jossey-Bass.

Schneider, R. J., & Kropf, N. P. (1992). *Gerontological social work.* Chicago: Nelson-Hall.

Shulman, L. (1995). Supervision and consultation. In R. Edwards (Ed.-in-Chief), *Encyclopedia of social work* (vol. 3, pp. 2373-2379).

Shulman, L. (2005). *The skills of helping individuals, families, groups, and communities.* New York: Wadsworth.

Silverstone, B., & Burack-Weiss, A. (1983). *Social work practice with the frail elderly and their families.* Springfield, IL: Charles C Thomas.

Thompson, K. H. (1994). Role theory and social work practice. In R. R. Greene, (Ed.), *Human behavior: A diversity framework* (pp. 93-114). Hawthorne, NY: Aldine De Gruyter.

Tice, C. J., & Perkins, K. (1996). *Mental health issues and aging: Building on the strengths of older persons.* Pacific Grove, CA: Brooks/Cole.

Walker, A., Pratt, C. A., & Eddy, L. (1995). Informal caregiving to aging family members. *Family Relations, 44*, 402-411.

Walsh, F. (2006). *Strengthening family resilience*. New York: Guilford Press.

White, M., & Epston, D. (1990). *Narrative means to therapeutic ends*. New York: W. W. Norton.

3

Assessment and Functional Age

with Sandra Graham

The first part of this chapter provides a general introduction to the geriatric assessment process. The second part presents information to use in assessment of the biological aspects of functional age. Chapter 4 will discuss psychological age; and chapter 5 social age and spirituality.

Introduction to Assessment

Clinical social work is a method of helping individuals, families, or groups cope more effectively with problems in social functioning. It is a humanistic process that rests on a body of specialized knowledge and professional expertise (Shulman, 2005). According to Northen (1995), a distinguishing feature of clinical social work is

> adequate appraisal of a person's biological, psychological, and social attributes, capacities, and resources as well as problems; the structure, and process of families and other groups; and the interconnectedness of people with their environments. Assessment goes beyond diagnosis of a problem or illness to a broader appraisal of the interrelationships between physiological, emotional, and sociocultural factors and the external environmental conditions that influence well-being. (p. 12)

The purpose of an assessment, whether the difficulties center around an individual, family, group, or community, is to bring together the various facets of the client's situation in an orderly, economical manner (Cournoyer, 2000; Kadushin & Kadushin, 1997; Meyer, 1993). An assessment aims to identify and explain the nature of a problem, to appraise it within a framework of specific elements, and to use that appraisal as a guide to action (Perlman, 1957). Thus, assessment is a social work procedure used to examine the client's issues for purposes of selecting interventions or treatment modalities.

Because language can convey both negative and positive messages, theorists are rethinking the use of terms such as *diagnosis* and *assessment*

(Laird, 1993). For example, Dean (1993) cautioned that practitioners who assume the role of expert diagnostician–"someone who does something to the client"–may limit client participation in the helping process. She suggested that practitioners use assessment approaches that get as close as possible to client meaning by asking the following four questions:

1. Which theoretical concepts increase understanding of the client?
2. Which theories are useful in talking to clients and which only work when talking to colleagues?
3. Is the theory relevant given the client's cultural background and economic status?
4. Has the assessment process preserved the unique aspects of clients' experiences? (p. 63)

At the same time, Meyer (1993) argued that assessment must involve critical thinking, a process that requires that the practitioner use relevant knowledge and informed judgments to produce a statement of the problem. She attributed the diminished interest in assessment to confusion about the difference between assessment and classification, and a reluctance to use universal assessment norms. Meyer contended that assessment is not about rigid classification. Rather, assessment should involve the use of a body of knowledge that helps the practitioner better understand and individualize a client.

Multilevel Geriatric Assessments

Assessment of an older adult involves getting to know the person–his or her motivations, strengths, challenges, and capacity to change. Assessment is (a) a cross-sectional study of the client's situation and his or her traditional mode of behavior and (b) an evaluation of what psychological, biological, sociocultural and spiritual factors can contribute to positive change. Assessment encompasses how clients engage with people and their environments. The evaluation of an older adult, as with that of other age groups, is a method of looking at the presenting problem(s), determining what the dynamic issues are, and mutually selecting interventions to alleviate or eliminate the problem (Butler, Lewis, & Sunderland, 1998).

The assessment of the older adult can be used to match a client with needed services and care along a continuum of care (Hooyman, Hooyman & Kethly, 1981; figure 5.1). This approach may be termed *triage*. For clients whose functional abilities suggest the greatest independence, little care may be needed. Such older adults are able to live with relative independence (should they so desire) and can benefit from health-promotion and disease-prevention programs. For elders who experience many challenges to their functional abilities or who are quite frail, services and care arrangements are more extensive. Services needed may include skilled nursing care and interventions by interdisciplinary professional teams.

Geriatric Social Work Assessment and Functional Age

Historical Background

Geriatric assessments tend to focus on older adults' functional status. "*Functional status* is the quality of overt behavior as evaluated by social-normative and subjective criteria" (Lawton, 1991, p. 31). Although evaluating functional status is currently a prototype for geriatric assessments, both the scientific and practice communities have long been concerned with how to obtain a comprehensive assessment of an older adult's functional capacities. As long ago as the late 1800s and early 1900s, there was interest in measuring health status. At that time, information was obtained through health surveys. Questions generally dealt with the number of persons who were sick and unable to report to work on a given day. This information represented the first approach to concepts of disability or dysfunction. As the concept of disability was refined, questions about the duration of an illness and issues relevant to the classification of types of dysfunction emerged.

Early longitudinal studies of functional capacity focused on differences in scores on a single trait, such as cardiovascular disease or intelligence. However, gerontologists needed a composite or a global indicator of overall function. Their goal was to develop an index that would classify large amounts of information about interrelated changes associated with aging. They hoped that such an index could be used to predict such things as employment capabilities, the likelihood of survival, or the capacity for independent living.

In the last four decades, the range of available measures of biological, mental, and social functioning has been greatly expanded (Kane & Kane, 1981). *Multidimensional assessment procedures*, those that combine the major domains of a comprehensive evaluation within a single instrument, such as OARS Instrument developed by the Duke Center for the Study of Aging and Human Development (1978) at Duke University, have remained useful in resource planning and in gathering medical, functional, and psychosocial information (see *Handbook of Geriatric Assessment* by Fillenbaum, Gallo, Fulmer, Paveza & Reichel, 2000).

A Geriatric Social Work Approach

A social work approach to a functional assessment is different from those of other disciplines. Although it encompasses an understanding of the biological, social, and psychological dimensions of aging, a social work assessment of an older adult is process oriented and includes context variables such as sociohistorical time and spirituality. That is, it is an interactional procedure in which social worker and client engage in a dialogue over time. Many social workers may use diagnostic tools, such as the *Diagnostic and Statistical Manual of Mental Disorders* (DSM-IV: American Psychiatric Association, 1994), Beck et al.'s (1961) *Inventory for Measuring Depression*, or the *Mini-Mental State Exam* (MMSE; Folstein, Folstein & McHugh, 1975), as a useful adjunct to their own professional judgment. However, diagnostic tools do not replace other professional forms of clinical assessment. More important, such scales do not use the information-processing skills usually associated with social work method; nor do they recognize the interactional role of the practitioner in shaping the assessment process.

For example, geriatric social work assessments emphasize client competence. Specific measures of a clients' competence may involve a listing of illness, pains and discomfort, medications, hospitalizations and so forth; an enumeration of *activities of daily living* (ADL), including the ability to dress, groom, and feed oneself; and a measure of *instrumental activities of daily living* (IADL) involving a client's ability to take care of bathing, dressing, and feeding themselves. Clients also must be able to get up and down off a chair or bed as well as use the toilet unassisted (Kane & Kane, 1981).

Environmental Press

Social workers are interested in more than measures of ADL or IADL They are concerned with clients' *everyday competence*, or a general picture of older people's ability to care for themselves, manage their affairs, and live independent, quality lives in their homes and communities (Tinetti & Powell, 1993; Willis, 1996). For this more global understanding of a person's functional competence, practitioners need highly skilled interviewing and listening skills. Assessment may begin by observing clients in their home environment. The social worker's principal goal is to learn about a client's sense of *self-efficacy*, the perceived power to be effective in one's environment (Bandura, 1986). For example, does the client have a sense of security at home? Or is he or she fearful about slipping or falling? Does the client have the capacity to prepare dinner or is he or she likely to burn food on the stove? (Greene & Kropf, 1993; Tinetti & Powell, 1993).

A dynamic approach to assessing functional age is not an automatic formula-ridden method to be used solely as an experimental or research tool. Rather, social workers assess a client's confidence and ability to function in a given environment (Greene & Watkins, 1998). The concept of environmental press can be used to understand an older adult's competency in meeting the demands—or press—of his or her environment (figure 3.1). From the perspective of environmental press, competence is defined "as the theoretical upper limit of capacity of the individual to function in the areas of biological health, sensation-perception, motoric behavior, and cognition" (Lawton, 1982, p. 38). Factors the social worker might assess are:

- *biological health,* or the absence of disease states;
- *sensory-perceptual capacity,* which includes the primary processes of vision; audition; olfaction; gestation; somesthesis (bodily perception); and kinesthesis (the ability to sense the position, orientation, and movement of one's body parts);
- *motor skills,* which encompass muscular strength and complex coordination;
- *cognitive capacity,* or the individual's capacity to comprehend, process, and cope with the external world;
- *ego strength,* or an internal psychological strength (Lawton, 1982, pp. 37–38).

Social work assessment is an evaluation of the "factors at play in the person-problem-situation complex" (Perlman, 1957, p. 171) wherein social worker has obtained substantive knowledge about a client's physical health, mental health, emotional health, social supports, physical environment, functional abilities, coping styles, and formal service usage (Morrow-Howell, 1992).

Social work assessment generally examines person-environment fit. *Person-environment fit* refers to the extent to which there is a match between the individual's adaptive needs and the qualities of the environment (Greene, 1999/2008). Social workers who use the ecological perspective as a conceptual framework examine older clients' behavior as a "complex outcome of person-environment transactions at multiple systems levels" (Greene & McGuire, 1998, p. 9). For example, practitioners may examine if care or opportunities in the health care arena are

Figure 3.1
The Environmental Press–Competence Model

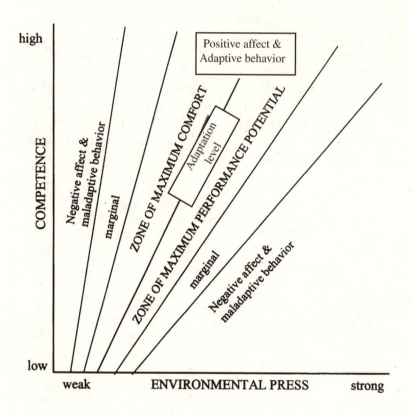

Source: Lawton, M. P. & Nahemow, L. (1973). Ecology and the aging process. In C. Eisdorf, & M. P. Lawton (Eds.). The psychology of adult development and Aging (pp. 619-674). Washington: American Psychological Association. (P. 661)

compatible with an older adult's needs, resources, and demands (Berkman & D'Ambrioso, 2006; Berkman & Harootyan, 2003). If so, there is a goodness of fit (Coulton, 1981). The determination of goodness-of-fit and what interventions and resources are needed leads to the development of the treatment plan.

Assessment as a Plan for Intervention

The important aim of geriatric social work assessment is to reach a mutually acceptable intervention plan with reasonable, attainable treatment goals (McInnis, 2002). The idea that the client has agreed to the assessment and helped to formulate the intervention plan is sometimes called a *contract*. Assessment should also provide a mutual understanding of what difficulties can be reversed or ameliorated and a picture of what kind of services and or supports are needed (Butler, Lewis, & Sunderland, 1998). Social work assessments are also characterized by collaboration of the client and social worker. A social worker's understanding of the client's story or point of view is critical to a mutually acceptable treatment plan.

The Functional Age Concept

Because of the person-environment point of view of the functional age concept, the author of the text adopted it to use as a guide in the assessment of older adults. The concept addresses *aging* as the regular (behavioral) changes that occur in mature genetically representative organisms living under representative environmental conditions as they advance in chronological age. *Chronological age*, the most commonly used definition of aging, is simply based on the passage of time or the number of years that have passed since the person's birth. Because chronological age is only a measure of calendar years, it does not provide an understanding of an individual's bodily changes or those of his or her abilities or limitations; nor does it consider the important differences between individuals in their patterns of aging (Kastenbaum, 1993; Hooyman & Kiyak, 2004). Although the usefulness of chronological age is questionable, it continues to be used as a criterion for determining time for retirement and for receiving age-related benefits and services such as social security and Medicare (Butler, Lewis, & Sunderland, 1998).

The approach to aging adopted here examines the individual's relative performance capacities adopted from Birren (1969). He was one of the first gerontologists to address the issue of how to appraise an individual's level of functioning in a given environment relative to others of his or her age. His interest in age-associated changes and their effect on a person's capacity to cope effectively with his or her living conditions led to his description of *three kinds of aging*: biological, psychological, and social. He defined *biological age* as the physiological age-related changes and the functional capacities of vital organ systems that contribute to life expectancy; *psychological age* as the adaptive capacities of the individual and his or her ability to adjust to environmental demands; and *social age* as the roles and habits of individuals as they interact with other members of society. These definitions guide the text's assessment content as well as (Crowther et al., 2002) conceptualization of *positive spirituality* as a necessary component of health and well-being.

Biological Aspects of Functional Age

Introduction

Of all the areas of information in which the geriatric social worker must be knowledgeable, the biological aspects of aging seem the most forbodding or out of reach. Many social workers feel that this information is difficult to learn and requires special abilities. Many erroneously believe that the biologic problems of aging are entirely out of their area of professional expertise, and they "abandon" these issues to other allied health professionals. Yet, social workers who are not familiar with the basic biological factors associated with aging are at a decided disadvantage, because they are not properly prepared to assess their elderly clients or to work effectively with other professionals.

Aging is a normal biopsychosocial process of change that occurs in all organisms over their life spans. Four areas of aging (biological, psychological, sociological, and spiritual) interact with each other in a complex way that is increasingly understood. This means that a client's physical symptoms can be determined by multiple factors. The practitioner who raises questions about these interrelationships is more likely to arrive at a realistic and accurate appraisal of the client's situation.

Because social workers often make home visits and develop a long-term therapeutic relationship with their clients, they are in an ideal position to obtain information about the client's total situation. Assessment relevant to biological functioning should not be overlooked, and information about factors such as nutritional habits, ease of mobility, availability and use of medication, and understanding of and follow through with medical-health regimes should be obtained.

Clearly, the geriatric social worker cannot become an expert on bio-medical problems; nor is this desirable. However, it is important to be well informed. This chapter suggests some of the key biological issues in aging of which the social worker should be aware. It is recognized that this is a rapidly growing field of study and information can soon become outdated. For this reason, a list of assessment questions is provided at the end of the chapter to serve as a guide to obtaining current client information (see Berger, 1994, and Schneider & Rowe, 1996 to supplement this section).

Biological Age

Biological Aging refers to those changes in the structure and functions of body organs and systems that occur over time. Biological processes may have profound affects on psychological and social age. Behavioral and psychological changes that take place because of the biological changes associated with dementia are examples (see chapter 4). Biological age is the process most closely associated with the individual's capacity for survival. Biological age, in the strictest sense, is a measure of the functional capacity of the vital life-limiting organ systems and is a predictor of whether the individual seems "older" or "younger" than other persons of the same chronological age (Birren & Renner, 1977); e.g., "He has the heart of a forty year old"; or "She has the stamina of a woman half her age."

Physiological changes play a primary but not exclusive role in determining biological age. Physiological aging includes all time-dependent changes in structure and function of the organism, eventually contributing to diminished efficiency (of organ systems) and increased vulnerability to disease and death. Physiological changes associated with advancing age should be differentiated from disease-related changes. Normal aging is characterized by the general progressive loss of some physiological capacities (table 3.1). These include, for example, a reduction in lung capacity, a slowing in the speed of response and reaction time, a reduction in the capacity for withstanding stress, and an increase in healing time. However, there is a difference between these age-related biological changes and those related to a specific disease. For example, calcification of the arterial system is a disease; while a reduction in peak cardiac output a normal aging process. It has been shown that cerebral blood flow and oxygen consumption do not decline simply as a function of aging but in proportion to the degree of actual vascular disease.

Table 3.1
Normal Aging

Heart	Grows slightly larger, and oxygen consumption during exercise declines
Arteries	Stiffen with age, and fatty deposits build up
Lungs	Decline in terms of breathing capacity
Brain	Loses some cells and some may become damaged; the number of connections between cells may regrow
Kidneys	Become less efficient; if urinary incontinence occurs, it may be managed through exercise and behavioral techniques
Muscles	May decline without exercise
Skin	Becomes less elastic and more lined and wrinkled
Hair	Turns more gray and thins
Height	Declines slowly to as much as 2 inches by age 80 years
Eyesight	Declines, with loss of peripheral vision and decreased ability to judge depth
Taste, touch, and smell	Decrease; taste decreases, sensitivity to touch lessens, and the ability to smell declines
Hearing	Lessens, with loss of hearing acuity
Personality	Maintained; stability is expected

Source: Retrieved February 13, 2006, from these three web pages:
http://www.dpa.org.sg/PAGE4AGE/newpage11.htm
http://www.webmd.com/hw/healthy_seniors/tn722.asp
http://www.merck.com/mrkshared/mmg/sec1/ch1/ch1a.jsp

Clearly, physiological functioning and health status are important factors in how a person functions in old age. However, given the complexity and heterogeneity of the geriatric population, there are marked individual differences in the onset and rate of physical change with age. In addition, organs and subsystems within the individual age differently (Schneider & Rowe, 1996). Although chronological age and health status are correlated to some extent with chronic ailments and physical disabilities occurring more frequently in the old, it is necessary to remember that there are always variations and exceptions to this general pattern of more diseases among the elderly. The social worker can play a crucial role in alerting the client family and physician to a perceived difficulty that requires further exploration (Merck & Co., Inc., 2005. *The Merck Manual of Geriatrics*. http://www.merck.com/mrkshared/mmg/sec1/ch7/ch7a.jsp)

Assessing Biological Age

Biological age is, to a large degree, a reflection of changes in various bodily systems and an indication that these changes can affect the physical and psychological functioning of the older adult (table 3.2). During assessment, the social worker focuses on how these biological and physiological processes interact with and influence personality and social behavior. Practitioners must first be generally aware of how the basic physiological systems function and how they may change with age. In addition, social workers should be prepared to ask their older clients if they may consult with their physician. This section highlights the major characteristics of the eight organ systems, with special emphasis on those issues of greatest concern to social work practice.

The Reproductive System and Human Sexuality. Because society has been willing to accept the myth that older people are feeble, unproductive, and asexual, and researchers have generally been reticent to investigate sexuality among older adults, stereotyping and folklore have obscured our understanding of this activity in later life. Practitioners may erroneously assumed that older people do not have sexual desires or are too frail or sick to engage in this activity (Altschuler & Katz, 1996; Butler & Lewis, 2002) . However, from the studies that have been conducted on sexuality and aging, one fact has clearly emerged: Most older people continue to have sexual needs and interests on into their eighties and possibly beyond, and those healthy older persons who want to maintain their sexual activity are able to do so (Butler, Lewis & Sunderland, 1998).

Table 3.2
Biological-Age Assessment Checklist

I.   Common Physical Symptoms

- Pain
- Fatigue
- Shortness of breath
- Swelling of ankles
- Change in skin-pallor
- Constipation-diarrhea
- Incontinence or bladder problems
- Bowel control
- Fainting, dizziness
- Bleeding
- Other (client's self-report)

II.   Physical Limitations

- Hearing loss-hearing aid
- Vision loss-glasses, cataracts, glaucoma
- Dentures
- Gait-cane, walker, wheelchair
- Prosthetic devices
- Posture

III.   Cognitive Ability, Judgment, and Communication

- Use of telephone
- Knowledge of news events
- Financial management
- Memory
- Intellect
- Orientation: use of calendar, appointments

IV.   Medical Regimes

- General medical history
- Chronic illnesses
- Acute illnesses
- Prescription drugs and over-the-counter drugs (i.e., laxatives, aspirin)
- Special diets: low sodium, low sugar, low fat, low cholesterol

V.   Daily Living Habits

- Alcohol and drug use
- Water intake
- General nutritional requirements, vitamins, and protein
- Eating and self-feeding skills and general appetite

- Grooming: shaving, hair, teeth, nails, skin, clothes
- Bathing/washing
- Caffeine use
- Smoking
- Smoking
- Alcohol Consumption
- Exercise/activity: regular, exertion level
- Sleep patterns: difficulties, naps, average number of hours, sleeping pills, day-night reversals, insomnia
- Sexual activities: desires, changes, outlets

VI.   Mobility and Safety

- General speed of motion
- Home environment (manipulation of) lighting, stairs, bathtub, location of toilet and bedroom
- Architectural barriers: accessing ramps, curbs
- Ability to handle emergencies: fire, medical
- Safety: lighting, security of carpets

VII. Home Management

- Housecleaning
- Kitchen activities: i.e., open cans and meal preparation
- Ability to shop for groceries

As with other physiological systems, there are a number of age-related changes in human sexual physiology and performance. Although these changes are usually minimal and a natural part of the aging process, they can have a major effect on the older client who may not understand their implications. The geriatric social worker can play a significant role by correcting misconceptions and providing information.

Older men, age, and sexuality. The older man may experience a slower physiological response to sexual stimuli and take longer to obtain an erection. While these changes occur after a young man reaches the height of his sexuality, they are more pronounced and identifiable in those over fifty. For most older men, the refractory period (the capacity for erection following ejaculation) is longer than for younger men. However, there is generally greater control of ejaculatory demand, which means that the older man can remain erect and make love longer before coming to orgasm (Butler & Lewis, 2002; Butler, Lewis & Sunderland, 1998).

The most important point is that the older man does not lose his facility for erection as he ages unless there are other physical or emotional problems. In other words, impotence is never a consequence of chronological age alone. If older men lose interest or become impotent, a number of factors could be involved and should be assessed, including (a) general ill health and disease (e.g., diabetes); (b) vascular insufficiency; (c) hypertension; (d) prostate enlargement and other genitourinary problems; (e) neurological disorders; (f) excessive drinking or alcoholism; (g) drugs and prescribed medication (e.g., major and minor tranquilizers, antidepressants, and antihypertension medications); (h) depression; (i) fatigue; (j) long periods of abstinence; and (k) social expectation of impotence in age.

Older women, age, and sexuality. While sexual function in women has been less fully researched, evidence suggests that older women experience fewer changes than do men. The capacity for orgasm continues on into old age, and, if in reasonable health, the older woman can expect to continue sexual activities until late in life. Unfortunately, because of the differences in life spans between men and women, sexual partners may not be available.

There are some physiological changes in the older woman during and after menopause.These generally include the effects of gradual hormone reduction, such as thinning of the vaginal walls, a reduction of length and diameter of the vagina and major labia, and a decrease in vaginal secretions. As with the male, these normal age-related changes need not affect the pleasure of sexual intercourse, and cultural expectations and psychological reactions play a major role in this regard.

It is important to recognize that the human sexual function is highly idiosyncratic and that the ways in which sexuality is expressed are very diverse (Butler & Lewis, 2002). The task of social workers is to recognize and support the view that love and intimacy are important throughout life and to seek an acceptable way of discussing this highly personal subject with their clients. Sexual problems in later life include those that may occur at any age and are an equally important aspect of human relationships. In that sense, they should not be ignored in the counseling relationship. Many clients need to be reassured that their continued sexual interest is "natural," others may be concerned that a partner is not available, some may be misunderstood by family and friends, and still others may be in settings, such as nursing homes, where the expression of sexuality is not acceptable. All are entitled to understanding and support of their sexual feelings.

Clients who have had disfiguring surgery, such as mastectomy or colostomy, or have a major illness or have had a heart attack may need considerable reassurance about their sexuality. In addition, they may require realistic medical information and suggestions for how to best continue sexual activity. Such clients can be encouraged to speak with their physician.

Any discussion with the client should take into account the fact that human sexuality encompasses more than sexual intercourse. Intimacy may be manifested in many ways, including listening, conversation, holding hands, or giving a hug or a gift. The ability to achieve intimacy involves the emotional flexibility to be able to redefine relationships and to invest in new sources of love and friendship. Those elderly persons who have been able to establish consistent relationships and have an intimate friend on whom they can depend for support generally are better adjusted and have higher morale and life satisfaction.

Age and the Nervous System. The nervous system consists of the brain, the spinal cord, and the related nerve cells and fibers throughout the body. The nervous system keeps people in contact with the world outside their bodies and, along with the endocrine system, provides most of the control functions for the body. A person's nervous system receives literally thousands of bits of information from the different sense organs, integrates them, and determines the response to be made. The rate at which nerve fibers conduct information becomes less efficient with age (Berger, 1994).

Sleep disturbance: A common nervous disorder. Sleep complaints are among the most common in older adults. Sleep difficulties may contribute to an increased risk of falls, difficulty with concentration and memory, and overall decreased quality of life (Ancoli-Israel & Ayalon, 2006). Because sleep disturbance has such a profound effect, it is suggested that medical doctors take interventions to optimize sleep quality (Dew et al., 2003).

Wakefulness and sleep, in large part, are controlled by brain activity, although they can, of course, be influenced by environmental factors. Certain sleep changes are common in later life and may be related to changes in biological rhythms. In general, older people sleep less, sleep lighter, and awaken earlier and more easily. They also have a greater tendency to awaken throughout the night. Because many older people retire early when fatigued, they may waken at 3:00 A.M. and then fear they have insomnia when, in fact, they have had an adequate night's sleep (Schneider & Rowe, 1996).

However, complaints about sleep disturbances should be evaluated from a biopsychosocial perspective. Changes in sleep patterns may be related to illness, chronic pain, anxiety, depression, drug dependence, and the need for more activity during the day. Too many catnaps during the day can result in day-night sleep reversal. A discussion with the client about his or her specific habits can often lead to a better understanding and a solution. Consultation with the physician may also prove helpful.

Parkinsonism. Parkinson's disease is a result of a deficiency of dopamine and a loss of brain cells and associated lesions in the brain. It is characterized by rigidity of the body, tremors, and slowness of movement. It may also be accompanied by involuntary movement of the fingers, shaking head, stooped posture, shuffling gait, and depressed stare. Parkinson's needs to be diagnosed by a health care professional. Major breakthroughs in the drug treatment of Parkinson's have occurred over recent years, which may relieve many of the most common symptoms. However, the social worker should be alert to possible side effects such as confusion. As these symptoms may mimic other medical and psychiatric difficulties, consultation is advised. Because Parkinson's disease has no cure and an individual will need treatment the rest of his or her life, it is also important for the social worker to be sensitive to the physical implications as well as the embarrassment and depression that may accompany the disease (Centers for Disease Control and Prevention, 2006; http://www.cdc.gov/aging/).

Alcoholism in older adults. Alcohol is a central nervous system depressant that inhibits cortical control and impairs intellectual functions. Alcoholism is a condition resulting from excessive ingestion of or idiosyncratic reaction to alcohol. Alcoholism can shorten life expectancy, cause heart disease, damage the brain, contribute to falls and accidents, and lead to chronic impotence in men by damaging the central nervous system and upsetting hormonal balance. Chronic alcoholism can also contribute to vitamin and protein deficiencies, liver dysfunction, and general deterioration of the personality. Age-related physiological changes affect the risk associated with alcohol as do emotional and social problems such as bereavement (*http://www.americangeriatrics. org/products/positionpapers/alcohol.shtml*). Therefore, this damaging disease should be addressed in assessment. In fact, the American Geriatrics Society recommends that all patients sixty-five years of age or older be asked about their use of alcohol. Among the assessment clues for the clinical presentation of alcoholism in old age are insomnia, impotence, problem with control of gout, rapid onset of confusion, uncontrollable hypertension, and unexplainable falls. In addition, studies have found that victims of elder abuse may be related to the abuse of alcohol or other drugs (Choi & Mayer, 2000).

Mental Illness. Mental illness is now understood to be a result of biological, psychological, and social influences (Sullivan, 1998). In making correct assessments and providing appropriate treatment, of all the difficulties associated with advancing age, mental illness presents the greatest challenge for geriatric practitioners (Zarit & Zarit, 1998). The most recent and widely accepted description of mental disorders that may affect older adults is found in the American Psychiatric Association's DSM-IV (1994). These diagnostic categories and definitions offer a means of clarifying symptoms and standardizing terms and are discussed in greater detail in chapter 4.

Skeletal and Muscular Systems. The skeletal and muscular systems reach maximum size and strength when the individual is in his or her early to mid-twenties. With age, as cells are reduced in number and size, bones tend to lose density and become more brittle, joints tend to become less mobile (stiffer), and the cartilage between segments of the spinal column degenerates. These changes, which do not occur at the same rate for everyone, bring about a reduction in height and flexibility, which can contribute to a hunched-over look known as *kyphosis*, a curvature of the spine.

As changes in the skeletal and muscular systems take place, related physical difficulties may occur. Osteoarthritis and bursitis are common diseases; whereas a general loss of muscle strength and tone are age-related common complaints. Lack of protein deposition in the bones causes osteoporosis with consequent weakness of the bones, particularly in women. Osteoporosis is a disease in which bones become fragile and more likely to break. If not prevented or if left untreated, osteoporosis can progress painlessly until a bone breaks *http://www.niams.nih.gov/bonr/hi/overview.htm*). Again, the social worker should not attribute these problems simply to "old age," as proper medical care can often alleviate painful symptoms. Expediting an appropriate referral can be an important social work role.

Endocrine System. The endocrine system comprises all internal glandular activity and secretions. The hormones that are secreted play a major regulatory function in metabolism, blood clotting, and body temperature. Malfunctioning of the endocrine system can contribute to high blood pressure, arthritis, arteriosclerosis, and diabetes.

Diabetes, a disease of the endocrine system, is usually hereditary, especially for those who develop it at an early age. Diabetes is characterized by high levels of blood glucose resulting from defects in insulin production. Type 1 diabetes is commonly called juvenile-onset diabetes. Type 2 diabetes which may account for about 90 percent to 95 percent of diagnosed cases of diabetes, is associated with older age, obesity, and family history. Type 2 diabetes is usually an adult-onset form of the disease but may occur among children. Lifestyle interventions such as diet and exercise may prevent or delay occurrence (http://www.cdc.gov/diabetes/pubs/general.htm).

Mild diabetes is common in old age, especially for people who are overweight; however, diet can often reduce blood glucose levels and symptoms can be controlled. When improperly treated, diabetes can cause impotence, mental confusion, or depression. Testing for this disease is simple and should be part of a general physical examination that all elderly clients should receive regularly.

Genitourinary System. The purpose of the genitourinary system is to bring about the interchange of nutrients and cellular waste between the tissues and circulating blood. Kidney function shows a decline with age, which can lead to a buildup of waste products in the body. This can have many side effects, including confused mental states and eventual renal failure. The effect of acute or chronic renal failure depends to a great extent on the water and food intake of the person, which means that dietary habits and medication play an important role.

Dialysis of uremic patients with artificial kidneys has been an available treatment for about fifty years. It is now developed to the point that many patients can live normal life spans. However, there are many psychosocial, economic, political, and ethical questions involved that can affect clients and professionals alike. Older people, particularly women, may have difficulty with bladder control because of poor muscle control. This condition may cause embarrassing "leakage" and sometimes results in social isolation. As the client may not feel free to discuss the subject, the social worker should be alert to this physical condition and the fact that research has proven exercise, medications, or a simple operation helpful (McIntosh, Frahm, Mallett & Richardson, 1993) .

Circulatory System. With age, the circulatory system, which comprises the heart and vascular system, is characterized by a general decline in its capacity to circulate blood. This is due to a buildup of fatty deposits along the walls of the blood vessels that can, when associated with degenerative changes in the arterial walls, obstruct and narrow the passages. These disease processes can lead to coronary heart disease and difficulties in other organs of the body, especially the brain, kidneys, liver, and gastrointestinal tract.

As hardening (arteriosclerosis) and narrowing (atherosclerosis) of the vessel walls interferes with blood flow, strokes may eventually occur. The stroke, which is, in effect, a blocked or ruptured vein in the brain, can lead to temporary or permanent paralysis, confusion, clouding of memory, loss of speech (aphasia), dementia (see discussion of multiinfarct dementia), unconsciousness, and death. Treatment involves a combination of medical care including physical therapy, recreation, and therapeutic and social services; the social worker is an important member of this multidisciplinary team.

Respiratory System. Changes in the respiratory system with age are closely related to the ability to transfer oxygen to the blood. This capacity declines as the older person has decreased elasticity of bronchial tubes and may breathe faster as a result. These "normal" age-related changes in the respiratory system may be exacerbated by smoking and diseases, such as bronchial pneumonia and tuberculosis.

Digestive System. The primary function of the digestive system is to provide the body with a continual supply of water and nutrients. Obviously, the physical and mental well-being of the older person is closely linked to the digestive function, and disease or changes associated with aging may affect nutrition. Calorie needs tend to decrease as people age because of decreased activity, changes in metabolism, and a decrease in cell mass. However, the nutritional requirements relative to vitamins, minerals, and proteins do not alter. In fact, there is some evidence that as older people experience a decline in digestive secretions and in intestinal absorption, more nutrients may be necessary.

Obtaining information about nutritional habits and dietary prescriptions is an important part of a multifaceted assessment. Unfortunately, many older people may not be able to shop for and prepare a proper diet. Others may not want to cook for one person or eat alone. Low income, a lack of knowledge of balanced nutrition, and dulled taste and smell may also interfere with proper nutrition. Lack of proper nutrition can have a ripple effect, leading to deterioration in physiological and mental processes. Social workers can be of assistance to the client and medical team in sorting out these difficulties. An assessment of the client's biological age involves an evaluation of physiological processes and is designed to detect medical problems and their psychosocial effects.

> Ms. Scott, a tiny single woman eighty-nine years old, came to the attention of a social worker when she fell on the escalator of a subway station. At that time she was taken to a hospital. An observant emergency room clerk noted her disheveled appearance and agitated behavior and notified the social service department.

Before she was released that day, Ms. Scott was referred to a social worker at a home health care agency. At first, Ms. Scott was reluctant to accept the referral. When the social worker called to offer an appointment, Ms. Scott sounded weak and confused, and her voice was barely audible. During the social worker's second call Ms. Scott stated that she was unable to get out and that there was no food in the house. Ms. Scott finally allowed the social worker to visit when she offered to bring her some groceries.

When the worker arrived, she found Ms. Scott dressed (in the middle of winter) in a sleeveless summer housecoat with a stained apron on top. Her apartment was cold, dirty, and disorganized, with clothes, shoes, and newspapers in the middle of the floor. The hot water in the kitchen sink was running and was about to overflow. Ms. Scott did not seem to notice. The social worker also observed a college degree on the wall and many fine china cups and plates. When she asked about them, she was able to piece together the following background information: Ms. Scott had moved to the Washington, D.C., area at the age of 21 to become a government worker during World War II. She was viewed as a bright and capable worker, received several promotions, and held responsible positions in her 44-year career. While working, she attended a university at night and earned a degree in business administration. Despite several offers, she had elected not to marry. Ms. Scott had had an active social life. She had a circle of friends, mostly single women, with whom she traveled to Europe, Latin America, and the Orient. She was interested in theater, concerts, and opera, and she wrote poetry. She was a member of the Toastmistress Club and had been president for many years. She did volunteer work at her church and was an active member of the women's auxiliary. Her income allowed her to do what she pleased. She always dressed in expensive clothes and furnished her apartment in good taste, but she ate all her meals out. She also played the stock market and followed it carefully. She often became depressed when the market went down and was in high spirits when the market did well.

Although Ms. Scott had an excellent pension and savings, she indicated that she was reluctant to spend her money for services. She wanted to save it "for a rainy day." Ms. Scott said that she valued her independence and freedom more than anything in life. She also valued her friends and found comfort in them. Her best friend is a 91-year-old woman who lives in the same building. She is homebound but very alert, and Ms. Scott visits her daily. Ms. Scott has no family in the area. Her nephew, who was 59 and lived nearby, died 6 months earlier of cancer. He was very helpful to her, and she was very fond of him. Ms. Scott cried bitterly when she talked about him. She felt his death was untimely because he was young and that she should have been the one to die because she is old and "miserable."

After several assessment interviews, it became clear that Ms. Scott's problems began when she started having difficulty with her dentures. She made several visits to the dentist, who said she would need a new plate that would cost $2,500. Ms. Scott who was "shocked" by the cost, never went back. When she realized she could no longer eat "gourmet meals" in her favorite restaurants, she began to subsist on coffee and donuts. Gradually, she became malnourished, depressed, and disoriented. Friends and neighbors, noticing these changes, encouraged her to "take better care of herself." It was not until her accident that she was able to accept help.

Based on this assessment, the goal of treatment was to help Ms. Scott cope with her losses and physical changes and to accept minimal services in order to help her to be able to remain independent in her apartment. To the extent possible, geriatric social workers should focus on the promotion of well-being. Research of the 1990s has supported the view that aging is not synonymous with decline, and there are many ways to preserve and even improve peoples' mental and physical functioning.

Rowe and Kahn (1998), in their book *Successful Aging*, contend that fears about functional decline are exaggerated. They state that,

> The losses experienced in the course of what we have called "usual aging" are a combination of the inevitable and the preventable, more often the latter. People often blame aging for losses that are in fact caused by lifestyle---overeating and poor nutrition, smoking, excessive use of alcohol, lack of regular exercise, and insufficient mental (cognitive) exertion. The couch-potato syndrome, all too common in spite of public ridicule and good resolutions, has both physical and mental effects. (p. 44)

In addition, physical activity and exercise are known to improve an individual's ability to perform activities of daily living and thereby maintain independence, preserve quality of life, and increase longevity. In a recent meta-analysis, regular exercise and religious attendance (see chapter 5) were important factors accounting for an additional 3.1 to 5.1 years over a life time (Hall, 2006).

References

Altschuler, J. & Katz, A. D. (1996). Sexual secrets of older women: Countertransference in clinical practice. *Clinical Gerontologist, 17* (2), 51-67.

American Psychiatric Association. (1994) *Diagnostic and statistical manual of mental disorders*. Washington, DC: Author.

Ancoli-Israel, S., & Ayalon, L. (2006). Diagnosis and treatment of sleep disorders in older adults. *American Journal of Geriatric Psychiatry, 14* (2), 95-103.

Bandura, A. (1986). *Social foundations of thought and action: A social cognitive theory*. Englewood Cliffs, NJ: Prentice-Hall.

Beck, A. T., Ward, C. H., Mendelson, M., Mock, J., & Erbaugh, J. (1961). An inventory for measuring depression. *Archives of General Psychiatry 4*, 561-571.

Berger, K. S. (1994). *The developing person through the life span*. New York: Worth Publishers.

Berkman, B., & D'Ambrioso, S. (Eds.) (2006). *The Oxford handbook of social work in health and aging*. New York: Oxford University Press.

Berkman, B., & Harootyan, L. (2003). *Social work and health care in an aging society*. New York: Springer.

Binstock, R. H., George, L. K., Schulz, J. H., Myers, G. C., Marshall, V. W., & Birren, J. E. (1996). *Handbook of aging and the social sciences*. San Diego, CA: Academic Press.

Birren, J. E. (1969). Principles of research on aging. In J. E. Birren (Ed.), *The handbook of aging and the individual*. Chicago: University of Chicago Press. (Abridged in *Middle Age and Aging*. B. Neugarten (Ed.), Chicago: The University of Chicago Press, 1968.)

Birren, J. E., Lubben, J., Rowe, J. C., & Deutchman, D. E. (Eds.). (1991). *The concept and measurement of quality of life in the frail elderly*. San Diego, CA: Academic Press.

Birren, J. E., & Renner, V. J. (1977). Research on the psychology of aging: principles and experimentation. In J. E. Birren & K. W. Schaie (Eds.), *Handbook of the psychology of aging*. New York: Van Nostrand Reinhold Company.

Brink, T. L. (1979) *Geriatric psychotherapy*. New York: Human Services Press.

Butler, R. N., & Lewis, M. (2002). *The new love and sex after sixty*. New York: Ballantine Books.

Choi, N.G. & Mayer, J. (2000). Elder abuse, neglect, and exploitation: Risk factors and prevention strategies. *Journal of Gerontological Social Work, 33* (2), 5-25.

Cournoyer, B. (2000). *The social work skills workbook* (3rd ed.). Belmont, CA: Thompson Brooks/Cole.

Crowther, M. R., Parker, M. W., Achenbaum, W. A., Larimore, W. L., & Koenig, H. G. (2002). Rowe and Kahn's Model of successful aging revisited: Positive spirituality—The forgotten factor. *The Gerontologist, 42,* (5), 613-620.

Dean, R. G. (1993). Teaching a constructivist approach to clinical practice. In J. Laird (Ed.), *Revisioning social work education: A social constructionist approach* (pp. 55-76). New York: Haworth Press.

Dew, M. A., Hoch, C. C., Buysse, D. J., Monk, T. H., Begley, A. E., Houck, P. R., Hall, M., Kupfer, D., & Reynolds, C. F. (2003). Healthy older adults' sleep predicts all-cause mortality at 4 to 19 years of follow-up. *Psychosomatic Medicine, 65*, 63-73.

Espino, D. V., Avril, C. A., Bradley, J., Johnston, C. L., & Mouton, C. P. (1998). Diagnostic approach to the confused elderly patient. *American Family Physician, 57*, 1358-1367.

Eyde, D. R., & Rich, J. (1983). *Psychological distress in aging: A family management model*. Rockville, MD: Aspen Publishers.

Fillenbaum, G., Gallo, J.J., Fulmer, T., Paveza, G. J., & Reichel, W. (2000). *Handbook of aging and human development*. Rockville, MD: Aspen Publishers.

Folstein, M. F., Folstein, S., & McHugh, P. R. (1975). Mini-mental state: A practical method for grading the cognitive state of patients for the clinician. *Journal of Psychiatric Research, 12*, 189-198.

Germain, C. B., & Gitterman, A. (1996). *The life model of social work: Advances in theory and practice*. New York: Columbia University Press.

Greene, R. R. (1999/2008). *Human behavior and social work practice* (3rd. ed.). New Brunswick, NJ: Aldine de Gruyter.

Greene, R. R., & McGuire, L. (1998). Ecological perspective: Meeting the challenge of practice with diverse populations. In R. R. Greene & M. Watkins (Eds.). *Serving diverse constituencies: Applying the ecological perspective* (pp. 1-28). New York: Aldine de Gruyter.

Greene, R. R., & Watkins, M. (1998). *Serving diverse constituencies: Applying the ecological perspective*. New York: Aldine de Gruyter.

Hall, D. E. (2006). Religious attendance: More cost-effective than lipitor? *Journal of American Board of family Medicine, 19*(2), 103-109.

Hartman, A., (1978). Diagrammatic assessment of family relationships. *Social Casework, 59*, 465-476.

Hartman, A., & Laird, J. (1983). *Family-centered social work practice*. New York: Free Press.

Hooyman, N., & Kiyak, H.A. (2004). *Social gerontology: A multidisciplinary perspective*. Boston: Allyn & Bacon.

Kadushin, A. & Kadushin, G. (1997). *The social work interview: A guide for human service professionals*. New York: Columbia University Press.

Kahn, R.L., Goldfarb, I., & Pollack, M. (1964). The evaluation of geriatric patients following treatment. In P. H. Hoch, & J. Zubin (Eds.), *Evaluation of psychiatric treatment*. New York: Grune and Stratton.

Kane, R.L., & Kane, R. A. (1981). *Assessing the elderly: A practical guide to management.* Lexington, MA: D.C. Health.

Kastenbaum, R. (1993). *Encyclopedia of adult development.* Westport, CT: Greenwood Press..

Katz, S. (1983). Assessing self-maintenance: Activities of daily living, mobility, and instrumental activities of daily living. *Journal of the American Geriatric Society, 31,* 721-727.

Laird, J. (1993). Family-centered practice: Cultural and constructionist reflections. In J. Laird (Ed.), *Revisioning social work education: A social constructionist approach* (pp. 77-110). New York: Haworth Press.

Lawton, M. P. (1982). Competence, environmental press, and the adaptation of older people. In M. P. Lawton, P. G. Windley, & T. O. Byerts (Eds.), *Aging and the environment: Theoretical approaches* (pp. 33–59). New York: Springer.

Lawton, M. P. (1991). Functional status and aging well. *Generations, 15,* 31-36.

Merck & Co., Inc. (2005). *The Merck Manual of Geriatrics.* Retrieved October 1, 2005, from *http://www.merck.com/mrkshared/mmg/sec1/ch7/ch7a.jsp*

Masoro, E., & Austad, S. (2005). *Handbook of the biology of aging.* San Diego, CA: Academic Press.

McIntosh, L. J., Frahm, J.D., Mallett, V.T. & Richardson, D. A. (1993). Pelvic floor rehabilitation in the treatment of incontinence. *Journal of Reproductive Medicine, 38* (9), 662-666.

Meyer, C. (1993). *Assessment in social work practice.* New York: Columbia University Press.

McInnis, K. (2002). *Social work with elders: A biopsychosocial approach to assessment and intervention.* Boston: Allyn & Bacon.

Morrow-Howell, N. (1992). Multidimensional assessment of the elderly. *Families in Society, 73,* 395-406.

Northen H. (1995). *Clinical social work knowledge and skills.* New York: Columbia University Press.

Perlman, H. H. (1957). *Social casework. A problem-solving process.* Chicago: University of Chicago Press.

Pinderhughes, E. (1995). Direct practice overview. In R. L. Edwards (Ed.-in-Chief), *Encyclopedia of social work.* (Vol. 1, pp. 740-751). Washington, DC: NASW Press.

Rowe, J. W., & Kahn, R. L. (1998). *Successful aging.* New York: Pantheon.

Schneider, E. L., & Rowe, J. W. (1996). *Handbook of the biology of aging.* San Diego, CA: Academic Press.

Shulman, L. (2005). *The skills of helping individuals, families, groups, and communities.* New York: Wadsworth.

Tinetti, M. E., & Powell, L. (1993). Fear of falling and low self-efficacy: A cause of dependence in elderly persons [Special Edition]. *Journal of Gerontology, 48,* 35-38.

Willis, S. L. (1996a). Assessing everyday competence in the cognitively challenged elderly. In M. Smyer, K. Schaie, W. Kapp, & B. Marshall (Eds.), *Older adults' decision making and the law.* New York: Springer.

Willis, S. L. (1996b). Everyday cognitive competence in elderly persons: Conceptual issues and empirical findings. *The Gerontologist, 36,* 595-601.

Zarit, S. H. & Zarit, J. M. (1998). *Mental disorders in older adults: Fundamentals of assessment.* New York: Guilford.

Zarit. S., Reever, K., & Bach-Peterso, J. (1980). Relatives of the impaired elderly: Correlates of feelings of burden. The Gerontologist, 20, 649-655.

4

Psychological Aspects of Functional Age

This chapter discusses the psychological aspects of functional age including development across the life course, the adaptive processes of older adults, the sensory processes of aging, and the major mental illnesses of later years.

Introduction

Despite the ever-growing body of scientific knowledge associated with the processes of growing old, there are still myths about the psychological aspects of aging. Although there is no evidence that the normal processes of aging produce substantial changes in personality, a common notion about age-related personality change (even among professionals) is that as individuals grow older, they become more rigid, irritable, demanding, and set in their ways.

Another myth about the psychological aspects of aging is that aging is associated with reverse development and decline. Before 1940, social scientists (a) believed that individuals did not develop after reaching maturity and (b) generally confined themselves to understanding the early stages of life. In subsequent decades, life-span theorists rejected this view. They pointed out that, although there may be limits to the growth of physical attributes such as height, other qualities such as creativity and abstract reasoning do not fit this model. For example, according to Borysenko, (1996), the last stage of life involves developmental tasks that require the older adult to

- respond to loss and change by using these opportunities to reevaluate life circumstances and create new fulfilling pathways,
- remain physically, psychologically, intellectually, and spiritually active and as emotionally connected as possible,

- come to terms with death while focusing on what else one can still do for oneself and others,
- bring careful reflection, perspective, and balance to the task of life review,
- accept dependence on others and diminished control of one's life,
- affirm and work out one's financial, spiritual, and emotional legacy to the next generation,
- accept death of spouse (partner) and need to create a new life,
- accept one's own life and death. (p. 243)

Thus, development unfolds continuously throughout the life span from conception until death, and does not cease with the attainment of physical maturity.

As theorists increasingly questioned whether the life cycle follows an inherent, fixed trajectory, the concept of lifelong development further evolved to encompass the life course model adopted here. The life course assumes that the family status and position that people experience in later years of life is molded by cumulative life history and by the specific historical conditions affecting their lives at earlier times (Hareven, 1996). This approach is particularly useful in social work with the aged and their families because it examines intergenerational relationships such as mutual support as they are shaped by environmental circumstances such as poverty, oppression, violence, or immigration (Hareven 1996).

Psychological Age and Adaptability in the Older Adult

Psychological age provides an understanding of the psychological adaptations of adulthood, and explains how an aging client has faced problems of daily living throughout the life course. The assessment of *psychological age* and the related concept of adaptability involve an evaluation of an individual's lifelong adjustment coping strategies and how these strategies have been affected by recent events. The psychological age approach has several benefits. Because the concept encompasses past and present adaptive issues, its use during assessment allows the social worker "to start where the client is." The psychological age approach has the added benefit of avoiding unnecessary labeling. While there are settings that base assessment on the classification of mental disorders defined by the American Psychiatric Association in the *Diagnostic and Statistical Manual of Mental Disorders*, (DSM–IV;1994), social workers also need to be able to arrive at a clear picture of the whole person.

The practitioner is not restricted to using diagnostic categories. Rather, he or she gathers information related to life history, present difficulties, critical incidents, economic circumstances, living conditions and routine activities of daily living, and psychological and interpersonal attitudes. The psychological aspects of a geriatric evaluation include a general appraisal of personality functioning, such as a client's ability to handle his or her own affairs, level of contact with reality, judgment, problem-solving capacity, sense of self-esteem, appropriateness of affect, and interpersonal skills. This information enables the practitioner to better understand the client's coping strategies and intervention needs. It provides a full picture of psychological age or how the elderly client is adapting to life changes, stress, and loss. The psychological age perspective also suggests appropriate intervention strategies that draw on the client's strengths and resources.

Psychological age may be defined as a person's relative capacity to adapt to his or her environment across the life course, and it encompasses intellectual, behavioral, affective, and psychiatric aspects of human behavior. Distinguishing what constitutes adaptive behavior or the relative capacity to be well functioning in a given society is a complex task. Among the behaviors considered adaptive, are those that (a) contribute to effective modes of dealing with reality; (b) lead to a mastery of the environment; (c) resolve conflict; (d) reduce stress; or (e) establish personal satisfaction (Greene, 2007). Select theoretical perspectives on adaptability are described below and a summary of definitions is provided in table 4.1.

Birren: Origins of Functional Age

Birren (1959) was among the pioneers addressing the question of adaptability in adulthood. In his study of functional age, Birren developed a research strategy to appraise an individual's level of functioning in a given environment relative to others his or her age. His research on the functional capacities of older adults led to the delineation of three kinds of aging: biological age, social age, and psychological age. He defined psychological age as the age-related adaptive capacities of the individual, encompassing the ability to adapt to and modify familiar as well as unfamiliar environments. By equating psychological age with adaptability and recognizing that mastery of the environment is a vital personality function, Birren set the stage for the discussion of adaptation in later life.

Table 4.1
A Summary of Definitions of Adaptability

Author	Adaptability Definition
Birren	Adaptability is akin to psychological age and manifests itself in the capacity to adjust to and modify the environment.
Erikson	Adaptability is directly related to the strength of one's ego and the support of social institutions.
Peck	Adaptation requires "deep" active effort to make life more secure and meaningful through ego differentiation.
Pfeiffer	Adaptation is the process of meeting an individual's biological, psychological, and social needs under changing circumstances.
Lawton	Adaptation is akin to individual competence achieved by successfully meeting the demands of environmental press.
Germain	Adaptation is a continuous active process characterized by positive person-environment fit.
Atchley	Adaptation is the maintenance of internal and external patterns throughout the life course.

Erikson: Stages of Life

Erickson's (1950) discussion of adaptiveness throughout the eight stages of life focuses on how an individual solves a series of psychosocial crises. Through the resolution of these crises, an individual develops his or her coping strategies. Erikson's perspective suggests that adaptability involves the strengthening of a person's ego as an outcome of the relatively successful resolution of the challenges of each developmental stage.

Erikson believed that at each life stage people develop a new orientation toward themselves and toward their world. For example, Erikson termed the polarity of the psychosocial crisis of late adulthood *integrity versus despair*. He contended that older people who have achieved a sense of integrity appreciate the continuity of past, present, and future experiences. They also accept their life cycle and experience a sense of being complete (integrity). On the other hand, older people who experience a sense of despair feel that time has been too short and want a second chance at life. They find little meaning in human existence, and they have lost faith in themselves and others (despair). Such individuals have little sense of world order or spiritual wholeness. As a result, they are fearful of death.

Erikson was also concerned with how social organizations influence adaptability. He was sensitive to the idea that if societal institutions become fragmented and unresponsive, they may contribute to a disturbance in personal identity. He proposed that in every society there is a crucial coordination between the developing individual and his or her human environment. His optimistic vision of mental health emphasizes the growth of the healthy personality and stresses the need for socioeconomic, ethnic, and institutional factors to meet human needs. This person-environment image makes Erikson's theory consistent with effective social work practice with the older adult.

Peck: Adaptive Tasks of Old Age

Peck (1968) thought that there were three major psychological adaptive tasks in old age: (a) transcending the work role, referring to the ability to secure a sense of self-worth by engaging in activities beyond the "job"; (b) transcending the body, concerning the capacity to adjust to the decline in physical powers that accompany old age; and (c) transcending the ego, relating to the ability to face the immediate and certain prospects of death with a "deep, active effort to make life more secure, meaningful, or happy for those who go on after one dies" (Peck, 1968, p. 91). Peck concluded that the developmental tasks of old age can vary greatly from one adult to another and that the timing of life stages cannot necessarily be tied to chronological age.

Pfeiffer: Aging and the Adaptation to Loss

Pfeiffer (1977) added another dimension to understanding the adaptive tasks of later life. He proposed that although losses can occur at any age, adaptation to loss is one of the principal tasks facing an older adult. Most elderly people face multiple losses, including the loss of a spouse, partner, friend, or colleague; a decline in physical health, body tone, or hair; and loss of status, prestige, or income. The task becomes one of "replacing" some of the losses with new relationships, "retraining for lost capacities," or "making do with less" (p. 651). While growth is usually conceived of as obtaining something more than existed previously, people are confronted with and tested by loss and separation throughout life. Thus, loss—whether of a possession, a function, an ideal, or a relationship—is a part of the developmental process (Carr, 1975).

Another important task in later life, suggested by Pfeiffer (1977), is an identity review. An identity review involves self-reflection and reminiscence in the face of approaching death, and it is an evaluative backward glance at one's life. An individual weighs his or her accomplishments and failures and comes to a reasonably positive view of life's worth. This process of enhancing self-esteem has been incorporated in a number of treatment modalities discussed later in the text. Another major task of later life proposed by Pfeiffer is the ability to remain active to retain function. Pfeiffer assumed that to age successfully older people must maintain their physical and social activity and find suitable intellectual and emotional stimulation. Pfeiffer concluded that when maintenance of these critical functions does not occur, aging is less successful.

Lawton: Meeting Environmental Demands

Lawton's work represents a departure from stage theories that examine life segments or predetermined life tasks. Whereas Erikson, Peck, and Pfeiffer focused on the psychological adaptive tasks, Lawton emphasized an ecological view of the connection between the physical and psychological characteristics of aging (Hooyman & Kiyak, 1999; Willis, 1991). In a series of seminal works (1982, 1987), Lawton developed a model of competence, environmental press, and adaptation. He defined *everyday competence* as a person's ability or potential to carry out activities necessary for living independently within the demands of their social and physical environment—including the home, the neighborhood, the community, and the larger society. He termed the demands of the social and physical environment *environmental press* (see chapter 3, figure 3.1)

Depending on a person's living arrangements and the quality of his or her surroundings, the demands of environmental press can range from weak to strong. When the pressure of the environment is strong or oppressive, such as living in an abusive home situation, environmental press is high and produces a negative effect on an individual's functioning. On the other hand, when an individual's needs for safety and care are met, press is low and a person's psychological well-being is enhanced. At the same time, the greater a person's competence, greater the ability to manage environmental press (Lawton & Nahemow, 1973). A social worker's consideration of how environmental press influences an older adult's daily life covers issues of biological, social, and psychological age, suggesting intervention strategies from micro- to macrolevels (Lawton & Nahemow, 1973, chaps. 9 to 11).

Germain: Adaptation to the Environment

Germain (1994) is another theorist who proposed an ecological definition of adaptation. A major assumption of this perspective is that person and environment form a unitary, inseparable unit and mutually influence each other (Bronfenbrenner, 1979). This concept of adaptiveness examines the *goodness of fit* between a person and his or her environment, or the match between person and environment over time.

Germain (1994) outlined four capacities that she believed to be significant to adaptation that are relatively free of cultural bias: (1) *human relatedness*, sustaining personal relationships and emotional support; (2) *competence*, acting effectively on one's environment; (3) *self-esteem*, feeling capable, significant, effective, and worthy; and (4) *self-direction*, taking responsibility for oneself, making decisions, and pursuing purposive action (pp. 45-48).

Whereas most people are able to adapt to later life with relative success, others can experience stress and difficulty that lead to problems of living. Although there are differences in emphasis, the definitions of adaptability discussed here clearly point out that the relationship of the individual to his or her environment is the crux of assisting older adults and their families to meet these challenges. Because an ecological perspective views a person's capacity to interact with the environment, and to strive for competence as innate, it also offers a strengths-based practice perspective.

Atchley: Maintaining Continuity

Atchley (1999) is a gerontologist with a long-standing interest in why—despite significant changes in health, function, and social circumstances—older adults maintain their customary lifestyle patterns throughout the life course. He linked his conception of adaptability to continuity theory. *Continuity theory* examines adult development as a process in which the older adult adapts to changing internal and external circumstances. The theory assumes that the major goal of adult development is adaptive change (Atchley, 1999). Adaptation is a consequence of lifetime learning, personal growth, and a considerable investment in one's internal and external life patterns.

Atchley (1999) outlined the following principles: Continuity theory is constructionist, that is, people actively interpret their own experiences and individualize their ideas. These subjective ideas about reality form meaningful patterns and allow a person to adapt and have "coherence in their life stories" (p. 7). Internal thinking patterns that are maintained include self-concept, personal goals, worldview, philosophy of life, coping strategies, and moral frameworks. External patterns involve social role, activities, relationships, living arrangements, and geographic location (see chapter 5).

Strength and Resilience in Older Adults

Other theories that stem from the strengths perspective also address adaptability and are increasingly popular in guiding social work practice with the aged (Greene & Cohen, 2005; Lewis & Harrell, 2002). Risk and resilience theory is an emerging theory that has roots in developmental theory and the strengths-based movement (Greene, 2002, 2007; Saleebey, 1997). The theory also comes under the umbrella of positive psychology, an area of psychology that focuses on how people maintain well-being despite adversity. *Resilience* can be defined as markedly successful adaptation following an adverse event (Greene, 2007; table 4.2). In using this concept in assessment, social workers would determine what *protective factors*—events and conditions that help individuals to reduce risk and enhance adaptation—exist in the client's internal and external environments. Practitioners would also explore a client's "self-righting capacity" or natural capacity to heal (Garmezy, 1993, p. 129). This leads to an evaluation of what adverse events may threaten a person's self-reliance and how he or she is managing specific external and/or internal demands. When a practitioner learns what abilities and assets a client possesses, this knowledge may be used to further effective adaptation.

Understanding Sensory and Cognitive Processes in the Older Adult

The ability of older persons to acquire new information, to alter behavior, and to develop new skills is related to cognitive and sensory process. While an in-depth discussion is beyond the scope of this text, this section presents an overview of the major and most pertinent cognitive and sensory functions.

Sensory Processes

It is generally accepted that all five senses tend to decline in old age. However, the level of functioning of a particular individual depends on his or her state of health and the adaptive strategies he or she has evolved to optimize performance.

Table 4.2
Definitions of Resilience

Rutter	Resilience is concerned with individual variations in response to risk.
Palmer	Resilience is a process in which the development of substantive character is made up of greater or lesser periods of disruption and the development and use of greater or lesser competencies in life management.
Borden	Resilience is the ability to maintain continuity of one's personal narrative and a coherent sense of self following traumatic events.

Vision. With age the eye undergoes many structural changes; as a result, visual difficulties tend to increase. In general, starting at the age of forty-five, the eye gradually becomes less flexible, and in old age it becomes less able to distinguish levels of brightness, less color sensitive, and more sensitive to glare. Many older persons adapt to these changes by wearing glasses, using large-print reading materials, and not driving at night.

Hearing. With advancing age there are physiological changes in the auditory system, changes usually associated with disturbances in the inner ear and related neural pathways. These disturbances produce functional changes in hearing. Significant hearing loss occurs in 30 percent of all older people, more often in men. Sounds in the higher frequency ranges are harder to hear, the intensity level within the range of pitch that older people can hear needs to be greater, and there is more difficulty making fine distinctions in hearing speech. Helping an older person to accept a hearing loss and compensate for it is an important social work function. Interventions may take the form of educating a person about the advantages of wearing a hearing aid or installing an amplifier on the telephone.

Taste, smell, and somesthetic sensitivity. The number of taste buds tends to decrease starting in childhood, and a sensitivity to taste declines particularly in the sixties. The inability to enjoy the sense of taste is often compounded for those whose health requires them to eliminate salt and other spices, making it even more difficult to enjoy food. The staff of nutrition programs can help older people adjust to this difficulty by offering attractively prepared foods and companionship at mealtime.

The sense of smell also tends to decline with age. This decline can result in a lessening of the ability to distinguish unpleasant odors or smoke. The social worker can be most helpful in this instance by evaluating safety aspects of the client's living conditions. Somesthetic (touch, vibration, temperature, kinesthesis, pain) also tends to decrease with age. Losses in these areas are by no means universal and are often related to specific physical problems or diseases. Therefore, changes should be considered in light of a multifaceted assessment.

Cognitive Processes

Intelligence is a term that refers to the capacity and the ability to effectively perform and learn cognitive and behavioral tasks. *Memory* refers to the ability to retain information about specific events that have occurred at a given time and place. It is a process of storing and retrieving facts or information, involving short and long-term capacities. *Short-term memory* refers to recall after a relatively brief delay or time period; *long-term memory* refers to recall of events that occurred in the past and have not been frequently rehearsed. Of interest to the social worker is how the capacity to recall events affects the client's activities of daily living and functional capacities. *Learning* refers to the ability to acquire general knowledge about the world and can occur at all ages. It involves the ability to store knowledge and develop intellectual skills (Hoffman, Paris & Hall, 1994).

Recognizing the Major Psychiatric Disorders of Later Life

When older adults experience a mental illness, there are usually many changes throughout the family (see chapter 6). Families may have numerous questions including, Why is my relative behaving this way? What causes mental illness? What is the chance of recovery? or How do I find the best treatment? (Hatfield, 1998, p. ix). Because mental illness can affect the quality of life of millions older adults and their families, geriatric social workers must be able to recognize the major psychiatric disorders that may be associated with later life and realize treatment potentials (Pinquart & Soerensen, 2001). The symptoms of depression and dementia and the means of assessing and treating these disorders are described in the following section (Liebowitz et al., 1977).

Depression

Depression is one of the most common psychiatric disorders in people over sixty-five years of age (NIA, 1999). In 1991, the magnitude of the problem led the National Institutes of Health to hold a Consensus Development Conference on Diagnosis and Treatment of Depression in Later Life. The Consensus Panel found that the seriousness of late-life depression constituted a public health concern. The panel also concluded that even though depression among older adults may be accompanied by other illnesses, such as vascular disorders, depression is not a normal aging process and can be diagnosed and successfully treated. Several efficacious treatments are available for geriatric depression but seem to go underused. These include interpersonal, brief psychodynamic, problem-solving, and cognitive-behavioral therapies (Gallagher-Thompson et al., 2000). In addition, when depression goes untreated, it leads to a greater use of health care services and accompanied cost in medical care (Leibowitz et al., 1977).

The fact that there are increased impairments in physical, mental, and social functioning among depressed elders is supported by recent studies (IOM, 2003; U.S. Department of HHS, 1999). Despite being associated with excess morbidity and mortality, depression often goes under diagnosed and treated. A Report of the Surgeon General (1999) attributes this problem to the fact that depression is difficult to discriminate from many of the other disorders facing older adults.

The term *depression* is generally used to refer to a wide variety of feelings ranging from a mild indifference to a state of complete demoralization. *Depressive illness*, according to the DSM–IV (American Psychiatric Association, 1994), is a mood disorder (table 4.3). The most common everyday signs of depression include an empty feeling; tiredness or lack of energy; loss of interest or pleasure in everyday activities, including sex; sleep problems; problems with eating, a weight gain, or a weight loss; a lot of crying; aches and pains that won't go away; a hard time focusing, remembering, or making decisions; feeling that the future looks grim, feeling guilty, feeling helpless, or feeling worthless, being irritable; or thoughts of death or suicide, or a suicide attempt (National Institute on Aging, 1999). Practitioners may observe or ask clients if they

- feel guilty or worthless
- are very tired and slowed down
- feel nervous or "empty"
- become restless or irritable
- think that no one likes or loves them
- believe life is not worth living (NIMH, *http://www.nimh,nih.gov/healthinformation/depoldermenu.cfm*)

Table 4.3
DSM–IV Criteria for Major Depressive Episode

A. Five (or more) of the following symptoms have been present during the same 2-week period and represent a change from previous functioning; at least one of the symptoms is either (1) depressed mood or (2) loss of interest or pleasure.   ·

Note: Do not include symptoms that are clearly due to a general medical condition, or mood-incongruent delusions or hallucinations.

(1) depressed mood most of the day, nearly every day, as indicated by either subjective report (e.g., feels sad or empty) or observation made by others (e.g., appears tearful). Note: In children and adolescents, can be irritable mood.

(2) markedly diminished interest or pleasure in all, or almost all, activities most of the day, nearly every day (as indicated by either subjective account or observation made by others).

(3) significant weight loss when not dieting or weight gain (e.g., a change of more than 5% of body weight in a month), or decrease or increase in appetite nearly every day. Note: In children, consider failure to make expected weight gains.

(4) insomnia or hypersomnia nearly every day.

(5) psychomotor agitation or retardation nearly every day (observable by others, not merely subjective feelings of restlessness or being slowed down).

(6) fatigue or loss of energy nearly every day.

(7) feelings of worthlessness or excessive or inappropriate guilt (which may be delusional) nearly every day (not merely self-reproach or guilt about being sick).

(8) diminished ability to think or concentrate, or indecisiveness, nearly every day (either by subjective account or as observed by others).

(9) recurrent thoughts of death (not just fear of dying), recurrent suicidal ideation without a specific plan, or a suicide attempt or a specific plan for committing suicide.

B. The symptoms do not meet criteria for a Mixed Episode.

C. The symptoms cause clinically significant distress or impairment in social, occupational, or other important area of functioning.

D. The symptoms are not due to the direct physiological effects of a substance (e.g., a drug of abuse, a medication) or a general medical condition (e.g., hypothyrodism).

E. The symptoms are not better accounted for by bereavement (i.e., after the loss of a loved one, the symptoms persist for longer than 2 months or are characterized by marked functional impairment, morbid preoccupation with worthlessness, suicidal ideation, psychotic symptoms, or psychomotor retardation).

Treatment for depression generally includes a combination of psychotherapy and medication depending on the severity of the depression (Scogin, 2001). For a mild depression, nondrug therapies are as effective as antidepressant medication; for mild-to-moderate depression, nondrug therapies are sometimes sufficient, but some older adults may also need antidepressant medication; for moderate-to-severe depression, medications are needed (American Psychiatric Association, 1998; NIA, 1999). Depression may be triggered by difficult life events such as death of a loved one.

Social workers need to be aware that clinical depression is not *grief*—a normal reaction to loss. In addition, older adults cannot treat depression on their own and often need to be encouraged by their families or friends to seek professional help (Mental Health America, 2007; Wyeth-Ayerst Connexions, 1997). Social workers can play a significant role in reaching out to depressed older adults and in screening for depression among a well elderly population (Dorfman et al., 1995).

Confusion

Confusion is a relatively frequent phenomenon among older adults. Confusion may be a symptom of delirium or dementia, but it also occurs with depression and psychoses. Confusion may be attributed to a number of causes including medications, diseases such as diabetes, and infections (Espino, Avril, Jules-Bradley, Johnston, & Mouton 1998). Therefore, geriatric social workers need to be prepared to assist older adults and their families to sort out the difficulty about what has caused the confusion.

The social worker generally acts as a member of an assessment team or in conjunction with a person's primary physician. Because social workers often see clients in their familiar surroundings, they need to be aware of general symptoms and changes in functional status: Are the cognitive or behavioral changes of recent onset or have they been developing over a period of months? Has the patient had a change in his or her functional activities? What chronic medical problems exist? What is the patient's level of alertness? (Espino et al., 1998, p. 1360). Depending on their work setting, geriatric social workers may also give a brief mental-status type of examination. (The Mental Status Questionnaire of Kahn et al. 1960, presented in table 4. 4 is probably the most widely used and appropriate to include in social work interviews). An assessment for confusion in an older adult is not complete until there is a full physical exam and laboratory tests.

Table 4.4
Mental Status Questionnaire

1. Where are we now?

2. Where is this place located?

3. What is today's date?

4. What month is it?

5. What year is it?

6. How old are you?

7. What is your birthday?

8. What year were you born?

9. Who is President of the United States?

10. Who was President before him?

Modified from R. L. Kahn, L. Goldfarb, & M. Pollack (1964). The evaluation of geriatric patients following treatment. In P. H. Hoch & J. Zubin (Eds.), *Evaluation of psychiatric treatment*. New York: Grune & Stratton.

Dementia

Dementia is described by the DSM–IV (American Psychiatric Association, 1994) as a significant change in the level of cognitive function or memory (table 4.5). Approximately 4 million people or 10.9 percent of the population over sixty-five years of age have Alzheimer's disease (Administration on Aging, 1999). As Alzheimer's disease progresses, individuals experience an irreversible decline in mental functioning (table 4.6). A person gradually loses their capacity to reason, communicate, and carry out the simple tasks of daily life. Alzheimer's disease is devastating to individuals who have the disease and seriously disrupts the lives of those who care for them (*http://www.alzinfo.org*).

The risk of dementia increases with age: the chance of developing a dementing illness roughly doubles every year after age sixty-five. Over the age of eighty-five, 47 percent of the elderly exhibit a dementing illness (Soniat & Pollack, 1993). One in ten individuals over sixty-five and nearly half of those over eighty-five are affected. One percent of those age sixty to sixty-four are affected with dementia; 2 percent of those age

Table 4.5
DSM–IV Diagnostic Criteria for Dementia of the Alzheimer's Type

F. The development of multiple cognitive deficits manifested by both
    (1) memory impairment (impaired ability to learn new information or to recall previously learned information);
    (2) one (or more) of the following cognitive disturbances:
    (a) aphasia (language disturbance),
    (b) apraxia (impaired ability to carry out motor activities despite intact motor function),
    (c) agnosia (failure to recognize or identify objects despite intact sensory function),   ,
    (d) disturbance in executive functioning (i.e., planning, organizing, sequencing, abstracting).

G. The cognitive deficits in Criteria A1 and A2 each cause significant impairment in social or occupational functioning and represent a significant decline from a previous level of functioning.

H. The course is characterized by gradual onset and continuing cognitive decline.

I. The cognitive deficits in Criteria A1 and A2 are not due to any of the following:

    (1) other central nervous system conditions that cause progressive deficits in memory and cognition (e.g., cerebrovascular disease, Parkinson's disease, Huntington's disease, subdural hematoma, normal-pressure hydrocephalus, brain tumor);
    (2) systemic conditions that are known to cause dementia (e.g., hypothyrodism, vitamin B12 or folic acid deficiency, niacin deficiency, hypercalcemia, neurosyphilis, HIV infection);
    (3) substance-induced conditions.

J. The deficits do not occur exclusively during the course of a delirium.

K. The disturbance is not better accounted for by another Axis I disorder (e.g., Major Depressive Disorder, Schizophrenia)

---

sixty-five to sixty-nine; 4 percent of those age seventy to seventy-four; 8 percent of those seventy-five to seventy-nine; 16 percent of those age eighty to eighty-four; and 30 to 45 percent of those age eighty-five and older. Cognitive impairments that "cause anguish to millions of caregivers" eventually mean that an older adult can not undertake daily activities such as preparing meals, managing finances, using the telephone, or driving without getting lost (table 4.6). These are often the psychosocial aspects of dementia for which families seek help (Small et al., 1997, p. 1363, chap. 11).

Table 4.6
Stages of Alzheimer's Disease

Stage I	**No impairment** (normal function)
	Unimpaired individuals experience no memory problems and none are evident to a health care professional during a medical interview.
Stage II	**Very mild cognitive decline** (may be normal age-related changes or earliest signs of Alzheimer's disease)
	Individuals may feel as if they have memory lapses, especially in forgetting familiar words or names or the location of keys, eye glasses or other everyday objects. But these problems are not evident during a medical examination or apparent to friends, family or co-workers.
Stage III	**Mild cognitive decline** Early-stage Alzheimer's can be diagnosed in some, but not all, individuals with these symptoms
	Friends, family or co-workers begin to notice deficiencies. Problems with memory or concentration may be measurable in clinical testing or discernible during a detailed medical interview. Common difficulties include:
	Word- or name-finding problems noticeable to family or close associates
	Decreased ability to remember names when introduced to new people
	Performance issues in social or work settings noticeable to family, friends or co-workers
	Reading a passage and retaining little material
	Losing or misplacing a valuable object
	Decline in ability to plan or organize.
Stage IV	**Moderate cognitive decline** (Mild or early-stage Alzheimer's disease)
	At this stage, a careful medical interview detects clear-cut deficiencies in the following areas:
	Decreased knowledge of recent occasions or current events
	Impaired ability to perform challenging mental arithmetic-for example, to count backward from 100 by 7s
	Decreased capacity to perform complex tasks, such as marketing, planning dinner for guests or paying bills and managing finances
	Reduced memory of personal history
	The affected individual may seem subdued and withdrawn, especially in socially or mentally challenging situations.

Stage V   **Moderately severe cognitive decline** (Moderate or mid-stage Alzheimer's disease)

Major gaps in memory and deficits in cognitive function emerge. Some assistance with day-to-day activities becomes essential. At this stage, individuals may:

Be unable during a medical interview to recall such important details as their current address, their telephone number or the name of the college or high school from which they graduated

Become confused about where they are or about the date, day of the week, or season

Have trouble with less challenging mental arithmetic; for example, counting backward from 40 by 4s or from 20 by 2s

Need help choosing proper clothing for the season or the occasion

Usually retain substantial knowledge about themselves and know their own name and the names of their spouse or children

Usually require no assistance with eating or using the toilet.

Stage VI   **Severe cognitive decline** (Moderately severe or mid-stage Alzheimer's disease)

Memory difficulties continue to worsen, significant personality changes may emerge and affected individuals need extensive help with customary daily activities. At this stage, individuals may:

Lose most awareness of recent experiences and events as well as of their surroundings

Recollect their personal history imperfectly, although they generally recall their own name

Occasionally forget the name of their spouse or primary caregiver but generally can distinguish familiar from unfamiliar faces

Need help getting dressed properly; without supervision, may make such errors as putting pajamas over daytime clothes or shoes on wrong feet

Experience disruption of their normal sleep/waking cycle

Need help with handling details of toileting (flushing toilet, wiping and disposing of tissue properly)

Have increasing episodes of urinary or fecal incontinence

Experience significant personality changes and behavioral symptoms, including suspiciousness and delusions (for example, believing that their caregiver is an impostor); hallucinations (seeing or hearing things that are not really there); or compulsive, repetitive behaviors such as hand-wringing or tissue shredding

Tend to wander and become lost.

Stage VII   **Very severe cognitive decline** (Severe or late-stage Alzheimer's disease)

This is the final stage of the disease when individuals lose the ability to respond to their environment, the ability to speak and, ultimately, the ability to control movement.

Frequently individuals lose their capacity for recognizable speech, although words or phrases may occasionally be uttered.

Individuals need help with eating and toileting and there is general incontinence of urine. Individuals lose the ability to walk without assistance, then the ability to sit without support, the ability to smile, and the ability to hold their heads up. Reflexes become abnormal and muscles grow rigid. Swallowing is impaired.

---

http://www:alz.org/aboutAD/stages.asp prepared by Barry Reisberg, Clinical Director, NYU School of Medicine, Silberstein Aging and Dementia Research Center.

Delirium

Among the other diagnoses the medical team makes is the distinction between (a) Alzheimer's and vascular-type dementia and (b) delirium. Delirium is a transient disturbance in consciousness and cognition (American Psychological Association, 1994). Because some of the underlying causes of delirium may be a medical condition that is treatable, it is important to take notice of these changes and make this distinction quickly. Dementia is a generic term characterized by multiple cognitive losses but may be due to general medical conditions, vascular changes, Parkinson's disease, or human immunodeficiency virus (HIV disease). These too have treatable dimensions.

The following example suggests questions to explore in assessment when symptoms of depression and forgetfulness are mentioned (tables 4.7 and 4.8):

John called a family service agency for help for his mother, Mary, age 70. Mary was described as very depressed. "She has not left her apartment in 3 months." Although no medical cause could be found, Mary complained that her heart and lungs were failing. Mary's immediate family consisted of her husband, Harold, age 73, and two grandchildren, David, 19, and Rebecca, 17. Mary and Harold adopted David and Rebecca after their daughter, Barbara, died of a severe asthma attack and Barbara's husband deserted the family. At that time, this "new" family unit moved from Russia to Washington, D.C. to be near John.

During the social worker's original home visits, the family indicated that they had little interaction or family plans (for cooking or cleaning). David and Rebecca went their own way, usually to the mall, and ignore

Table 4.7
Interviewing a Client with Alzheimer's Disease

How to Talk to Someone with Alzheimer's

DOs

- Approach from the front, make eye contact, and introduce yourself
- Speak slowly, calmly, use friendly facial expression
- Use short, simple, familiar words
- Show that you are listening and trying to understand
- Ask one question at a time and allow time for a reply
- Make positive rather than negative suggestions
- Identify persons by name rather than by using pronouns
- Make suggestions if the person has difficulty choosing
- Empathize, have patience and understanding, touch or hug if it helps

DON'TS

- Don't talk about the person as if he or she weren't there
- Don't confront or correct, if it can be avoided
- Don't treat the person as a child, but as an adult

Source: Robert W. Griffith, MD, How to Talk to Someone with Alzheimer's, Health and Age, October 20, 2005 http://health and age.com/module/cms/cms_index/index.cfm

their "old fashioned" and "forgetful" grandmother. David said he was rarely at home and often ate out. Harold said he went to the senior center every day. He said my wife was depressed before when we lived in Russia, and "it will pass."

Conclusions

This chapter has emphasized the life-cycle approach to understanding psychological development and mental health status in old age. It has suggested that adaptiveness in later life, as in all stages of the life cycle, requires that people feel in control over their environment. Social work interventions that are directed toward enhancing the strengths of older people and developing their capacities can contribute to this process. This point of view has important implications for preventive social work practice. A sense of personal well-being can also be enhanced by programs that encourage interpersonal relationships, reduce unnecessary stress, and strengthen social support systems.

Table 4.8
A Study of Depression

I.   The diagnosis of mental disorder

1.   What behaviors, symptoms, lead John to believe his mother is depressed?
2.   What signs of "pathological" behavior does the social worker observe? (use DSM–IV)
3.   What does Mary say about "her depression," eating, sleeping habits, weight loss, sad feelings?
4.   What is the duration of the depression?
5.   Have there been other episodes of depression (as suggested by Harold)?
6.   If so, when, under what circumstances, and what was the treatment and the response to it?
7.   Given that no medical reasons have been found for her physical complaints, what are the symbolic meanings?
8.   Does Mary appear to have cognitive losses?

II. Indications of lifelong adjustment patterns

1.   What type of wife, grandmother, mother, has Mary been over the years? How does her family remember her? How does she recall her past life?
2.   Does Mary feel her life has been worthwhile? What does Mary think about having a "new" family to care for?
3.   How do family members describe their relationships? For example, is communication open? Do all members feel they are heard? How do they resolve conflict, deal with crises?
4.   How has Mary faced other major biopsychosocial and spiritual tasks and life transitions?
5.   How did Mary adapt to previous losses in her life, the death of Barbara, her move to Washington?

III. Present situation and family response

1.   How does Mary spend her day? Specifics.
2.   Does Mary take care of her own needs? For example, does she dress each day, fix her meals?
3.   With whom does Mary interact? How? Specifics.
4.   What has the family responses to Mary's behavior been?
5.   What, if anything, have they tried to do so far about her depression? What was the response?
6.   How do other family members feel about her behavior?

References

Administration on Aging. (1999). *Alzheimers disease: Administration on aging fact sheet.* http://www.aoa.gov/fact sheet/alz.html.

American Psychiatric Association. (1994). *Diagnostic and statistical manual of mental disorders (DSM-IV).* Washington, DC: Author.

American Psychiatric Association. (1998). *Let's talk facts about depression* [Brochure]. Washington, DC: Author.

Beers, M. H., & Berkow, R. (Eds.). (2006). *The Merck manual of diagnosis and therapy* (17th ed.). Hoboken, NJ: John Wiley & Sons.

Birren, J. E. (1959). Principles of research on aging. In J. E. Birren (Ed.), *The handbook of aging and the individual*. Chicago: University of Chicago Press. (Abridged in *Middle Age and Aging*. B. Neugarten [Ed.], Chicago: The University of Chicago Press, 1968.)

Bloom, M. (1984). *Configurations of human behavior*. New York: Macmillan.

Borden, W. (1992). Narrative perspectives in psychosocial intervention following adverse life events. *Social Work, 37*, 125–141.

Bronfenbrenner, U. (1979). *The ecology of human development*. Cambridge, MA: Harvard University Press.

Carr, A.C. (1975). Bereavement as a relative experience. In B. Schoenberg et al.(Eds.), *Bereavement: Its psychosocial aspect*. New York: Columbia University Press.

Dorfman, R. A., Lubben, J. A., Mayer-Oakes, A., Atchison, K., Schweitzer, S. O., De-Jong, F. J., & Mathias, R. E. (1995). Screening for depression among a well elderly population. *Social Work, 40*, 295-304.

Erikson, E. (1950). *Childhood and society*. New York: W. W. Norton.

Espino, D. V., Avril, C. A., Jules-Bradley, M. D., Johnston, C. L., & Mouton, C. P. (1998). *American Family Physician, 57*, 1358-1367.

Gallagher-Thompson, D., McKibbin, C. Koonce-Volwiler, D., Menendez, A., Stewart, D., & Thompson, L. W. (2000). Psychotherapy with older adults. In C. R. Snyder & R. E. Ingram, (Eds.), *Handbook of psychological change: Psychotherapy processes & practices for the 21st century* (pp. 614-637). New York: John Wiley & Sons.

Germain, C. B. (1994). Human behavior in the social environment. In F. G. Reamer (Ed.), *The foundation of social work knowledge* (pp. 88-121). New York: Columbia University Press.

Greene, R. R. (1983). Step on a crack, break an old man's back. *Gerontology and Geriatrics Education, 3*(4), 307–12.

Greene, R. R. (2002). *Resiliency theory: An integrated framework for practice, research, and policy*. Washington, DC: NASW Press.

Greene, R. R. (2007). *Social work practice: A risk and resilience perspective*. Monterey, CA: Brooks/Cole.

Greene, R. R., & Cohen, H. L. (2005). Social work with older adults and their families: Changing practice paradigms. *Families in Society, 86*(3), 367–373.

Hareven, T. K. (1996). *Aging and generational relations over the life course: A historical and cross-cultural perspective*. New York: Aldine de Gruyter.

Hatfield, A. B. (1998). *Coping with mental illness in the family: A family guide*. Arlington, VA: National Alliance for the Mentally Ill.

Hoffman, L., Paris, S. & Hall, E. (1994). *Developmental psychology today*. New York: McGraw-Hill.

Hooyman, N. R., & Kiyak, H. A. (1999). *Social gerontology: A multidisciplinary perspective*. Boston: Allyn & Bacon.

Institute of Medicine. (2003). *Unequal treatment: Confronting racial and ethnic disparities in health care*. Washington, DC: National Academy Press.

Kahn, R. L., Goldfarb, A. J., Pollack, M. & Peck, A. (1960). Brief objective measures for the determination of mental status in the aged. *American Journal of Psychiatry, 117*, 326-328.

Karel, M., & Hinrichsen, G. (2000). Treatment of depression in late life: Psychotherapeutic interventions. *Clinical Psychology Review, 20*(6), 707–729.

Kiyak, A. H. & Hooyman, N. R. (1999). Aging in the twenty-first century. *Hallyn International Journal of Aging, 1*(1), 56-66.

Lawton, M. P. (1982). Competence, environmental press, and the adaptation of older people. In M. P. Lawton, P. G. Windley, & T. O. Byers (Eds.), *Aging and the environment: Theoretical approaches* (pp. 33-59). New York: Springer.

Lawton, M. P. (1987). Contextual perspectives: Psychological influences. In L. W. Poon (Ed.), *Handbook for clinical memory assessment of older adults*. Washington, DC: American Psychological Association.

Lawton, M. P., & Nahemow, L. (1973). Ecology and the aging process. In C. Eisdorfer & M. P. Lawton (Eds.), *Psychology of adult development and aging* (pp. 619-674). Washington, DC: American Psychological Association.

Lebowitz, B. et al. (1997). Diagnosis and treatment of depression in late life: Consensus statement update. *JAMA, 278*, 1186-1190.

Lewis, J. & Harrell, E. B. (2002). Older adults. In R. R. Greene (Ed.), *Resiliency theory: An integrated framework for practice, research, and policy* (pp. 277-292). Washington, DC: NASW Press.

Lowy, L. (1991). *Social work with the aging: The challenge and promise of the later years*. New York: Harper and Row.

Maddi, S. (1972). *Personality theories*. Homewood, IL: Dorsey Press.

National Institute on Aging. (1999). *National Institute on Aging Age Page. Depression: A serious but treatable illness*. http://www.nih.gov/nia/health/pubpub/deprestl.htm.

Mental Health America. (2007). www.MentalHealthAmerica.net

Palmer, N. (1997). Resilience in adult children of alcoholics: A nonpathological approach to social work practice. *Health and Social Work, 22*, 201–209.

Peck, R. (1968). Psychological developments in the second half of life. In B. Neugarten (Ed.), *Middle age and aging*. Chicago: University of Chicago Press.

Pfeiffer, E. (1977). Psychopathology and social pathology. In J. E. Birren and K. W. Schaie (Eds.), *Handbook of psychology of aging*. New York: Van Nostrand Reinhold.

Pinquart, M., & Soerenson, S. (2001) How effective are psychotherapeutic and other psychosocial interventions with older adults? A meta analysis. *Journal of Mental Health and Aging, 7*(2), 207-243.

Saleebey, D. (1997a). Is it feasible to teach HBSE from a strengths perspective, in contrast to one emphasizing limitations and weakness? Yes. In M. Bloom & W. C. Klein (Eds.), *Controversial issues in human behavior in the social environment* (pp. 33–48). Boston: Allyn & Bacon.

Saleebey, D. (1997b). *The strengths perspective in social work practice*. New York: Longman.

Scogin, F., Shackelford, J., Rohen, N., Stump, J. Floyd, M., McKendree-Smith, N., & Jamison, C. (2001). Residual geriatric depression symptoms: A place for psychotherapy. *Journal of Clinical Geropsychology, 7*(4), 271-283.

Small, G. W. (1997). Diagnosis and treatment of Alzheimer Disease and related disorders. *JAMA, 278*, 1363-1371.

Thomas, H. (1980). Personality and adjustment to aging. In J. E. Birren and H. B. Sloane (Eds.), *Handbook of mental health and aging*. Englewood Cliffs, NJ: Prentice-Hall.

U. S. Department of Health and Human Services, Public Health Service. (1993). *Depression is a treatable illness: A patient guide* [Brochure]. Washington, DC: U. S. Government Printing office.

U.S. Department of Health and Human Services, Substance Abuse and Mental Health Services Administration. (1999*). Mental health: A report of the Surgeon General*. Rockville, MD: Center for Mental Health Services, National Institutes of Health, National Institute of Mental Health.

Willis, S. L. (1991). Cognition and everyday competence. In K. W. Schaie (Ed.), *Annual review of gerontology and geriatrics*, (vol. 11, pp. 80-109). New York: Springer.

Wyeth-Ayerst Connexions. (1997). *Talking: Understanding depression* [Brochure].

5

Sociocultural and Spiritual Aspects
of Functional Age

with Harriet Cohen

Throughout the assessment process, social workers focus on biopsychosocial and spiritual factors that account for a client's relative functional capacity. The first part of the chapter explores the social context of how people age and introduces the concept of social age as the major vehicle for evaluating an older client's situational and environmental circumstances. Living arrangements, household composition, marital status, income, modes of transportation, use of technology, and patterns of activity, such as socializing and hobbies, are all encompassed in a client's social milieu (Atchley, 1999, Kiyak & Hooyman, 1999). During the process of exploring the social context of how a client ages, the practitioner may focus on any level of social influence--from client's immediate interpersonal environment (microsystem) to the less immediate social systems of which he or she is a part (macrosystem), such as religious and other cultural institutions. The social worker also inquires about the tasks a client undertakes to function socially and explores how the client interacts with family, friends, and support networks including religious institutions. The total assessment provides an understanding of the client's social age—the roles and social habits of an individual in relationship to other members of his or her social structure as well as his or her spiritual life.

Social Age: The Aging Individual in a Social Context
Age Stratification

Gerontologists have long recognized that a person's age has a powerful influence on how they are treated in society. For example, decades ago Neugarten (1968) proposed that age is an underlying dimension of social organization in all societies and that the relations between individuals and between groups are regulated by age differences. Social scientists have underscored this perspective contending that all societies employ age as a social variable by which they prescribe and evaluate what is considered to be appropriate behavior (Binstock & George, 2005). The idea that age is a major factor in determining how people interact and how political and economic resources are allocated is known as *age stratification* (O'Rand, 1996).

Age-based or assigned roles specify the person's rights and responsibilities, what is expected of him or her, and what he or she can expect in return (Marshall, 1996). This means that what an individual believes he or she should do and, in some instances, are able to do is closely linked to what society expects. According to classical role theory, role behavior and a person's entitlements and privileges are considered to be a social product defined through social interaction (Kluckhohn, 1951),

> "I just don't feel old enough to retire, but I guess it's time." "My family says I'm too old to live in this big house alone, perhaps I should consider moving to an apartment." "My daughter doesn't think 1 should get married again (at my age). I guess she's right."

Every society has expectations regarding age-appropriate behavior. These expectations are internalized as an individual grows up and grows old. Therefore, people generally know at what age they are expected to work, marry, raise children, retire, and even "grow old" and die (Riley, 1994; Rowe & Kahn, 1998). These expectations are such a pervasive element of social organization that people are often cognizant of subtle variations in age-appropriate behavior and the timing of major life events. They also, if asked, can give a fairly accurate assessment of their own adherence to these patterns.

From this point of view, aging consists of (a) passages from one socially defined position (status) to another throughout the recognized divisions of life, from infancy to old age, and (b) the obligations, rights, and expectations (roles) that accompany these various positions (Riley & Riley, 2000). Socialization is the process by which a person takes on a succession of roles and changing role constellations, learning the behaviors appropriate to his or her sex, social class, ethnic group, and age. Socialization, which occurs at all stages of the life cycle, is a learning process through which individuals acquire knowledge, skills, attitudes and values, motivations, and the cognitive and affective patterns that relate them to their sociocultural world.

At each stage of life, as people perform new roles, adjust to changing roles, and relinquish old ones, they are, in effect, attempting to master new social situations. New circumstances that may occur in later life and require major role changes include becoming a grandparent, entering retirement, and becoming widowed. How each of these roles is carried out is related to the norms of society and the older person's psychological reactions. Adopting new roles, such as grandparenthood, may often be fulfilling. On the other hand, giving up well-established and valued roles such as that of spouse can be painful.

Successful role performance at all stages of life is a complex phenomenon involving the interplay between psychological adaptations and societal expectations. The relative success that an individual has in moving into a new role or, where necessary, in giving up an old one is central to social functioning (table 5.1). However, given the major changes that are occurring in today's society, we can expect that the roles older adults assume are evolving and being "recreated" (Blundo & Greene, 1999/2008).

Age Integration

Although role theory has primarily focused on the effect of societal expectations on an individual's behavior, the theory also recognizes that individuals have an influence on and are the harbingers of societal change (Thompson & Greene, 1994). For example, more than thirty years ago, Lipman-Blumen (1976) predicted that the individual and his or her "changing sex roles are a sound barometer of a more pervasive change within a society" (p. 67). Role behavior, then, cannot be understood simply by examining the prescriptions or expectations for role performance. *Sex typing*, a process in which male and female children are socialized into adopting male and female adult roles, is an example. While a child may be introduced to various expectations, he or she develops a unique behavioral standard (Bem, 1987).

Over the past several decades, there also has been increased sensitivity to the way in which given roles provide for differential treatment and opportunity in the U.S. social structure (Moen, 1992, 1994). Complex social change has led to a "revolutionary (reexamination of) the degree to which individuals have formal attachments to social structure" (O'Rand, 1996, p. 191). Among the social and demographic changes that are frequently cited are the number of women in the workforce, the increase in two-wage-earner families, delayed marriage and childbearing, and increased survivorship (Greene, 2005). As O'Rand (1996) pointed out, the revolution in longevity and the revolution in gender have challenged old norms and philosophies about role performances. Inequalities exacerbated by race and ethnicity also are increasingly confronted. In fact, the phenomenon of flexibility in role expectations has become so common that the hegemony of a few values, norms. and mores that formerly constrained the actions of family, neighbor, friend, and stranger has given way to a variety of competing standards (Binstock & George, 2005).

The various factors that have brought about more fluidity of roles are predicted to bring about a more age-integrated society that is more congruent with the diversity of lives over time (Riley, 1994). Riley and Riley (1994) projected an age-integration model in which the life course has multiple tracks or life trajectories in the areas of education, work, and leisure. They did not view these education, work, and leisure roles as sequential but as co-occurring. According to Kiyak and Hooyman (1999), the twenty-first century will see "a work-retirement continuum for a population with a longer life span [that] will involve lifelong education and training" (p. 63).

Assessing Role Performance

When assessing a client's role performance it is important to remember that role is both (a) a prescribed pattern of behavior expected of an individual in a given situation and (b) an outcome of the way an individual interprets or construes his or her own performance. This paradoxical idea can be more clearly understood by examining the situation of a person who becomes seriously ill. The individual who becomes ill must not only learn to deal with the physical and psychological changes accompanying the illness but also learn how to assume the role of patient (Goffman, [1967] 2005; Parsons, 1951). As the individual takes on the patient role, many of the behaviors in this well-defined situation are well-known; others reflect the unique meaning a person brings to the role and the cultural norms of the particular group in which the role is enacted. Stated another way, role performance is an outcome of the individual's conception of his or her role (how I see myself as patient), others' reactions or responses (how we see and treat you as patient), and the cultural expectations for that role by the participants (how our group believes patients should act). This suggests that any particular role is an organized enterprise related to other roles.

Role performance can change when an individual does not follow defined patterns of reciprocal claims and obligations. People in mutually supportive roles are usually expected to be thankful and to give something back in return. The sick role allows the patient temporary relief from normative behaviors that are incumbent on those who are well (only exceptional patients think of others), but the patient will be thoughtful again when he or she recovers. However, role performance can be transformed when the patient has Alzheimer's disease. For the cognitively less aware Alzheimer's patient, the norms for role performance are suspended. This may add to the family's sense of loss and grief (Pearlin et al., 1996).

Role expectations also may vary with cultural values. Culture shapes group meaning of "what is a good old age," and influences an individual's experience of such seemingly private matters as bodily changes associated with illness (Fry, 1996). Culture is produced by persons who live in it, and includes knowledge, beliefs, art, morals, laws, customs, and any other capabilities and habits acquired by members of society. It is a road map for living. Birth cohort is another social factor that influences patterns of aging and reaction to illness. A cohort refers to a group of people born in a particular year or era, e.g., the Eisenhower generation or the baby boomers. Because a cohort is in a particular stage of life in a particular historical context, many members of the cohort may share certain beliefs and values (Uhlenberg & Miner, 1996). For example, clients who grew up on farms during the Depression and had to leave school at an early age to work may perceive work roles differently than a cohort that has grown up during the information age with its use of technology. Therefore, social workers must consider how clients are affected by the far reaching social changes in areas such as sexual attitudes, fertility rates, and labor force participation,

A social worker's evaluation of role performance is illustrated in the following case study:

Miss V., a semi-retired schoolteacher age 75, was referred to a family service agency by one of her former students, Mrs. P. explained that her favorite teacher had been in perfect health until she had undergone surgery for a hip replacement; now she was requesting part-time homemaker service and transportation to the doctor for Miss V Mrs. P. indicated that Miss V was a proud, self-reliant woman who would have difficulty asking for help for herself.

When the social worker visited Miss V., who had agreed to be seen at her apartment, she seemed to be a strong, bright, competent, independent person. She explained that she was a retired Hebrew school teacher who chose never to marry, but to "give her whole life to her students." She went on to say that she had taught for over 50 years at a Jewish day school and had seen many of her students grow up and later send their own children to the academy. Many of her students continued to be devoted to her and visit her often.

Miss V. lived alone in a neighborhood that was no longer considered safe. Her apartment building had no elevator and no air conditioning. She lived on the third floor, and walking up three flights of stairs had become a problem. She had lived in this apartment for 35 years because it was within walking distance of the school as well as near public transportation. Furthermore, the rent was very low. Although

Miss V. had an adequate income from social security, pension, and interest from savings, and could afford to move to other housing, she refused, stating that "she wanted to be close to her doctors."

Miss V. gradually recovered from the hip surgery; however, over the next few years, Miss V.'s health deteriorated seriously. She developed heart trouble, became diabetic, lost 20 pounds, developed great difficulty walking, and lost her vision to the point that she could no longer read. During that time, her situation necessitated home health care, with an RN visiting weekly, a health aide providing personal care, and a homemaker doing light housekeeping and shopping twice a week, all of which she accepted begrudgingly.

The social worker became very concerned about Miss V.'s deteriorating health, and shared her concerns with Miss V. She was hoping to get Miss V. "to accept" her situation and consider an alternative, more protective living arrangement. Miss V. would have no part of moving away from the academy and said she did not want to be treated as if she were sick.

Later that same month, on one of her routine visits, the visiting nurse found Miss V. dehydrated and confused, and hospitalized her. Miss V. remained in the hospital one week and was discharged to a nursing home. In the nursing home, her health improved, but she became very depressed. Her main complaint was that she had to wait for the nurses to bring her the medication that she herself knew how to take. "I have been taking this medicine alone for years, and know exactly when and how much to take." Against everyone's advice, she decided to return to her apartment. She insisted that she could manage alone with the help of the health aide and Meals-on-Wheels until she regained her health. In her own home, Miss V. continued to be depressed, expressing suicidal thoughts. She indicated that she valued her freedom and independence more than life. Now she felt she had "lost control and was dependent on others for everything." Her former students, demoralized by her poor health and frail appearance, gradually stopped visiting. Miss V. wondered if she should "have given up everything for them." She had always pictured herself in old age as a "white-haired woman walking with a cane, active with many interests."

The social worker, recognizing that Miss V.'s depression might stem from her feelings of helplessness in the patient role, began to put Miss V. to work on her own behalf. The social worker asked Miss V. to think of the time in her life she would most want to re-create. Miss V. said that although she knew she could no longer teach at school, she wished she could once again have students come to her home for tutoring. She wondered aloud if they had deserted her because she "had nothing to offer." The social worker said, "I wonder if you would want to teach Hebrew once again?" During the social worker's next visit, she learned that Miss V. had mentioned to a number of families that she was planning a course in conversational Hebrew. Many remembered her abilities and referred students.

As Miss V. began to see herself once again in the teaching role, her depression lifted. She was able to accept the health and other professional services she needed to remain in her apartment. She continued to enjoy teaching a few students each week until she died at age 80.

Miss V. is an example of growing phenomenon termed aging in place, older adults who want to remain in the community despite increasing frailty (Ivry, 1995). In the situation of Miss V., it is clear that her conception of self throughout her adult life was that of teacher. Therefore, the loss of such a central role was experienced as damaging to her self-esteem and life satisfaction When others no longer recognized and counted on her to teach, she experienced a sense of personal loss, which was reflected in depression (figure 5.1) The role of the geriatric social worker is to provide the clinical and support services necessary to help such clients continue to live as independently as possible.

Figure 5.1
Impact of role loss. F. Elwell & A. Maltbie-Crannell (1981).
The impact of role loss upon coping resources and life satisfaction of the elderly.
Journal of Gerontology, 36, 223-232

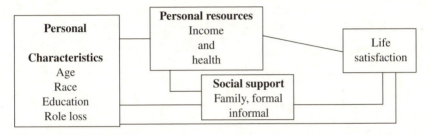

Social Networks

The ability to relate and connect with others is a critical aspect of human development throughout the life course (Bowlby, 1969; Germain, 1991) While social support is important at any time, it becomes even more so during difficult life transitions (Pearlin et al., 1996). Therefore, social workers need to assess a client's support network. An assessment of an individual's social network, which can be augmented through social network mapping (figure 5.2; table 5.1), focuses on who provides social support; kind of support available; gaps in relationship resources; opportunities for reciprocal exchanges; presence of negativism and stress, which produces criticism; barriers to using available resources, and priority of social support in relation to other challenges (Miley, O'Melia, & DuBois, 1998, p. 340).

The assessment examines the structure and the content of a person's social network. *Structure* includes the number of ties, types of ties (kin. friends, neighbors), and the interconnectedness of ties. *Content* examines the kinds of assistance the elderly person receives (grocery shopping, house cleaning) and gives (babysitting, volunteer work). Clients are asked who provides them with help for the tasks they cannot do for themselves and whether they are satisfied with the assistance.

Social workers should also assess the quality of social supports. In the situation of Miss V., there were many professionals involved in her

Table 5.1
Assessment of Social Relationships

1. Is there any one person you feel close to, whom you trust and confide in, without whom it is hard to imagine life? Is there any one else you feel very close to?
2. Are there other people to whom you feel not quire that close but who are still important to you?
3. For each person named in (1) and (2) above, obtain the following:

   a. Name
   b. Gender
   c. Age
   d. Relationship
   e. Geographic proximity
   f. Length of time client knows individual
   g. How do they keep in touch (in person, telephone, letters, combination)
   h. Satisfaction with amount of contact-want more or less? If not satisfied, what prevents you from keeping in touch more often?
   i. What does individual do for you?
   j. Are you satisfied with the kind of support you get?
   k. Are there other things that you think he or she can do for you?
   l. What prevents him or her from doing that for you?
   m. Are you providing support to that individual? If so, what are you giving?

4. Now thinking about your network, all the people that you feel close to, would you want more people in it?
5. Are there any members of your network whom you would not want the agency to contact? If so, who? Can you tell its why?
6. Are you a member of any groups or organizations? If so, which ones?
7. Are you receiving assistance from any agencies? If so, what agency and what service(s)?

Source: Biegel, Shore, and Gordon (1984).

care; however, she had lost those social supports that provided emotional satisfaction. After Miss V.'s retirement and the decline of her health, she experienced a decline in social participation. As she became more isolated, she felt alienated and depressed. For this reason, the social worker's interventions were aimed at trying to repair social attachments and community ties.

Culturally sensitive social work practice also suggests that knowledge of a client's cultural patterns, ethnic background, and traditions constitutes a fundamental part of an assessment of social supports (Delgado & Tennstedt, 1997; Mokuau & Browne, 1994). These—in addition to formal supports and the informal supports of family, friends, and voluntary organizations—play a critical supportive role (Canda & Furman, 1999). The most common type of voluntary organizations among older adults is religious affiliation (Schneider & Kropf, 1992). As a member of the Jewish community, Miss V. shared in a tradition that stresses

Figure 5.2
Social network map.

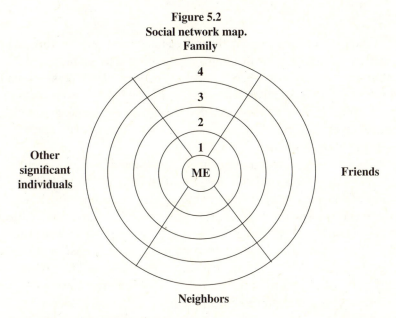

With permission from D. Biegel, B. K. Shore, and E. Gordon. Building Support Networks for the Elderly. Beverly Hills, CA: Sage Publications, 1984, p. 29.

continued learning and old age as a time of continued leadership. Miss V. undoubtedly experienced increasing distress as she was less able "to live up to" these cultural values. At the same time, ethnic communities can often serve as powerful support networks for the elderly. In helping Miss V. to reestablish her ties to the Jewish educational community, the social worker had effectively established a network of professional, social, and emotional support.

Spiritual Age

Although spiritual beliefs and practices have long been a central part of individual and family life, mental health practitioners have not always attend to how it contributes to adaptive functioning. Given the societal dislocations of the twenty-first century, there is a renewed interest in issues of the spiritual in mental health practice (Greene, 2007; Lifton, 1999; Walsh & Pryce, 2003).Therefore, the newly revised Functional-Age Model of Intergenerational Treatment has added this component to the original model developed by Greene in 1986.

Definitions

Although the terms are sometimes used interchangeably, it is important for the sake of clarity to distinguish between the terms faith, religion, and spirituality (Joseph, 1988). *Faith* may be viewed as a person's inner system of beliefs about the meaning of life and relationship with the transcendent or God. Faith may be developed over the course of a lifetime or may be experienced as a conversion event related to a life crisis such as an illness or the loss of a loved one.

Religion is the external communal expression of a person's faith. It includes institutionalized practices, codified beliefs, ethical codes, and various forms of worship that unite one to a moral community. Religion also has been defined as the outward expression of an individual's faith or inner system of beliefs. Religion is also characterized by rites and rituals may of which support people during times of crisis, such as end-of-life ceremonies. As older adults the face losses of friends and family associated with old age, rituals can be a help in overcoming adversity.

Spirituality differs from faith and religion and refers to how a "person seeks to transcend the self in order to discover meaning, belonging, and relatedness to the infinite" (Conrad, 1999, p. 64). It may be likened to meditation , tranquility, and a contemplative atmosphere. Spirituality has also been liken to resilience—or a person's ability to transcend adversity and grow. For example, Canda and Furman (1999), have stated that religion involves "adaptive and transformational properties" (p. 54); whereas Angell, Dennis, and Dumain (1998) have proposed that "spirituality is a fundamental form of resilience [and] serves as a modifiable resource that can be drawn upon during times of personal crisis" (p. 616). The transcendent, adaptive, transformational, and often religious qualities that are most associated with resilience may be tapped during social work interventions.

This text as do several other social work textbooks leans toward the more universal aspects implied in spirituality, leaving questions of specific religious practice alone (Hutchison, 1999; Canda, 2002). Separating the concepts of religion and spirituality provides the practitioner a way to engage the client in exploration and support of this important aspect in their lives without presuming a particular religious stance.

Individual Assessment

Theoretical Frameworks. In assessing a client's connection with his or her faith community or spiritual life it is helpful to have a theoretical framework. Developmental theorists have conceptualized the phases of faith and spiritual formation and growth (Fowler, 1995; Westerhoff, 1983). For example, Fowler (1995; Table 5.2) has described six stages of faith development in which the individual grows from a more concrete understanding of faith to a more transcendent expression of his or her spirit. These definitions are useful to us as they reveal possible

Table. 5.2
Fowler: Stages of Faith

Stage I   Intuitive-Projective Faith

Stage I is most typical in children three to seven years of age. At this age, a child has a fantasy-filled life and a quick *imagination*, usually uninhibited by logical thought. Gradually the child becomes more self-aware and connected to the perceptions of others. As this awareness develops, children become cognizant of family and cultural moral and faith-based expectations. Towards the end of the phase, they attempt to sort out and clarify what is real and what only seems to be. Adults may retain powerful images in the way of memories from this stage.

Stage II   Mythic-Literal Faith

Stage II is a time when children begin to take on the stories, beliefs, and observances that symbolize belonging to their community. Beliefs are usually understood through literal interpretations as are moral rules and attitudes about *justice*. *Story* becomes the major vehicle for understanding what is right and wrong and for giving coherence to experience. At the end of Stage II, clashes and conflicts in literal teachings may occur.

Stage III   Synthetic-Conventional Faith

Stage III comes to ascendancy in adolescence and may or may not remain permanent. Personal relationships and *"conformity"* interrelate with faith values. Faith may become part of *personal identity*. Some teenagers experience nihilistic despair about their personal principles. They may also feel an intimacy with a Supreme Being. At the end of this stage, the individual begins to make their own commitments, and take on their own beliefs and values.

Stage IV   Individuative-Reflective Faith

In Stage IV, a person must begin to *take seriously* their responsibilities for *their commitments,* beliefs, and attitudes. This stage common in the mid-thirties or forties is characterized by the development of the self and the capacity for self-reflection. During Stage IV, some individuals will become disillusioned and experience the pressure for a multileveled approach to life truth.

Stage V   Conjunctive Faith

Those individuals who have struggled with their own reality emerge in Stage V with the capacity to live with paradox and apparent contradictions. They may experience a fuller sense of social justice, meaning, and transcendence.

Stage VI   "All Inclusive Faith"

Individuals who reach Stage VII are rare and experience a universal, fulfilled human community. They are ready for fellowship.

Table 5.3
Framework for Spiritual Assessment

Initial Narrative Framework

1. Describe the religious/spiritual tradition you grew up in. How did your family express its spiritual beliefs? How important was spirituality to your family? Extended family?

2. What sort of personal experiences (practices) stand out to you during your years at home? What made these experiences special? How have they informed your later life?

3. How have you changed or matured from those experiences? How would you describe your current spiritual or religious orientation? Is your spirituality a personal strength? If so, how?

Interpretive Anthropological Framework

1. Affect: What aspects of your spiritual life give you pleasure? What role does your spirituality play in handling life's sorrows? Embracing life joys? Coping with life's pain? How does spirituality give you hope for the future? What do you wish to accomplish in the future?

2. Behavior: Are there particular spiritual rituals or practices that help you deal with life's obstacles? What is your level of involvement in faith-based communities? How are they supported? Are there spiritually encouraging individuals with whom you maintain contact?

3. Cognition: What are your current spiritual/religious beliefs? On what are they based? What beliefs do you find particularly meaningful? What does your faith say about personal trials? How does this belief help you overcome obstacles? How do your beliefs affect your health [mental health] practices?

4. Communion: Describe your relationship to the Ultimate. What has been your experience of the Ultimate? How does the Ultimate communicate with you? How have these experiences encouraged you? Have there been times of deep spiritual intimacy? How does your relationship help you face life challenges? How would the Ultimate describe you?

5. Conscience: How do you determine right or wrong? What are your key values? How does your spirituality help you deal with guilt (sin)? What role does forgiveness play in your life?

6. Intuition: To what extent do you experience intuitive hunches (flashes of creative insight, premonitions, spiritual insight)? Have these insights been strength in your life? If so, how?

Hodge, D. R. (2001). Spirituality assessment: A review of major qualitative methods and a new framework for assessing spirituality. *Social Work*, 46(3), 203-207. p. 208.

interconnections between religious and social work sources of help and healing. Hodge (2001; Table 5.3) provides another means of exploring a client's spiritual life including daily experiences of joy and interpersonal connections. He asks about spiritual beliefs and practices that can be incorporated into a client assessment.

Self-definitions. Social workers may find that clients raise religious and or spiritual issues during the helping process. Learning what religion means to the client or how they express their spirituality may suggest helping strategies. According to Walsh and Pyrce (2003), religion and spirituality are an integral part of the identity of many older adults. Because religious and spiritual beliefs comprise such an important part of the lives of older clients, social workers need a clearer understanding of how clients incorporate these values into their lives if the social worker is to really "meet clients where they are." "By providing older adults the opportunity to define the concepts of religion and spirituality from their perspectives, we can understand the concepts and values that have guided their lives in the past and will likely guide their decisions and perspectives in the future" (Cohen, Thomas, & Williamson, in press).

Family Assessment

A family's presenting problem may not ostensibly be related to spirituality. However, Walsh and Pryce (2003) have suggested that spirituality may emerge as a source of distress or an avenue for healing. It can also be incorporated into a family assessment, learning how a family blends principles of faith with other aspects of life. Practitioners may want to inquire about:

- How important religion or personal spirituality is in current life?
- Has adversity or trauma wounded the spirit?
- Has religion or spirituality contributed to problem resolution?
- Does the client family have spiritual resources on which to call?
- Are there additional spiritual resources on which the family may draw?
- Does the family want to connect or reconnect with their spiritual roots (summarized from p. 399).

* Hodge (2000; figure 5.3) has developed a spiritual ecomap for times when the practitioner wants to actively gather information about the role of spirituality in the family. Similar to the original Hartman ecomap, the family is asked to confer with the social worker and complete a self-assessment of how they relate to various aspects of their faith traditions.

Figure 5.3
Spiritual Ecomaps

God/
Transcendence   Transpersonal
Faith   Beings
Community

Spiritual
Leader

Father's
Spiritual
Tradition

Family Household

Mother's
Spiritual
Tradition

Rituals

Hodge, D. (2000). Spiritual ecomaps: A new diagrammatic tool for assessing marital and family spirituality. *Journal of Marital and Family Therapy, 26,* p.222

The ecomap depicts:

- Rituals. Codified spiritual practices. The social worker might ask, "What particular rituals or practices nurture your spiritual/family life? This may be most helpful in the aftermath of trauma or a crisis.
- God/Transcendent. Connection with a higher being. The social worker may want to know if the client's feelings of self-mastery are enhanced by this connection. This feeling of connection may help a family overcome adversity or stay steadfast in caregiving.
- Faith community. A group involvement with a similar belief system. The practitioner might ask if the client family attends a particular house of worship or participates in any activities. These social supports may

prove helpful during times of great stress such as visiting a family who has a chronically ill member.

- Spiritual leader. The groups' moral role model and teacher. The social worker might ask, "Does your family seek guidance from your minister, rabbi, spiritual elder? In this way, the practitioner learns what possible solutions a client is considering.
- Parent's spiritual traditions. The intergenerational belief system (s) transmitted in the family. The practitioner may learn what beliefs pass from generation to generation and how they help the family cope.
- Transpersonal beings. The spiritual universe. Social workers might learn how a particular culture /religion views spirits, mystical experiences, or creative insights. In this way, the social worker can draw on these spiritual resources including music and artistic expressions (pp. 220-224).
- Parent's spiritual traditions. The intergenerational belief system (s) transmitted in the family. The practitioner may learn what beliefs pass from generation to generation and how they help the family cope.
- Transpersonal beings. The spiritual universe. Social workers might learn how a particular culture /religion views spirits, mystical experiences, or creative insights. In this way, the social worker can draw on these spiritual resources including music and artistic expressions (pp. 220-224).

Because there is a strong positive association between religious and spiritual practices and mental health social workers should learn more about a client's inherent healing potential (Walsh & Pryce, 2003). The social worker might also learn that a client finds that the communal nature of religion provides them with fellowship and a social support system. Similarly, the more private nature of spirituality may offer a client the means of stress reduction or a positive meaning system (McInnis-Dittrich, 2002). Moreover, Dunbar, Mueller, Medina, and Wolf (1998) have proposed that psychological and spiritual growth can contribute to a client's life affirmation, the redefinition of relationships, and the reckoning with death.

Cohen et al. (in press) recommend techniques for assessment:

- Be open and nonjudgmental in hearing about the beliefs and values important to older adults;
- Encourage older adults to share their stories and personal understanding of religion or spirituality;
- Understand, acknowledge and embrace the expertise of the older adult in terms of their own world view;
- Remember the importance of the social worker's role as advocate for the religious and spiritual needs of clients;

- Recognize cultural and ethnic variations and its historical significance for older adults;
- Listen to the words, phrases, and terms older adults use when referring to their religious or spiritual beliefs; and
- Make sure you understand what these words mean for the client (p. XXX).

Communal Helping

For some older adults and their families, their house of worship may be a source of help during crisis. For example, the National Survey of Black Americans (Taylor & Chatters, 2003) explored mental health and help-seeking among African Americans. They found that African Americans underutilize mental health services, and tend to seek help through their social networks which include the black church and African-American pastors. Farris (2006) has recommended that social workers' assessments explore how African-American pastors may work as part of the mental health team.

Figure 5.4
The Resiliency Model

Stressors
Adversity
Life Events

Resilient
Reintegration

Biopsycho-
Spiritual
Homeostasis

Reintegration
Back to
Homeostasis

Protective Factors

Reintegratio
n with loss

Disruption   Reintegration   Dysfunctional
Reintegration

Richardson, G. E. (2002). Metatheory of resilience and resiliency. *Journal of Clinical Psychology, 58*(3), 307-321.

Completing the Assessment: Functional Age

Although each component of biopsychosocial and spiritual functioning has been described separately in chapters 3 through 5, assessment requires that all aspects of functioning be appreciated as complementary. An integrated holistic assessment of the older adult's ability to function in his or her environment will lead to an effective treatment plan.

Social workers can better grasp the interrelatedness of biopsychosocial and spiritual factors by examining Richardson's (2002) resiliency model in which he proposed that at a given point in time a person "has adapted physically, mentally, and spiritually to a set of circumstances whether good or bad" (p. 311). But, when daily stress "bombards" the individual, it disrupts their internal and external balance, resulting in challenges as well as opportunities. Coping with this process of disruption requires that people grow and develop insight. This transformation, or what Richardson called *resilient reintegration,* may occur naturally or with therapeutic intervention (figure 5.4).

Figure 5.5
Continuum of Care

1. Continuum of Need

Independent	Moderately dependent	Dependent
(Little or no need)		(Multiple needs)

2. Continuum of Services

Health promotion/ disease prevention	Screening and early detection	Diagnosis and pre-treatment evaluation	Treatment	Rehabilitation: skilled nursing services	Continuing care and hospice

3. Continuum of Service Settings

Own home, apartment etc.	Friend or relative's home apartment, etc.	Congregate living situation	Subacute care facility (e.g., day hospital)	Acute-care facility (e.g., hospital)	Skilled long-term care facility (e.g., nursing home)	Continuing care and hospice

4. Continuum of Service Providers

Nonservice	Self-care	Family friends	Paraprofessionals (support network)	Professionals

5. Continuum of Professional Collaboration

Single discipline	Multidisciplinary	Interdisciplinary

SOURCE. Hooyman, N., Hooyman, G., & Kethley, A. (1981, March). *The role of gerontological social work in interdisciplinary care.* Paper presented at the annual program meeting of the Council on Social Work Education, Louisville, KY.

Another schema that can help the social worker come to a holistic assessment is Hooyman, Hooyman, and Kethley's (1981; figure 5.5) Five Continua of Needs, Services, and Interventions. The five continua include: (1) a continuum of client need, or how independent or dependent an older adult is; (2) a continuum of services, that is, services suggested by need; (3) a continuum of service settings, or the degree of support for living the client requires; (4) a continuum of service providers, whether a person can manage without outside care, can conduct self-care, or requires professional care; and (5) a continuum of professional collaboration, whether the client requires the help from more than one discipline.

These continua help geriatric social workers visualize how to match a client with needed services and care along a *full* continuum of care that encompasses a range of activities and along a continuum of functional capacity—from those with the most capacity to those with the least (Vourlekis & Greene, 1992). To arrive at a holistic picture of the older adult's functioning and an intervention plan that is acceptable to the client (family), the social worker must synthesize the various elements of the functional age assessment. To complete the picture, the assessment of the individual is united with the family assessment to develop a comprehensive understanding of the client family (chapters 5 and 7) and integrate them into a treatment plan..

References

Angell, G. B., Dennis, B. G., & Dumain, L. E. (1998). Spirituality, resilience, and narrative: Coping with parental death. *Families in Society, 79,* 615–630.

Atchley, R. C. (1999). *Continuity and adaptation in aging*. Baltimore, MD: Johns Hopkins University Press.

Bem, S. L. (1987). Gender schema theory: A conceptual and empirical integration. In P. Shaver & C. Hendricks (Eds.), *Sex and gender* (pp. 251-71). Newbury Park, CA: Sage.

Biegel, D., Shore, B., & Gordon, E. (1984). *Building support networks for the elderly.* Beverly Hills, CA: Sage.

Binstock, R. H., & George, L. K. (2005). (5th ed.). *Handbook of aging and the social sciences*. San Diego: Academic Press.

Blundo, R., & Greene, R. R. (1999/2008). Social construction. In R. R. Greene, *Human behavior theory and social work practice*. New Brunswick: Aldine Transaction.

Bowlby, J. (1969). *Attachment and loss*. New York: Basic Books.

Canda, E. R. (2002).The significance of spirituality for resilient response to chronic illness: A qualitative study of adults with cystic fibrosis. In D. Saleebey (Ed.), *The strengths perspective in social work practice* (3rd ed., pp. 63-78). Boston: Allyn and Bacon.

Canda, E. R., & Furman, L. D. (1999). *Spiritual diversity in social work practice.* New York: Free Press.

Conrad, A. P. (1999). Professional tools for religiously and spiritually sensitive social work practice. In R. R. Greene, *Human behavior theory and social work practice* (pp. 63-72). New York: Aldine de Gruyter.

Delgado, M., & Tennstedt, S. (1997). Making the case for culturally appropriate community services. *Social Work, 22,* 246-55.

Dunbar, H. T., Mueller, C. W., Medina, C., & Wolf, T. (1998). Psychological and spiritual growth in women living with HIV. *Social Work, 43,* 144–154.

Eggebeen, D. (1992) From generation unto generation; Parent-child support in aging American families. *Generations, 16,* 45-50.

Elwell, F., & Maltbie-Crannell, A. (1981). The impact of role loss upon coping resources and life satisfaction of the elderly. *Journal of Gerontology, 36* (March), 223-232.

Farris, K. (2006). The role of African-American pastors in mental health care. In R. R. Greene (Ed.), *Contemporary issues of care* (pp. 159-182). New York: Haworth Press.

Fowler, J. (1995). *Stages of faith: The psychology of human development and the quest for meaning.* New York: Harper Collins.

Fry, C. L. (1996). Age, aging, and culture. In R. H. Binstock & L. K. George (Eds.), *Handbook of aging and the social sciences* (pp. 118-36). San Diego, CA; Academic Press.

Germain, C. B. (1991). *Human behavior and the social environment: An ecological view.* New York: Columbia University Press.

Goffman, E. ([1967] 2005). *Interaction ritual: Essays in face to face behavior.* New Brunswick, NJ: Aldine Transaction.

Greene, R. R. (2005). The changing family of later years and social work practice. In L. Kaye (Ed.). *Productive aging* (pp.107-122). Washington, DC: NASW Press.

Greene, R. R. (2007). *Social work practice: A risk and resilience perspective.* Monterey, CA: Brooks/Cole.

Hendricks, J., & Hendricks, C. D. (1977). *Aging in mass society.* Cambridge, MA: Winthrop.

Hodge, D. R. (2001). Spirituality assessment: A review of major qualitative methods and a new framework for assessing spirituality. *Social Work, 46*(3), 203-207.

Hodge, D. (2000). Spiritual ecomaps: A new diagrammatic tool for assessing marital and family spirituality. *Journal of Marital and Family Therapy, 26,* 229-240.

Hutchison, E. D. (1999). *Dimensions of human behavior: Person and environment.* Thousand Oaks, CA: Pine Forge Press

Ivry, J. (1995). Aging in place: The role of geriatric social work. *Families in Society, 76,* 76-85.

Joseph, M. V. (1988). Religion and social work practice. *Social Casework, 69,* 443–452.

Kiyak, A. H., & Hooyman, N. R. (1999). Aging in the twenty-first century. *Hallyn International Journal of Aging, 1* (1), 56-66.

Kluckhohn, C. (1951). Values and value orientations. In T. Parsons & E. A. Shils (Eds.), *Toward a theory of action.* Cambridge, MA: Harvard University Press

Koenig, H., Larson, D., & Weaver, A. (1998). Research on religion and serious mental illness. In R. Fallot (Ed.) *Spirituality and religion in recovery from mental illness: New directions for mental health services.* (pp. 81-95). San Francisco, CA: Jossey-Bass.

Koenig, H., McCullough, M., & Larson, D. (2000). *Handbook of religion and health.* New York: Oxford University Press.

Lifton, R. J. (1993). *The protean self: Human resilience in an age of fragmentation.* Chicago: University of Chicago Press.

Lipman-Blumen, J. (1976). The implications of family structure of changing sex roles. *Social Casework, 57,* 67-79.

Marshall, V. W. (1996). The state of theory in aging and the social sciences. In R. H. Binstock & L. K. George (Eds.), *Handbook of aging and the social sciences* (pp. 12-30). San Diego, CA: Academic Press.

Martin, P. Y., & O'Connor, G. G. (1989). *The social environment: Open systems applications.* New York: Longman.

Miley, K., O'Melia, M., & DuBois, B. (1998). *Generalist social work practice.* Boston: Allyn & Bacon.

Moen, P. (1992). *Women's two roles: A contemporary dilemma.* Westport, CT: Auburn House.

Moen, P. (1994). Women, work, and family: A sociological perspective on changing roles. In M. W. Riley, R. L. Kahn, & A. Foner (Eds.), *Age and structural lag: Society's failure to provide meaningful opportunities in work, family, and leisure* (pp. 151-70). New York: Wiley.

Mokuau, N., & Browne, C. (1994). Life themes of native Hawaiian female elders: Resources for cultural preservation. *Social Work, 39,* 43-49.

Neugarten, B. (Ed.) (1968). *Middle age and aging.* Chicago: University of Chicago Press.

O'Rand, A. M. (1996). The cumulative stratification of the life course. In R. H. Binstock & L. K. George (Eds.), *Handbook of aging and the social sciences* (pp. 188-207). San Diego, CA: Academic Press.

Parsons, T. (1951). *The social system.* New York: Free Press.

Pearlin, L. I., Aneshensel, C. S., Mullan, J. T., Whitlatch, C. J. (1996). Caregiving and its social support. In R. H. Binstock & L. K. George (Eds.), *Handbook of aging and the social sciences* (pp. 283-302). San Diego, CA: Academic Press.

Richardson, G. E. (2002). The metatheory of resilience and resiliency. *Journal of clinical Psychology, 58*(3), 307-321.

Riley, M. W. (1994). Aging and society: Past, present, and future. *The Gerontologist, 34,* 436-46.

Riley, M. W., Foner, A., Hess, B., & Toby, M. (1969). Socialization for the middle and later years. In D. A. Goslin, (Ed.) *Handbook of socialization, theory, and research.* Chicago: Rand McNally.

Riley, M. W. & Riley, J. W. (2000). Age integration: Conceptual and historical background. *The Gerontologist, 40*(3), 266-269.

Riley, M.W., & Riley, J. W. (1994) Structural lag: Past and future. In M. W. Riley, R. L. Kahn & A. Foner (Eds.), *Age and structural lag: Society's failure to provide meaningful opportunities in work, family, and leisure* (pp. 15-36). New York: Wiley.

Rowe, J. W., & Kahn, R. L. (1998). *Successful aging.* New York: Pantheon.

Schneider, R. L., & Kropf, N. P. (1992). *Gerontological social work: Knowledge, service settings, and special populations.* Chicago: Nelson Hall.

Shibutani, T. (1961). *Society and personality.* Englewood Cliffs, NJ: Prentice-Hall

Taylor, R., & Chatters, L. (2003). National survey of black Americans. In R. Taylor, & Chatters, L. (Eds.). *Religion in the lives of African Americans.* Thousand Oaks, CA: Sage.

Taylor, R., Ellison, C., Chatters, L., Levin, J., & Lincoln, K. (2000). Mental health services in faith communities: The role of clergy in black churches. *Social Work, 45,* 73-87.

Thompson, K. H., & Greene, R. R. (1994). Role theory and social work practice. In R. R. Greene (Ed.) *Human behavior theory: A diversity framework* (pp. 93-114). Hawthorne, NY: Aldine de Gruyter.

U. S. Bureau of the Census (1996). *Current populations report: 65+ in the United States, Special Studies* (pp. 23-190). Washington, DC: U.S. Government Printing Office.

Uhlenberg, P., & Miner, S. (1996). Lifecourse and aging: A cohort perspective. In R. H. Binstock & L. K. George (Eds.), *Handbook of aging and the social sciences* (pp. 208-28). San Diego, CA: Academic Press.

Walsh, F., & Pryce, J. (2003). The spiritual dimensions of family life. In F. Walsh (Ed.), *Normal family process* (pp. 337-372). New York: Guilford Press.

Westerhoff, J. (1983). *Building God's people.* New York: Seabury Press.

6

The Family as a Social System

with Harriet Cohen and Craig Campbell

This is the first of two chapters that discuss assessment of the family and its relationship to other social systems. Assumptions about how the family functions as a social system, as a set of reciprocal roles, and as a developmental unit are presented. Chapters 8 and 9 then describe how the assessment information can be used to implement the functional-age model of intergenerational treatment.

Assessment of a family involves viewing it as a system or group. The major goal of family assessments is to understand interactional patterns as they developed over time (Hartman & Laird, 1983). Structure, communication patterns, belief systems, and cultural milieu are among the internal factors that vary from one family to the next. Assessment also provides a picture of the way in which "individual symptoms" are intertwined with family functioning. The understanding of family difficulties allows social workers to collaborate with families in modifying those elements of family relationships that interfere with the management of life tasks.

General Systems Model

During the 1960s, general systems theory was first brought to the attention of the scientific community as a comprehensive theoretical model to describe all living systems (Bertalaffy, 1968). Since that time, the model has been modified and frequently used to examine social change. Perhaps, its most common use is in the area of family treatment. Systems theory is a model, an abstraction, or a visual representation that attempts to account for a complex reality.

As a model, it is not a description of the real world. It is only a way of looking at and thinking about selected aspects of reality. It is a map or transparency that can be superimposed on social phenomena to construct a perspective showing the relatedness of those elements that constitute the phenomenon (Anderson & Carter, 1978, p. 10).

Despite its abstraction, there are several benefits for the practitioner who adopts a systems approach. It permits practitioners to steer away from simplistic linear thinking (which assumes direct cause and effect between relationships) and allows them to integrate many sources of information into a comprehensible whole (Berger & Federico, 1982). Because the functional age model suggests that the social worker examine many aspects of human functioning, systems thinking can suggest avenues for integrating information. This might, for example, involve the realization that urinary incontinence is the reason for a client's social isolation.

Holistic thinking can also provide the practitioner with an understanding of family interactional processes. However, because systems theory is so abstract, before it can serve as a frame of reference for family therapy, its basic assumptions and terms must be defined (table 6.1). This chapter discusses the assumptions of systems theory and describes their use in the functional-age model to assess the family.

Basic Assumptions

Boundaries

One of the first tasks of the family-centered social worker is the delineation of family boundaries. A *boundary* defines the "edges" of the space or sphere in which the system is located, and it describes the extent of the system's organization. Boundaries enable the system to assume its identity and character. For example, a body may be viewed as a system with the skin as its boundary; a tree may be viewed as a system with its bark as a boundary, and so on. The family's organizational limits are also defined by its boundaries. From a family systems perspective, defining boundaries means that the social worker ascertains who is considered a member of the family group and who is not. This provides important information about who to include in treatment sessions.

Family Definition

Systems theory allows for a broad definition of *family*. According to Queralt (1996), "the many concepts of the family" may encompass remarriage and stepfamilies, shared-custody families, dual employment families, multigenerational extended families, families headed by gay and lesbian parents, cohabitation, interracial families, migrant families,

Table 6. 1
Basic Assumptions for Using Systems Theory Principles in Family Treatment

- The life of a family group can be studied as a whole system or as a structure of interlocking relationships.

- A family system is comprised of interrelated members who constitute a unit, or a whole.

- The life of the group is more than just the sum of its participants' activities.

- A biopsychosocial change in any one member affects the balance of the whole family group. Structural changes that occur at family transition points can also disturb its balance.

- Families under distress or in crisis seek to reestablish their internal balance.

- As family members interact, each member is socialized to the particular mores and emotional tone operating within that family system. The mores and emotional tone provide the family's organizational fiber, vary from family to family, and vary within each family over time.

- The family's organizational "limits" are defined by its boundaries or membership.

- Boundaries give the family its identity and focus as a social system, distinguishing it from other social systems with which it may interact.

- Transactions (movements) across family boundaries with other social systems influence the family's balance and functional capacity.

foster families, and child-free families (p. 344). The definition of family adopted here is borrowed from systems theory: The family is a *social system* comprising a number of people united by emotional ties and by some form of regular interaction (Buckley, 1967). By adopting this definition, the practitioner can decide to include in treatment those people most pertinent to gathering information and implementing successful interventions.

Family as a Collective

Systems theory suggests that to understand any social system, particularly a family, the practitioner cannot view each person in isolation but must learn how members function together as a whole. That is, a family is best understood by examining how family members relate to one another. Systems theory also assumes that the family group has properties of its own–over and above the simple addition of each member's contributions. Just as an understanding of each cell's function within the brain does not provide a complete picture of the workings of the human mind, an explanation of one family member's role does not provide a picture of the family group (Greene, 1989; chap. 7). As best expressed by Hartman and Laird (1983), the intrafamilial relationship system is an

> intimate constellation [that] shares a history. . .patterns of behavior, rules, symmetries, complementarities, and triangles. No matter how well we might come to know each of its members separately, with all its strengths, concerns, foibles, and styles of behavior, we would be unable to explain the family altogether. For the family is somehow a thing larger than the sum of its individual members; it emerges out of multiple sequences of permutations and combinations which it in turn works back upon, defining and shaping destinies. Making sense of this entity is the task of assessment. (p. 269)

The importance of belonging is evident when we look at the nature of family membership. Even in the rapidly changing U.S. society, family members are a given, and they remain a "permanent" part of the family group as visualized in a genogram (see Hartman & Laird, 1983; figure 6.1). A *genogram* is a tool for depicting the genealogical inner workings of the family, and serves as an intergenerational map. The map in Figure 6.1 outlines three generations of family relationships. In

Figure 6.1
A sample genogram

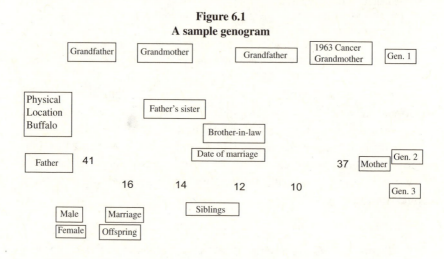

SOURCE. Adapted with permission from Hartman, A., & Laird, J. (1983). *Family-centered* social work practice. New York: Free Press.

addition to recording the genealogical tree, the practitioner uses it to obtain information on "ethnic and religious background, major family events, occupations, losses, family migrations and dispersal, identifications, role assignments . . . communication patterns" (Hartman & Laird, 1983, p. 215). Combined with the eco-map (see below), this information serves as the foundation for family intervention (chapter 8).

Family Functionality

Historically, social workers have proposed that family systems that are sufficiently organized or functional are better able to meet their needs or goals. A disorganized or dysfunctional family is said to be operating in a self-defeating manner. In a functional family, each member is given an opportunity to develop separately as a person, as well as to assume a unique identity through the process of individualization. Social workers often find that in a closed system—those with relatively impenetrable boundaries—changes are more difficult to achieve. Closed systems are less likely to seek help or outside resources. On the other hand, in a relatively open system that tends to be flexible and amenable to new ideas, change is much more possible to accomplish. Improving a family's communication patterns and resource base may make it more receptive.

Maintaining Family Balance

A major purpose of the family group is to sustain itself over time by meeting the needs of its members. For this to be accomplished, the family group constantly strives for and must achieve a sense of balance or *homeostasis*[1] both within itself and with other social systems (Berger & Federico, 1982). The model used in this text focuses on three major factors that can interrupt or interfere with family homeostasis and possible cause members to seek help: (a) changes in an older family member's biopsychosocial or spiritual functioning; (b) changes in family structure that occur at major transition points (chapter 7); and (c) changes in societal resources that interrupt family well-being. The assessment provides information about what disrupts the family social system and suggests intervention to reestablish or enhance family functioning.

Family Culture

As family members interact, each member is socialized to the particular mores and emotional tone operating within that family system. The mores and emotional tone provide the family's cultural and organizational fiber, varying from family to family as well as within each family over time.

Therefore, to be a culturally competent family therapist, a social worker should take a learning stance and become familiar with the *mores* of a particular family–the cultural expectations, customs, and norms by which the family lives, and the *emotional tone* or shades of intensity assigned to these family values (Hardy & Laszloffy, 1992; McGill, 1992, see chap. 11).

Family Diversity

Another area of learning for the culturally competent practitioner is the literature on diverse elders. The first distinction that should be made is the difference between a minority and an ethnic group. Members of an *ethnic group* think of themselves as being alike, having a sense of shared past and similar origins, and are so regarded by others. This sense of being distinct is most important when members of a given ethnic group are in contact with other groups (Green, 1999). Ethnicity provides group identity by sharing cultural characteristics passed from one generation to the other. However, this process does not transform culture into a static construct. An ethnic group is "a dynamic system constantly changing, adjusting, and adapting to the wider environment of which it forms a part" (Holzberg, 1982, p. 254).

A closely related concept to ethnic group, although not the same, is that of *minority group*. Many ethnic groups are singled out from others in the society in which they live for differential and unequal treatment. This minority-group standing often places members in a relatively less powerful position in society, and they may be denied access to societal resources, such as wealth, power, and prestige, that are available to others (Greene, 2002). The type and extent of denied resources may be different for different minority groups. For example, one of every twelve (7.5 percent) elderly Whites was poor in 2004, compared to 23 percent of elderly African-Americans, 13.6 percent of Asians, and 18.7 percent of elderly Hispanics (U. S. Census Bureau, 2005).

By virtue of minority group membership, minority elderly share common characteristics and life experiences with others of their reference group (i.e., history of slavery, immigration, alienation, minority status, etc.). The combination of ethnic characteristics, individual traits, and societal treatment of a given minority group, dictates the way minorities view the world, experience their surroundings, seek help, develop coping mechanisms, and adhere to conventional treatment modalities. Membership in a minority group may also indicate the way the family and the community are defined as well as the roles played in those systems.

Finally, minority aged bear a double burden—the devaluation in status associated with old age and the disadvantages imposed by their minority group status. Dows and Bengston (1978) called the plight of the minority aged "double jeopardy." Double jeopardy refers to the negative effects of being old and a member of a minority group concerning frequently cited indicators of quality of life. These indicators include income, health, housing, or life satisfaction. Both health status and health care assistance are of special concern for the minority elderly. This is not surprising given the extent of poverty among minority elderly. Native American older adults have the poorest health of all groups. In general, minority elders underuse health resources. Explanations for this behavior have changed through time. Researchers (see Berkman & Harootyan, 2003) have documented that health care behavior is a function of culture, and as a result, folk medicine was seen as the treatment of choice for many minority groups. By the 1960s, studies began to emphasize noncultural factors as major determinants of minority health care behavior. Studies done by Andersen et al., (1981), Gavira and Stern (1980), Scott (1974), Weaver (1973) and others pointed out other factors of importance including high cost of services, lack of insurance coverage, language barriers, and lack of available services.

Despite the many adverse elements inherited in the demographics of the minority aged, they exhibit a great deal of strength and resilience. Most important, they are survivors. Depending on the ethnic group, they may draw their strength from the family, spirituality, status within their own group, world view, or sense of belonging.

Although it is not possible to summarize the cultural variables of diverse ethnic groups without creating generalizations, there are some traits that appear to be critical to the well-being of minority elderly. Latino elderly as well as their children believe in the cultural value that older adults should be cared for within the nurturing environment of the family. Spirituality among Native Americans is a critical variable to preserve identity and promote healing (Green, 1999). The church has played a fundamental function throughout the history of black people, and as a result it is not surprising to see a strong religious commitment among black older adults (Fried & Mehrotra, 1998). Asian/Pacific Islanders from a perspective of Hinduism see old age as "the time for developing a philosophy and then adapting that philosophy into a way of life, a time for transcending the senses to find, and dwell with, the reality that underlies the natural world" (Fried & Mehrotra, 1998, p. 171).

Families of Choice

Like other aging Americans who are constrained by ageist stereotyping and misconceptions, older lesbians and gay men face similar problems of loss of family and friends, health concerns, increased isolation from community, fear of dependency, and reduced income. They may seek health and long-term care services from the same providers as their heterosexual counterparts (Zodikoff, 2006); however, older lesbians and gay men fear mistreatment, negative stereotyping, compromise in quality of care, and invisibility or fear of not having their non-heterosexual family configuration acknowledged. This triple discrimination of homophobia, heterosexism, and ageism may prevent older lesbians and gay men from searching for and accessing needed health care, support, and long-term care services.

Homophobia is an irrational fear of homosexuality. It is a mental health construct that represents a clinically phobic reaction to non-heterosexual people (Saulnier, 2002). Heterosexism as other "isms," denotes a cultural and sociopolitical perspective that marginalizes non-heterosexual people, such as lesbians and gays. Heterosexism bestows privilege, power, and dominance to heterosexual people and minimizes the value of lesbian and gay people (Neisen, 1990).

Current research indicates that older lesbians and gays are less likely to be living with life partners or children and are more likely to live alone than their heterosexual counterparts (Cahill et al., 2000). In contrast to the myth of loneliness, Cahill found that they are no lonelier than heterosexual elders or than GLBT (gay, lesbian, bisexual and transgendered) younger adults. Others have suggested that social networks, sometimes called "family of friends" or "families of choice" that older lesbians and gay men have developed may provide a buffer during times of loss and need (Barranti & Cohen, 2000; Butler, 2006; Healy, 2002). While older lesbian and gay men are more likely to live alone, they do not necessarily report feeling lonely and isolated. In studies of older gay men (Berger, 1996) and older lesbians (Clunis, Fredriksen-Goldsen, Freeman & Nystrom, 2005) older lesbian and gay men were found to be more similar to their heterosexual counterparts than different. They want companionship, are involved in satisfying sexual relationships, about a third of gay men having been married at some point in their lives and many have children, and as they get older, seek involvement in religious activities and social service organizations. In fact these lesbian and gay older adults may experience fewer adjustments to aging than their heterosexual counterparts (Friend, 1990). As they have learned to negotiate between the heterosexual society and homosexual communities, they have developed "crisis competence" (Kimmel, 1978) or "stigma management" (McFarland & Sanders, 2003). As older lesbians and gays have learned how to handle crises and losses associated with their rejection of heterosexuality, they have become more resilient. Older gays and lesbians have been "described as psychologically well adjusted, vibrant and growing older successfully" (Barranti & Cohen, 2000, p. 349). Through their adaptation, flexibility, and resiliency, they have cultivated coping skills in accepting

Family Resilience

Practitioners use systems theory to understand a family's organizational structure and communication patterns, refocusing attention from individual behavior to the dynamic interaction among family members. To help a family overcome a highly stressful event, Walsh (1998) has suggested that practitioners supplement systems theory with risk and resilience concepts (table 6.2). She suggested that this integration of theory allows the practitioner to learn how responsive the family unit is to stress, to understand the meaning members make of an adverse event, to foster a family's natural healing processes, marshalling a family's capacity to heal and grow (Walsh, 1998).

To accomplish this therapeutic task, an examination of family belief systems, organizational and communication patterns are included in assessment. Family organizational patterns stem from expectations about how family members should behave, and how the family is structured to carry out its tasks. Similar to systems theory, communication patterns are also involved as the family collectively deals with stress.

The family resilience concept draws on a crisis framework to understand family characteristics, dimensions, and properties that allow the family unit to overcome crises and adapt to stress. Such family resilience models involve an examination of family risk factors (the pileup of demands); family protective factors (resources and strengths); and the family's shared worldview (schema). The approach to family resilience stems from a systemic or relational view that enables practitioners to understand how families can better succeed.

Presenting Issues and Practice Strategies

Crisis Situations

People seek out mental health and social agencies for a variety of reasons. Clients come for help because they are "in need," "have a problem,"

Table 6.2
Key Processes in Family Resilience

Belief Systems
Making meaning of adversity
  • Affiliative value: resilience as relationally based
  • Family life cycle orientation: normalizing, contextualizing adversity and distress
  • Sense of coherence: crisis as meaning, comprehensible, manageable challenge
  • Appraisal of crisis, distress, and recovery: facilitative versus constraining beliefs
Positive outlook
  • Active initiative and perseverance
  • Courage and encouragement
  • Sustaining hope, optimistic view: confidence in overcoming odds
  • Focusing on strengths and potential
  • Mastering the possible; accepting what can't be changed
Transcendence and spirituality
  • Larger values, purpose
  • Spirituality; faith, communion, rituals
  • Inspiration: envisioning new possibilities, creativity, heroes
  • Transformation: learning and growth from adversity
Organizational Patterns
Flexibility
  • Capacity to change: rebounding, reorganizing, adapting to fit challenges over time
  • Counterbalancing by stability: continuity, dependability through disruption
Connectedness
  • Mutual support, collaboration, and commitment
  • Respect for individual needs, differences, and boundaries
  • Strong leadership: nurturing, protecting, guiding children and vulnerable members
  • Varied family forms: cooperative parenting/caregiving teams
  • Couple/coparent relationship: equal partners
  • Seeking reconnection, reconciliation of troubled relationships
Social and economic resources
  • Mobilizing extended kin and social support; community networks
  • Building financial security; balancing work and family strains
Communication Processes
Clarity
  • Clear, consistent messages (words and actions)
  • Clarification of ambiguous situation; truth-seeking/truth-speaking
Open emotional expression
  • Sharing range of feelings (joy and pain; hopes and fears)
  • Mutual empathy; tolerance for differences
  • Responsibility for own feelings, behavior: avoid blaming
  • Pleasurable interactions: humor
Collaborative problem solving
  • Creative brainstorming; resourcefulness
  • Shared decision making: negotiation, fairness, reciprocity
  • Conflict resolution
  • Focusing on goals: taking concrete steps, building on success, learning from failure
  • Proactive stance: reinventing problems, crises; preparing for future challenges

---

Adapted from *Strengthening Family Resilience*, by F. Walsh, 1998. New York: Guilford Press, p. 133. Copyright c 1998 by Guilford Press.

are "under stress," or are "in a crisis." While these terms are often used interchangeably, the concept of crisis, which is central to our model, can be more precisely defined: In simplest terms, it is a state of imbalance, or a critical period of disequilibrium (Rapoport, 1980). Crisis is a time of heightened vulnerability and threat. A crisis is a self-limiting period of upset when habitual problem-solving mechanisms do not meet the needs of an individual or family group. This may lead to less effective functioning and disorganization.

Family Adaptation

A *crisis* may be further defined as an event or circumstance that the family system cannot adequately handle. Factors that may have potential for disrupting family functioning should be identified early in assessment: Was there a stressful precipitating event? Were there rapid cognitive and affective changes in a family member, and have these changes been sustained for an extended period of time? (Bloom, 1963). This approach to crises presupposes that individuals and family systems strive to maintain a state of balance through their characteristic adaptive and problem-solving activities. When these adaptive patterns are not adequate to meet the situation, the individual and his or her family unit have difficulty functioning.

Because the family system is distinguished by a high level of interdependence, the practitioner can expect that a change in the behavior, status, or role of one member of the family can lead to changes throughout the whole group. For this reason, families are particularly vulnerable to disruption during transition points such as birth, marriage, divorce, or death. Families are also in a more precarious situation when faced with a biopsychosocial crisis in an older member, and they frequently come in for treatment at that time.

A decrease in functional ability can take place in the biological, psychological, or social sphere. Biological change may involve the onset of a disease, a stroke, or a hip fracture. Difficulties in psychological functioning may be brought about by a change of residence, the onset of dementia, or loss of a loved one. A diminution in social participation may be precipitated by inaccessibility of transportation or the fear of being incontinent in public. A spiritual crisis may also precipitate distress.

The older adult who has recently broken a hip may make "excessive" demands on his youngest son. The mildly confused mother may be viewed by her "anxious" daughter as an "appropriate" candidate for nursing home placement. A hospitalized stroke patient may be visited daily for many hours by a "concerned" daughter.

Crisis Resolution

Successful crisis resolution has been credited with preserving well-functioning systems and has become the goal of therapeutic intervention with persons and families in a state of temporary stress. The social work therapist needs to make a careful assessment of presenting issues. Is a family essentially well functioning and only temporarily derailed–needing help to get back on the right track? Or is a family less able to draw on and mobilize its own resources? The practitioner also should keep in mind that many families may not have sufficient resources upon which to draw. In either instance, the social worker should consider intervening with community resources and, where appropriate, with family counseling (chapters 8 and 9).

Crises often have a somewhat meteoric existence, appearing suddenly: their resolution is often equally speedy, even though devastating effects may linger. For example, an aging parent, after being stricken with a stroke and left paralyzed and confused, is confined to a nursing home following the emergency. The daughter continues to feel guilt about sending her mother to a nursing home, and the mother never really adjusts to her new situation. On the other hand, some crises are considered normal because they are a part of family development and, therefore, more predictable: for example, marriage, birth of a first child, children going to school, children leaving the home, retirement from a job, and death of a spouse. Even though such crises are to some extent predictable, they are nonetheless stressful. Because these events are often experienced as "points of no return," i.e., the family must establish a new equilibrium or balance.

Crisis Prevention

Some crises are neither predictable nor expected. Or, perhaps, the family knows that a problem is on the horizon but elects to put off thinking about it until it is a full-bloomed crisis situation (the ostrich maneuver). For example, the family may have observed changes in the older relative's physical health for some time. He or she may have become increasingly immobile but left to reside in a large two-story home. No one discusses the matter with the older person. "Suddenly" a serious incapacitating illness strikes. At the time of crisis, the family may seek help. This is not a time to assign blame, but to work with the family and older adult to resolve the crisis.

In this case, a hasty decision might be made to move the frail aged parent into the home of an adult child. The unaccustomed responsibility for the extra care for the parent might result in negative feelings on the part of the adult child, including feelings of resentment, martyrdom, and guilt. Crisis prevention and family-centered casework can be instrumental in circumventing or ameliorating such situations. A seemingly crisis-precipitating event does not have the same meaning and effect for every family, nor does every family handle a crisis in the same way. What may be troublesome to some families may be withstood by others without apparent disorganization. The family's capacity to deal with stress is the key to assessing how a crisis will be faced by a particular family.

Ecology of the Family

Older adults and their families also need to be understood in relationship to other social systems (Greene, 1999/2008; Hartman & Laird, 1983). Key to this assessment process is determining the goodness of fit between the family and its environment (Greene & Watkins, 1998). This assessment first proposed by Hartman (1977), allows for an understanding of how a family is connected to educational, religious, health, safety, recreational, political, economic, neighborhood, and ethnic systems (Greene & Watkins, 1998; see chapters 7 and 10). Assessment at the macrosystem level also explores how the large-scale societal context influences the client system.

A family's position relative to other social systems, another dimension of openness, can be better understood by adopting an ecological metaphor (Hartman & Laird, 1983). From this perspective, a family boundary is thought of as "separating" the family from other social systems with which it interacts, for example, family, school, church, and agency. In other words, the boundary gives the family its identity and focus as it carries out transactions with other systems. The more open the system, the more potential there is for exchanges with other systems. This allows for a greater use of outside resources and a greater capacity to mobilize for action. A family with a highly dense boundary is less likely to interact with other systems in the environment, restricting the interchange of materials, energy, and information (Berger & Federico, 1982).

Hartman & Laird (1975) developed a paper and pencil simulation of how a particular family relates to other social systems called an *eco-map* (figure 6.2). The eco-map used in assessment places the family of concern in a center circle and other circles, representing those environmental systems that influence the family, surround it. The practitioner then draws lines between the family and the various systems to delineate the quality of the relationship between them: A solid or thick line depicts a positive

Figure 6.2
Eco Map
Fill in connections where they exist. Indicate nature of connections
with a descriptive or by drawing different kinds of lines: for strong, for tenuous,
for stressful. Draw arrows along lines to signify flow of energy, resources, etc.
Identify significant people and fill in empty circles as needed.

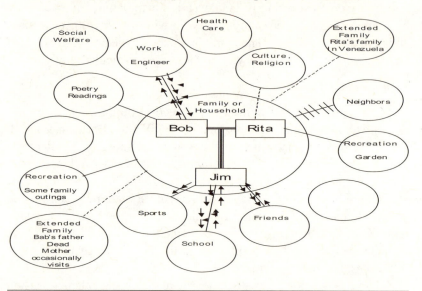

Hartman, A. (1978). Diagramatic assessment of family relationship. *Social Casework,*
59, 465-76.

or strong relationship, and a hatched line represents a stressful relationship (Hartman & Laird, 1983). This information suggests intervention
strategies that often involve the social worker helping the family seek
more community resources (see chapter 9).

Another way of describing a family-environment relationship or
the way in which a family interacts with other systems is to turn to the
ecological concept goodness of fit. The term *goodness of fit* refers to the
extent to which there is a match between an individual's needs and the
qualities of the environment, and it also may be used to examine the way
in which a family is affected by situational forces. For example, when
families experience the negative impact of discrimination, there is not
a goodness of fit between that family and its environment. The role of
social workers is to work for societal change and to improve a particular
family's access to needed resources.

Family Caregivers of Older People with Alzheimer's Disease

Social workers deal with many types of formal caregiving systems including families and medical, social welfare, community, political or economic systems. *Caregiving systems*, whether they be the family, a nursing home, or a day-care center are a form of social organization that involves the structuring of interpersonal relationships and the division of practical tasks. The social worker who understands that care is a truly collective action, depending upon direct and indirect contributions from a number of persons including self-care, is better prepared to work with the family and the long-term care system (Daatland, 1983). For example, those practitioners who work in nursing homes and think of the nursing home staff as a caregiving system are better able to act as intermediary among resident, family, and staff in the process of advocating for the older adult (Greene, 1982).

One of the most documented facts in gerontology is that the family system is the primary source of care for the frail or impaired elderly. In her seminal work, Brody (1985) suggested that family caregiving has become a normative event. For many families the situation may be highly stressful, especially when the older person has a debilitating illness. The following section examines some of the components of this stress, particularly as it relates to family members caring for relatives with Alzheimer's disease and suggests supportive interventions.

Family Caregiving

Family caregiving to a severely functionally impaired Alzheimer's patient is usually a progressively demanding, all-consuming task. At first, the individual with Alzheimer's disease experiences only minor and almost imperceptible symptoms. Gradually, however, the person becomes more forgetful. She or he may neglect to turn off the stove, misplace things, take longer than usual to complete routine tasks, or repeat already answered questions. Changes in personality, mood, and behavior including confusion, irritability, restlessness, and agitation are likely to appear. As the disease progresses, memory loss, poor judgment, and an inability to concentrate become more common. Gradually the older person may become unable to write, read, speak, or even eat. In the final stages, muscular twitching and repetitive movements such as lip smacking occur. The patient is finally confined to bed and becomes more prone to infections. In such situations, incontinence and excessive burdens on the family often lead to nursing home placement (see chapter 4). Social workers can be helpful in providing caregivers with information about the progression of the disease and offering support at critical transitions.

The care of an elderly person with Alzheimer's disease encompasses a range of duties. The daily management of activities such as planning a well-balanced diet, seeing that the person does not wander off, getting the person from a bed to a chair or from a chair to the bathroom, bathing, feeding, or even handling incontinence may be involved. Family caregivers usually have no training in these exacting caregiving skills and often develop strategies by trial and error, at great expense to themselves. Unlike child rearing, in which the level of the child's dependency gradually decreases, the caregiver for a family member with dementia faces continued or increased dependency, with no predictable end of the "36-hour day" (Mace & Rabins, 1999). Therefore, psychoeducational programs and support groups may be important social work interventions (chapter 9).

Practitioners can refer to Blum's (1991) work on courtesy stigma to help families understand how other families may cope with a relative with Alzheimer's disease. Blum identified phases that the intimates or caregivers of people with Alzheimer's disease navigate with their afflicted partners in the course of the illness. Phase one is *collusion* with the patient. Phase one becomes evident at the beginning of the disease when the client tries to mask the dementia symptoms from others. For example, a person may blame odd behavior on old age or lack of memory. As these episodes increase, the caregiver begins to collaborate in hiding the disease symptoms.

The next phase, *standing by*, is characterized by the intimate doing nothing to draw attention to any of the client's disruptive behavior. The caregiver's behavior may be viewed as a monitoring process with the caregiver only stepping in if needed. The next phase is *preventive passing*. This involves the caregiver trying to ward off potential problem situations. The caregiver may assume some of the client's normal tasks, often at the client's request. This phase is followed by active passing where the intimate takes a definite role in helping the client with her/his passing techniques.

The next phase is *covering*. Covering requires that the caregiver attempt to keep the client's symptoms invisible such as avoiding public outings to conceal the disease. Preventive covering involves the caregiver taking action to prevent disruptive client behavior such as the caregiver warning the client that she/he is about to make a mistake; whereas remedial covering are discreet attempts by the caregiver to correct or repair problematic behavior displayed by the client. As the client's disease worsens and she/he is less able to cooperate with the intimate, the caregiver must take on more power and responsibility in dealing with the client and the disease.

Realignment and colluding with outsiders then becomes necessary for the intimate to manage the client's behaviors and disruptions in public. This is not done immediately, rather incident by incident. Realignment originates with the caregiver seeking help. Voluntary disclosure usually begins with other relatives and friends as the primary caregiver seeks help with the client. Caregivers also disclose to get validation of the disease from others. This is often done with medical personnel, usually in hopes of identifying the disease. The combination of the client's disruptive behaviors, the advanced onset of the disease, and the contested disclosure of the disease often precipitates the realignment of the caregiver in seeking outside help.

Preemptive and remedial disclosure in public life involves a realignment of the caregiver with strangers in a public disclosure of the client's disease. The caregiver provides a preemptive disclosure to influence the reaction of strangers to the disruptive behavior. Remedial disclosure involves an explanation of the disruptive behavior after the fact. These can come in the form of an apology or as reassurance. This is also a method used by the caregiver to reassure others of the caregiver's competence or to respond to inexcusable social transgressions. By giving full disclosure that the client has Alzheimer's, the caregiver can control the stranger's definition of the situation, showing them that the client has no control to stop the disruptive behavior.

Gaining a better understanding of their relative's behavior and suggestions for how to better handle problems can often make a big difference. When the strain of caregiving becomes too great, family members may need to be helped to accept nursing home placement. On the other hand, social workers must be careful to evaluate how a family's traditional values and culture shape the perceptions of dementia caregiving, especially among clients whose cultures suggest they be cared for at home (Braun & Browne, 1998). In addition, because social workers usually see problematic situations, they may overlook the positive aspects of family transitions (Burack-Weiss, 1995; Motenko & Greenberg, 1995).

Caregiving and Family Stress

Family members who are involved in their relative's care can encounter their own problems. As it becomes evident that their relative will never get well, but will progressively become more dependent, they often experience powerful and, at times, conflicting emotions as they struggle to meet their relative's physical and emotional needs. Assuming the care of a dementia patient can, in short, result in family members' loss of freedom, privacy, mobility, energy, and time known as *caregiver burden.*

> Gone is the patient's ability to work and to love. Only fragments of familiar behavior and personality remain as sorrowful reminders to the family of what has been lost. The healthy spouse and family experience life as an ongoing funeral: the person they once knew is dying, a little at a time. The family grieves for the loss, yet there are no formalized rituals to help them through this time. (Kapust, 1982, p. 79)

Researchers have reported on the gender differences concerning caregivers' responses to stress. In general, female caregivers use more antidepressants, have more symptoms of stress, lower morale and higher levels of burden, and are less active than males in recreational and social activities. Conversely, male caregivers report of physical health symptoms and loss of financial resources. This may be attributed to a "getting the job done" approach where males caregiver by repairing the house, managing finances (Stoller, 1990; Stoller & Pugliesi, 1989) or driving the patient around.

The vast majority of services for demented elderly persons are provided by the spouse, together with adult daughters and daughters-in-law. Many of the daughters are "women in the middle" who find that they are caught between the needs of their parents and the demands of their children and husbands (Brody, 1981; Davenport, 1999; Lieberman & Fisher, 1999). In addition, they may have to adjust their work schedules, with some leaving paid employment to assume parent care (Brody, 1985). Fried and Mehrotra (1998) captured women's emotional struggles of competing values in the following way:

> ...the roles of paid workers and caregivers have been added to women's traditional roles of wives, homemakers, mothers, and grandmothers. Women face the challenge of how to balance the needs of their aging relatives, their own children, and their grandchildren while continuing to pursue their career interests. (p.97)

Social workers need to be aware that being a caregiver to a relative with dementia may "create a combination of positive feelings of fulfillment or accomplishment, and feelings of stress that can lead to depression and other negative symptoms" (Lawton, Rajagopal, Brody & Kleban, 1992,

p. 157). Numerous studies have identified the mental health problems that may result from the consequences of the emotional strain of caregiving. These include symptoms such as depression, anxiety, frustration, helplessness, sleeplessness, lowered morale, and emotional exhaustion. Because of these difficulties, there has been increased concern about the stress related to caregiving. Importantly, the characteristics of the caregiver and those of the elderly family member often influence the quality of relationships and the degree of burden that is felt. The ages, personalities, and health status of the persons involved, as well as the long-term quality of their relationship, are key factors. Severe memory loss or disorientation and urinary incontinence have been identified as especially likely to contribute to a sense of family burden (Robinson, 1983; Zarit, Reever & Bach-Peterson, 1980).

Assessment of Caregiver Stress and Burden

The assessment of the family's ability to cope with the demands of caretaking is critical to proper intervention. Several interview schedules have been used to measure caregiver strain (tables 6. 3 and 6.4) These interview schedules address a number of problematic behaviors that the client may display, as well as a range of feelings that the caretaker might experience. They suggest questions for assessment that can be incorporated into the social work interview. Assessment, which first focuses on the extent of emotional stress brought about by the burdens of caregiving, should include as many family members as possible.

The ongoing care of the Alzheimer's patient, as with all the severely impaired, puts a strain on the entire family system. In severe instances, stress can lead to interpersonal conflict and result in abuse, as seen in the following example:

In the spring of 1980, Mr. B. called a family service agency requesting socialization activities for his wife who was suffering from Alzheimer's disease. Mr. B., a 66-year-old retired man, had Parkinson's disease, and his right arm and leg were impaired. He explained that he was managing "rather well" and that he was doing the cleaning, cooking, shopping, and so forth. Mrs. B., age 72, was unable to help him or to care for herself. The couple had two children. A married daughter, who lived out of state, called the couple about once a month. A married son, who lived nearby, was interested and concerned. He visited the parents often and took them home for Sunday dinners.

The initial treatment goal was to help Mr. B. understand and cope with his wife's mental deterioration. The couple was also referred to a nutrition program and a home health care service in order to provide support to Mr. B., who was carrying the major burden of Mrs. B.'s care. As Mrs. B.'s mental condition deteriorated, Mr. B., who had formed a positive relationship with the social worker, was able to express his frustration and anger. He eventually volunteered the information that he had hit

Table 6.3
The Burden Interview*

---

1. I feel resentful of other relatives who could but who do not do things for my spouse.
2. I feel that my spouse makes requests which I perceive to be over and above what she/he needs.
3. Because of my involvement with my spouse, I don't have enough time for myself.
4. I feel stressed between trying to give to my spouse as well as to other family responsibilities, job, etc.
5. I feel embarrassed over my spouse's behavior.
6. I feel guilty about my interactions with my spouse.
7. I feel that I don't do as much for my spouse as I could or should.
8. I feel angry about my interactions with my spouse.
9. I feel that in the past, I haven't done as much for my spouse as I could have or should have.
10. I feel nervous or depressed about my interactions with my spouse.
11. I feel that my spouse currently affects my relationships with other family members and friends in a negative way.
12. I feel resentful about my interactions with my spouse.
13. I am afraid of what the future holds for my spouse.
14. I feel pleased about my interactions with my spouse.
15. It's painful to watch my spouse age.
16. I feel useful in my interactions with my spouse.
17. I feel my spouse is dependent.
18. I fell strained in my interactions with my spouse.
19. I feel that my health has suffered because of my involvement with my spouse.
20. I feel that I am contributing to the well-being of my spouse.
21. I feel that the present situation with my spouse doesn't allow me as much privacy as I'd like.
22. I feel that my social life has suffered because of my involvement with my spouse.
23. I wish that my spouse and I had a better relationship.
24. I feel that my spouse doesn't appreciate what I do for him/her as much as I would like.
25. I feel uncomfortable when I have friends over.
26. I feel that my spouse tries to manipulate me.
27. I feel that my spouse seems to expect me to take care of him/her as if I were the only one she/he could depend on.
28. I feel that I don't have enough money to support my spouse in addition to the rest of our expenses.
29. I feel that I would like to be able to provide more money to support my spouse than I am now.

Zarit, Reever, & Bach-Peterson. (1980). The burden interview, *The Gerontologist*, 20, 651.

Table 6.4
Caregiver Strain Questionnaire

I am going to read a list of things other people have found to be difficult in helping out after somebody comes home from the hospital. Would you tell me whether any of these apply to you? (GIVE EXAMPLES)

	(Yes = 1)	(No = 0)
Sleep is disturbed (e.g., because ____ is in and out of bed or wanders around at night)	_____	_____
It is inconvenient (e.g., because helping takes so much time or it's a long drive over to help)	_____	_____
It is a physical strain (e.g., because of lifting in and out of a chair, effort or concentration is required)	_____	_____
It is confining (e.g., helping restricts free time or cannot go visiting)	_____	_____
There have been family adjustments (e.g., because helping has disrupted routine; there has been no privacy)	_____	_____
There have been changes in personal plans (e.g., had to turn down a job; could not go on vacation)	_____	_____
There have been other demands on my time (e.g., from other family members)	_____	_____
There have been emotional adjustments (e.g., because of severe arguments)	_____	_____
Some behavior is upsetting (e.g., because of incontinence; ____ has trouble remembering things; or ____ accuses people of taking things)	_____	_____
It is upsetting to find ____ has changed so much from his/her former self (e.g., he/she is a different person than he/she used to be)	_____	_____
There have been work adjustments (e.g., because of having to take time off.	_____	_____
It is a financial strain	_____	_____
Feeling completely overwhelmed (e.g., because of worry about ____ ; concerns about how you will manage)	_____	_____
Total score (count yes responses)	_____	

Note. Scores range from 1 to 13. B. Robinson. (1983). Caregiver Strain Questionnaire. *Journal of Gerontology, 38,* 344-348.

his wife when "she refused to take a bath after forgetting to go to the bathroom." He said he was sure this would not happen again. He also said he was embarrassed by his lack of control, but became upset when "she wouldn't listen" to him. The social worker, hoping to reduce the pressure on Mr. B., said that she was sure the tension must be very great and suggested that home health care services be increased to at least twice a week. Mr. B. accepted this suggestion.

Several weeks later, the home health aide reported scratches on Mr. B.'s face and severe bruises on Mrs. B.'s arms. The nurse told the social worker she was considering a referral to protective services. The social worker followed up and invited the family (Mr. and Mrs. B., son and wife) to the office to discuss the problem. The family agreed, at the son's suggestion, to send Mrs. B. to a day-care center twice a week. He also offered to pay for this service. The long-range plan was to place Mrs. B. in a nursing home if and when day-care services were not adequate to meet her needs. The social worker also used the interview as an opportunity to reinforce the fact that Mr. B. had been a good provider and a caring husband for over 40 years. She suggested that it was undue stress in the care of his wife that led to "this situation." She thanked the son for his support and asked Mr. B. to advise her or his family when he felt under too much pressure so that help could be provided.

Mrs. B. was able to remain at home for almost a year as a result of these services–home health care three times a week and day–care twice a week. Mrs. B. gradually became incontinent, lost bowel control, and was severely disoriented. Mr. B. was able to discuss his feelings about a nursing home placement with the social worker. He came to the decision that this placement was responsible and meant he still cared about "what was best" for his wife. Following the nursing home placement, the caseworker continued to meet with Mr. B. for about 3 months. During that time, he dealt with his feelings of loss and spoke of his daily visits to the nursing home.

Assessment of Caregiver Resilience

Because the individual with Alzheimer's disease experiences continued decline over time, accompanied by increased care needs, taking care of loved ones with dementia is considered one of the most difficult caregiving situations. Nonetheless, the emphasis in current research on family caregivers for a relative with Alzheimer's disease is revealing a different picture of the caregiving situation (Riley, 2007). Primary caregivers for family members with dementia who have a greater identification with the caregiving role and are more enthusiastic about the role experience less depression and caregiver strain and is associated with resilience (Pierce, Lydon, & Yang, 2001).

Resilience is the ability to overcome the risks that accompany adverse events or stress. Resilience in the face of caregiving is also associated with effective problem solving, emotional coping, personal competence, and acceptance of self and life (Garity, 1997; Wagnild & Young, 1993; Table 6.5). Furthermore, resilience allows the caregiver to experience the rewards that can go together with the caregiving process. Social workers can foster this naturally occurring self-righting mechanism by using a strengths perspective in their interviews.

Table 6.5
Exploring Positive Attitudes Toward Caregiving

This questionnaire contains a number of statements related to opinions and feelings about yourself, your impaired relative, and your caregiving experience. Read each statement carefully, then indicate the extent to which you agree or disagree with the statement. Circle one of the alternative categories that are organized according to three subscales:

1. Loss/Powerless Subscale (LP), 2. Provisional Meaning (PM), 3. Ultimate Meaning (UM)

	SA STRONGLY AGREE	A AGREE	U UNDECIDED	D DISAGREE	SD STRONGLY DISAGREE
1. Loss/Powerless Subscale (LP)					
1. I miss the communication and companionship that my family member and I had in the past.					
2. I miss my family member's ability to love me as he/she did in the past.					
3. I am sad about the mental and physical changes I see in my relative.					
4. I miss the little things my relative and I did together in the past.					
5. I am sad about losing the person I once knew.					
6. I miss not being able to be spontaneous in my life because of caring for my relative.					
12. I miss not having more time for other family members and/or friends.					
13. I have no hope; I am clutching at straws.					
18. I miss our previous social life.					
19. I have no sense of joy.					
24. I miss not being able to travel.					
25. I wish I were free to lead a life of my own.					
30. I miss having given up my job or other personal interests to take care of my family member.					
31. I feel trapped be my relative's illness.					
34. We had goals for the future but they just folded up because of my relative's dementia.					
36. I miss my relative's sense of humor.					
37. I wish I could run away.					
41. I feel that the quality of my life has decreased.					
7. My situation feels endless.					
	SA STRONGLY AGREE	A AGREE	U UNDECIDED	D DISAGREE	SD STRONGLY DISAGREE
2. Provisional Meaning (PM)					
8. I enjoy having my relative with me: I would miss it if he/she were gone.					
9. I count my blessings.					
10. Caring for my relative gives me my life a purpose and a sense of meaning.					
14. I cherish the past memories and experiences that my relative and I have had.					
15. I am a strong person.					
16. Caregiving makes me feel good that I am helping.					
20. The hugs and "I love you" from my relative make it worth it all.					

Table 6.5 (cont.)

	SA STRONGLY AGREE	A AGREE	U UNDECIDED	D DISAGREE	SD STRONGLY DISAGREE
21. I'm a fighter. 22. I am glad I am here to care for my relative. 26. Talking with others who are close to me restores my faith in my own abilities. 27. Even though there are difficult things in my life, I look forward to the future. 28. Caregiving has helped me learn new things about myself. 32. Each year, regardless of the quality, is a blessing. 33. I would not have chosen the situation I'm in, but I get satisfaction out of providing care. 38. Every day is blessing. 39. This is my place: I have to make the best out of it. 40. I am much stronger that I think. 42. I start each day knowing we will have a beautiful day together. 43. Caregiving has made me a stronger and better person.					
3. Ultimate Meaning (UM) 11. The Lord won't give you more than you can handle. 17. I believe in the power of prayer: without it I couldn't do this. 23. I believe that the Lord will provide. 29. I have faith that the good Lord has reasons for this. 35. God is good.					

Farran, C., Miller, B., Kaufman, J., Donner, D., & Fogg, L. (1999). Finding meaning through caregiving: Development of an instrument for family caregivers of persons with Alzheimer's disease. *Journal of Clinical Psychology, 55*(9), 1107-1125.

The social worker's goal in working with caregivers of relatives with Alzheimer's disease is lessening caregiver stress. Assisting the family to obtain affordable respite service, whether in the form of homemaker, day-care, and so on, are examples. Education and support groups can also play a significant role in teaching caregivers specific management skills and techniques as well as providing an opportunity for them to express feelings and to obtain encouragement.

Older Adults Living Alone

In 2005, 21 percent of all those over seventy-five years of age lived alone, 5 percent were males and 16 percent were females US Census

Bureau, 2005 Annual Social and Economic Supplement). These older adults may have social relationships even when living by themselves. Often they have relatives and friends nearby. Many live in familiar neighborhoods and have a tendency to use community services. The following example exemplifies many of these points.

> Mrs. Walker, 78 years of age, moved to the East coast when she married her husband at age 20. They had only one son who was killed in a drive-by shooting. Her husband died 5 years ago after a long debilitating illness. Despite her personal losses, Mrs. Walker has kept in good spirit and very much connected with her neighbors. In fact, she keeps informed about on-going activities and distribution of food, clothing, medicine, etc. by the local agencies. She shares this information with her friends who are not as mobile. While financially she could move to an independent living facility and not bother with a run-down neighborhood, she refuses because of a sense of belonging that she experiences among her close friends, neighbors, and agency staff.

Note

1.   The terms balance, equilibrium, and homeostasis are used interchangeably in this text.

References

Alzheimer's Disease Fact Sheet. (1999). http://www.alzheimer.org/pubs/adfact.html

Anderson, R.E., & Carter, I. (1978). *Human behavior in the social environment.* Chicago: Aldine.

Berger, R., & Federico, R. (1982). *Human behavior: A social work perspective.* New York: Longman.

Berkman, B., & Harootyan (Eds.) (2003). *Social work and health care in all aging society: Education, policy, practice, and research.* New York: Springer.

Bertalanffy, L. (1968). *General systems theory, human relations.* New York: Brazillier.

Bloom, B. L. (1963). Definition aspect of the crisis concept. *Journal of Consulting Psychology, 27,* 498-502.

Blum, N. S. (1991). The management of stigma by Alzheimer family caregivers. *Journal of Contemporary Ethnography, 20*(3), 263-279.

Braun, K. L., & Browne, C. V. (1998). Perceptions of dementia, caregiving, and help seeking among Asian and Pacific Islander Americans. *Health and Social Work, 23,* 262-274.

Brody, E., *Women in the middle and family help to older people. The Gerontologist, 21* (1981), 471-480.

Brody, E. (1985). Parent care as a normative family stress. *The Gerontologist, 25,* 19-29.

Brody, E. (1985). *Mental and Physical Health Practices of Older People.* New York: Springer Publishing Company.

Buckley, W. (1967). *Sociology and modern systems theory.* Englewood Cliffs, NJ: Prentice-Hall.

Burack-Weiss, A. (1995). The caregiver's memoir: A new look at family support. *Social Work, 40,* 391-396.

Cox, C., & Monk, A. (1993) Hispanic culture and family care of Alzheimer's patients. *Health and Social Work, 18*(2), 92-106.

Daatland, S. O. (1983). Care systems. *Aging and Society, 3*, 1-21.

Davenport, D. S. (1999). Dynamics and treatment of middle-generation women: Heroines and victims of multigenerational families. In M. Duffy (Ed.), *Handbook of counseling and psychotherapy with older adults* (pp. 267 -280). New York: John Wiley & Sons, Inc.

Farran, C., Miller, B., Kaufman, J., Donner, D., & Fogg, L. (1999). Finding meaning through caregiving: Development of an instrument for family caregivers of persons with Alzheimer's disease. *Journal of Clinical Psychology, 55*(9), 1107-1125.

Fried, S. B., & Mehrotra, C. M. (1998). *Aging and diversity. An active learning experience.* Washington, DC: Taylor & Francis.

Garity, J. (1997). Stress, learning style, resilience factors, and ways of coping in Alzheimer family caregivers. *American Journal of Alzheimer's Disease* (July/August), 171–178.

Greene, R. R. (1982b). Life review: A technique for clarifying family roles in adulthood. *Clinical Gerontologist, 2*, 59-67.

Greene, R. R. (1982a). Families and the nursing home social worker. *Social Work in Health Care, 7*(3), 57-67.

Greene, R. R. (1989). A life systems approach to understanding parent-child relationships in aging families. In G. A. Hugston, V. A. Christopherson, & M. J. Bonjean (Eds.), *Aging and family therapy: Practitioner perspectives on Golden Pond* (pp. 57-70). New York: Hawthorne Press.

Greene, R. R. (1989). A life systems approach to understanding parent-child relationships in aging families. *Journal of Family Psychotherapy, 5*(1/2), 57-69.

Hardy, K. V., & Laszloffy, T. A. (1992). Training racially sensitive family therapists: Context, content, and contact. *Families in Society, 73*, 364-370.

Hartman, A., & Laird, J. (1983). *Family-centered social work.* New York: Free Press.

Howell, S. C. (1980). *Designing for aging.* Cambridge, MA: MIT Press.

Kapust, L. R. (1982). Living with dementia: The ongoing funeral. *Social Work in Health Care, 7*(4), 79-91.

Laird, J. (1993). Family-centered practice: Cultural and constructionist reflections. In J. Laird (Ed.), *Revisioning social work education: A social constructionist approach* (pp. 77-110). New York: Haworth.

Lawton, M. P., Rajagopal, D., Brody, E., & Kleban, M. H. (1992). The dynamics of caregiving for a demented elder among Black and White families. *Journal of Gerontology: Social Sciences, 47*(4) S156-S164.

Lieberman, M. A., & Fisher (1999). The effects of family conflict resolution and decision making on the provision of help for an elder with Alzheimer's disease. *The Gerontologist, 39*(2), 159-166.

Mace, N.L., & Rabins, P.V. (1999). *The 36-hour day.* Baltimore, MD: Johns Hopkins University Press.

McGill, D. W. (1992). The cultural story in multicultural family therapy. *Families in Society, 73*, 339-349.

Miller, D. (1981). The sandwich generation: Adult children of the aging. *Social Work, 26* (5), 419-423.

Morse, C., & Wisocki, P. (1991). Residential factors in programming for elderly. In P. A. Wisocki (Ed.), *Handbook of clinical behavior therapy with the elderly* (pp. 97-120). New York: Plenum.

Motenko, A. K., & Greenberg, S. (1995). Reframing dependence in old age: A positive-transition for families. *Social Work, 40*, 382-390.

Olsen, R. V., Hutchings, B. L., & Ehrenkrantz, E. (1999). The physical design of the home as a caregiving support: An environment for persons with dementia. *Care*

Management Journals, 1(2), 125-131.

Pierce, T., Lydon, J., & Yang, S. (2001). Enthusiasm and moral commitment: What sustains family caregivers of those with dementia. *Basic and Applied Social Psychology, 23*(1), 29-41.

Queralt, M. (1996). *The social environment and human behavior.* Needham Heights, MA: Allyn & Bacon.

Rappaport, R. (1980). Normal crisis, family structure and mental health. *Family Process, 2,* 68-80.

Robinson, B. (1983). Validation of a caregiver strain index. *Journal of Gerontology, 38* (3), 344-348.

Stoller, E. P. (1990) Males as helpers: The role of sons, relatives and friends. *The Gerontologist, 30,* 228-235.

Stoller, E. P., & Pugliesi, K.L. (1989). Other roles of caregivers: Competing responsibilities of supportive resources. *Journal of Gerontology: Social Science, 44,* S231-S238.

Wagnild, G., & Young, H. (1993). Development and psychometric evaluation of the Resilience Scale. *Journal of Nursing Measurement, 1*(2), 165–178.

Walsh, F. (1998). *Strengthening family resilience.* New York: Guilford Press.

Zarit, S., Reever, K.; & Bach-Peterson, J. (1980). Relatives of the impaired elderly: Correlates of feelings of burden. *The Gerontologist, 20*(6), 649-655.

7

Assessment: The Family as a Set of Reciprocal Roles and Developmental Unit

A family-centered assessment begins with the premise that the family is best understood as a social system with identifiable patterns of organization and communication. To complete an assessment, practitioners also need an understanding of role theory and how a family develops over the life course. This chapter discusses the role assessment from a family interactional perspective. It also describes the "interlocking tasks, problems, and relationships" of the intergenerational family system as it moves through time (Carter & McGoldrick, 1980, p. 11). The assessment of these various intertwined dimensions of family life provides a comprehensive picture of family life.

The Family as an Interactional System

In chapter 5, role performance was introduced as an outcome of the way a person conceives of his or her particular role, the response of others with whom it is enacted, and the cultural context in which it takes place. Viewing older clients from a role perspective leads to a dynamic understanding of their social age. However, the concept of role performance is more than a way of understanding the social dimensions of individual behavior. Individual role performances are linked to the family and form an interactive system. From this perspective, the family is a social system made up of multiple, reciprocal roles and statuses that produce discernible patterns of behavior and communication.

Role and Status

For the social worker to understand behavior from a role perspective, the concepts of role and status need to be defined. A *role* is "a set of expectations people share concerning behaviors to be performed as part of a specific situation" (Queralt, 1996, p. 30). *Status* is a structural term that indicates an individual's location in a given societal framework or group hierarchy. The more statuses a person acquires, the more roles he or she is obliged to play. A person may occupy several statuses (positions) concurrently, such as those of a citizen, attorney, wife, mother, sister, and so on. The person then assumes a set of corresponding roles that he or she plays out in daily life. As a particular status changes, so do the corresponding roles.

Roles are patterned with a partner in mind. An *obligation* is what a person feels bound to do for another by virtue of the role he or she occupies (i.e., a grandmother, I feel I should baby-sit for my grandchild). A *claim* consists of those things that are expected by virtue of the relationship (As your daughter, I expect you to baby-sit for your only grandson). "What constitutes a claim for one partner is an obligation for the other" (Shibutani, 1961, p. 47).

Satir (1972), a family therapist, illustrated the point that each role carries with it different expectations for behavior using the analogy of an individual wearing several hats. For example, a woman traditionally first dons her "self hat," the original hat that represents her primary role. This role is an integral part of her person–"she never removes this hat." Depending on what other activities she pursues and statuses she holds, other hats are stacked on the self hat; a wife hat, a mother hat, a daughter hat, a doctor hat, and so on. She puts on and takes off these various hats associated with her various statuses many times during any single day and appropriately shifts the roles that accompany them.[1]

Ascribed and Achieved Status

Expectations for role behavior often depend on whether the accompanying status is ascribed or achieved. An *ascribed* status is assigned by society, such as chronological age (year of birth) and gender. Society expects individuals to play roles appropriate to the statuses that it ascribes. A parent is expected to care for her child; an adult is expected to assume responsibility for his or her own behavior. Because of its relatively stable nature, an ascribed status is difficult to change. The more traditional a society, the more likely the negative reaction to individuals who do not fulfill an ascribed status and/or who deviate from the expected norm. An example might be if an adult child who is expected to care for an ailing parent does not do so.

Achieved status is attained by the individual. It is derived from a person's activity and effort, such as acquiring a college education or winning a political office. Society expects certain roles to be attached to achieved status, but if these expectations are not met, the individual may be shown a greater degree of tolerance than when roles are ascribed. Achieved roles are associated with highly valued social identity. They can be differentiated from ascribed roles by the freedom with which they are chosen and by the high esteem in which people who play them are held. The distinction between ascribed and achieved roles is highlighted during family transitions. Transitions may include a woman who has received a promotion at work, expects a child, or has an older parent in need of elder care.

Assumption of Roles and Group Culture

Children quickly begin to assume the various roles modeled around them. They copy the behavior of their parents and siblings and begin to internalize their roles and accept them as their own. Later, as more people enter their lives, additional role models influence behavior. Learning new roles is not completed by adulthood. Rather, it is a continuous process that occurs throughout life. In addition, learning new roles is influenced by the particular culture to which an individual belongs. Each new role is associated with culturally defined values and seemingly appropriate behaviors. This process of transmitting behaviors and customs from generation to generation, and that leads to a group-specific culture, is called *socialization*. Social work assessments need to address how cultural membership influences a client's role interpretation and performance (see chapter 10). What are the expectations for care in a particular culture? Who is "in charge" of end-of-life decisions?

Difficulties in Role Performance

As social workers use role theory to understand the internal workings of a family, they particularly need to assess which family members are experiencing difficulty in role performance (table 7.1). Many of the troubles faced by clients such as role pressure, role strain, role confusion, and role conflict are due to the stress surrounding role enactment.

Role Strain

The process of role enactment often proceeds in a relatively smooth, organized fashion. However, because role strain or conflict is inherent to the process of change, it is an expected aspect of family life. A person can experience role strain when family and circumstances bring about too many pressures, such as elder caregiving combined with job responsibili-

Table 7.1
An Intergenerational Family Focus: Assessment Questions

1. What is the problem?
   a. How does the family view the problem?
   b. How differently do individual members view the problem?
   c. How does the therapist's perception of the problem correlate or coincide with that of the family?

2. Who is the patient?
   a. Does the family recognize that the whole group is a unit of treatment?
   b. Does the family accept the fact that all its members need help?
   c. Is there an individual member around whom most of the complaints revolve?
   d. How are the family complaints portrayed by its members? Do their descriptions differ?

3. How and where did the problem originate?
   a. Has the problem originated in a recent change of roles and statuses within the family?
   b. Can the problem be traced (specifically) to the presence of triangular communication in the family?
   c. Is the problem contained inside the intergenerational network?

ties (figure 7.1). As seen in the following example, how individual family members cope depends on their personal capacities and the adaptability of the family system:

> A household is joined by an elderly aunt. She moves in with her nephew's family to recuperate from a stroke. On the surface, this appears to be straightforward. However, when it comes to the actual events, the seemingly simple plan becomes more complex. The nephew's daughter needs to give up her room to accommodate the aunt. The son resents "the intruder" and the daughter misses her privacy. The nephew's wife finds she needs to pay special attention to menus. As a person fully employed outside her home, she is used to cooking by cutting corners. Now she has to cook "proper" meals and serve them to the aunt in her room. She finds herself shopping for groceries on her lunch break. On several occasions when the nurse's aide did not show up, the niece has had to stay home from work. The nephew is obliged to spend a good part of his evenings visiting with his aunt, who likes to reminisce. He finds that the nightly visits are encroaching on his opportunity to decompress after a stressful work environment.

The family contacts a sectarian nursing home on the aunt's behalf. The social worker who makes several home visits learns that the aunt is a single, retired government worker. She has been accustomed to living by her own standards. Until this hospitalization, she had been an active member of the literary guild and local symphony board. While she was paralyzed on her left side, her biggest fear was to be institutionalized

Figure 7.1
Forms and Mechanisms of Stress Proliferation.

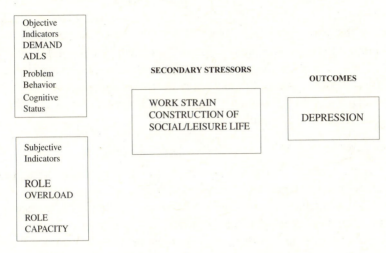

PRIMARY STRESSORS

Objective
Indicators
DEMAND
ADLS

Problem
Behavior

Cognitive
Status

SECONDARY STRESSORS

OUTCOMES

WORK STRAIN
CONSTRUCTION OF
SOCIAL/LEISURE LIFE

DEPRESSION

Subjective
Indicators

ROLE
OVERLOAD

ROLE
CAPACITY

BACKGROUND CHARACTERISTICS AND SITUATIONAL CONTEXT

Pearlin, L. I., Aneshensel, C. S., & Leblanc, A. J. (1997). The forms and mechanisms of stress proliferation: The case of AIDS caregivers. *Journal of Health and Social Behavior* *38*(3), 223–236.

with "old people who were out of their minds." She wanted to stay with her family.

Although seemingly not of crisis proportions, all the family members in this illustration were experiencing difficulties with changes in their respective roles. Their accustomed place(s) in the family and in society were being challenged (my independence, my room, my privacy, my job, my leisure). The social worker's sensitivity in recognizing the stress associated with the demands placed on each family member, whether they appear large or small, is the key to resolution through family-focused social work.

In assessing what risks a client may be experiencing in relation to their various roles, it is important for the social worker to remember that people have relationships and responsibilities related to the multiple roles in which they participate, "both within major institutions, such as family and occupation, and those within extended informal networks, such as those involving friendships or voluntary associations" (Pearlin, Aneshensel & Leblanc, 1997, p. 234). Therefore, caregiving responsibilities have the potential to negatively affect the mental and physical well-being of the caregiver, be disruptive to marital or family relationships, or cause problems in meeting work and other social responsibilities. "As a consequence, individuals may need to reconcile the changes and demands of one role with the requirements of a second role or domain of activity" (p. 234; figure 7.1).

Role Variability

Some systems therapists are reluctant to deal with emotions, preferring to focus on behavior; others are increasingly interested in individual meanings attached to family roles (White & Epson, 1992). Because a role usually is enacted according to its personal meaning, the meaning attached to a situation is an important aspect in assessment and treatment. The social worker's assessment may distinguish three degrees of role variability: (a) role as a welcome consequence; (b) role as learned art; and (c) role as life's necessity. Sometimes the acquisition of a new status is welcome and the person experiences pleasure in enacting the accompanying role. With the birth of her grandchild, the new grandmother acquires a new status. This usually is a welcome change in her life. At the same time, some grandmothers, who out of necessity have to assume the role of mother, may experience considerable stress (Burnette, 1997; Queiro-Tajalli & Smith, 1998). This form of kinship care is increasingly familiar to social workers in the field of child welfare.

At other times, a new status may not be so welcome, as in retirement. There are, of course, individuals who are delighted with this role since they have waited for this event for years and have plans to last three lifetimes. But then there are retired persons who may be at a loss as to how to enact the new role. Should they switch to another activity that produces income, do volunteer work, pursue hobbies, travel? Whether a person comes to retirement as an enthusiastic, reluctant, or unwilling participant, in most cases the status requires some adjusting. Even the enthusiastic retiree may find that life is quite different from the time when he or she was a 9-to-5 worker. Socialization into a corresponding and personally satisfying role often becomes a learned art. Longevity and the aging of the baby boomers will make this an increasing necessity (see chapter 1).

There are times when a new status is not welcome or wanted, such as widowhood. Accepting the status and role of a widow(er) is one of the most difficult of tasks. Acquiring the associated role(s) and accepting the loss of a loved one involves the process of grieving. The stages of disbelief, despair, and acceptance must occur before rebuilding can take place. Going through the process of grief is, of course, necessary to "normalize" the individual's life. Depending on the context of grief, resolution may occur through natural healing processes or require intervention.

Complementary Family Roles

The family plays a central part in negotiating the role changes facing its members' transitions from worker to retiree, from mother to mother-in-law, from mother to grandmother, or from spouse to widow. As family members shift and alter their relationships to meet the new needs of all family members, they establish a division of labor and a code of behavior. In addition, the process of defining the rights and duties associated with family membership results in a pattern of reciprocal claims and obligations. Understanding these patterns is a major element in family assessment.

Among all the issues related to family functioning and role structure, the complementarity of roles is of major importance. The principle of complementarity speaks to the way in which emotional needs are met within the family. It addresses the fit of role relationships and the health, growth, and creative adaptability of the family group. *Complementarity* exists when "the reciprocal role of a role partner is carried out automatically without difficulty, and in the expected way" (Strean, 1971, p. 320). To achieve complementarity of roles, one member of the family acts to provide something that is required by another. As a result, the other person has his or her needs fulfilled.

Discomplementarity reflects an unstable role structure and ambiguous role definitions and expectations. When complementarity fails, mutual needs are not adequately met, and the relationship is not fulfilling. Role partners disappoint each other, relationships are experienced as incomplete, and role participants may undergo feelings of anxiety, hostility, or tension. Social workers can explore five main reasons for failure in role complementarity: (a) *cognitive discrepancy*, occurring when one or both parties involved in the relationship are not familiar with the role requirements; (b) *discrepancy of goals*, referring to situations in which the immediate or ultimate goal of a role is unclear; (c) *allocative dis-*

crepancy, encompassing how the role is obtained—ascribed, achieved, assumed, or adopted; (d) *instrumental discrepancy*, occurring when the technical equipment, physical facilities, or instrumental prerequisites for role performance are not available to the actor; and (e) *discrepancy in cultural value orientations*, referring to variations in role expectations (Spiegel, 1968).

The following example is illustrative of many of the issues relevant to role complementarity:

> Mrs. B. was referred to the social worker at a nutrition site program for senior adults by a friend who discovered her crying and saying over and over again, "I can't take this anymore." Mrs. B., a youthful, athletic appearing woman of 65, indicated that she was upset about her husband, who is 75 years old and has Parkinson's disease. The event that precipitated her seeking help was the purchase of a hospital bed for her husband, which was made at the recommendation of his doctor. The bed was delivered that morning and she "suddenly realized that the marital relationship was over and that her husband was seriously ill."

In taking a history, the social worker soon learned that the marriage had been a stormy one for many years: Mrs. B. married when she was nineteen and Mr. B. twenty-nine. They had two children, whom they saw only on holidays. Throughout their marriage, Mr. B. was employed as a tailor and Mrs. B. as a seamstress. Mrs. B. described herself as the major breadwinner who contributed 85% of the household income because "my husband could not always find a job." She appeared very angry and resentful that she had to maintain this role. Mrs. B. "retired voluntarily" 2 years ago in order to care for her husband. She related bitterly that at work she felt, and was treated like, a real person. By contrast, she said that her husband verbally abused and criticized her constantly. Because Mr. B. was so irritable, friends no longer came to visit. Her social network was now virtually nonexistent. Furthermore, her income had diminished considerably. (The couple lived on Social Security; once again Mrs. B.'s amount was more than her husband's.)

Six months ago, Mrs. B. began sending her husband to a senior day-care program two days a week. During that time she would do errands, shop, take long walks, and swim at the Y, and felt that this was her only chance to do something for herself. Mr. B. did not like the program and would make upsetting remarks each morning as he left: "You only want to get rid of me." "Why don't you love me enough to take care of me yourself?" Shortly after she began seeing the social worker, Mrs. B. received a call from the director of the day-care service, who said the program could no longer meet Mr. B.'s needs. "His rapidly deteriorating physical condition and hostile attitude required too much staff time at the expense of other participants."

> Mrs. B. pleaded with the social worker to make them keep her husband. "Just tell them if they don't, I am going to put him in a nursing home." The social worker convinced the day-care director to keep Mr. B. for a "trial period" of 3 months. She also talked Mrs. B. into asking her husband to meet with the social worker and day-care staff in an effort to work things out. Unfortunately, there seemed to be "too many old scores to settle" in the marriage relationship, and Mr. B. entered a nursing home 3 months later.

The restoration of stability or equilibrium in the family system is a complicated process, particularly once complementarity is seriously threatened. In the example of Mr. and Mrs. B., there was a history of low complementarity of roles. Rather than growing and expanding, the relationship became less and less fulfilling and increasingly constricted, until it finally failed.

Hierarchy of Roles

Power is the ability of one person to influence another's behavior (Queralt, 1996). According to systems theorists, each family, even the most egalitarian, has a power structure known as a *hierarchy*, whereas role theorists (Parsons, 1951, 1954) considered power to be an underlying societal and family structure. The family was viewed as the main role-allocating agency for its members, socializing children into their expected roles and continuously guiding adult members in the adoption of new roles. This means that the family was understood to have considerable power to direct and control its members. As equity in role performance and power differentials have become important in the delivery of family treatment, the notion that there is a pecking order or ranking in families is increasingly under scrutiny (Davis, 1991; Thompson & Greene, 1994). As seen in the above illustration of Mr. and Mrs. B., what makes for role complementarity is bound to cultural, historical, as well as family contexts. Family-centered social workers need to be cautious about the meaning of roles (always receiving feedback from clients) need to recognize the historical time in which they are enacted. They also must be aware of their ideas about how families "should" function and must not avoid dealing with power issues that affect client well-being. This may become apparent in some ethnic families in which the eldest son has seemingly "taken over" decision-making. Does the older adult expect this as a consideration?

Communication and Interaction

No discussion of how to conduct a family assessment can be complete without giving serious attention to the topic of communication. Communication theory can be an important tool in understanding human interaction. The term *communication* has many meanings, and the study of communication systems is often highly complex, mathematical, or statistical. In social work practice, *communications* can be considered a system for transmitting information between two or more individuals. The cumulative exchanges serve as the basis for evolving relationships between people, each of whom receives, processes, and reviews information (Bloom, 1984; Marcus, 1974).

Because each family has an identifiable communication system, an analysis of the group's particular communication patterns can be made. These patterns develop through interaction over time and generate shared definitions of norms and roles for its members. This, in turn, influences the nature of relationships and results in the formation of a recognizable family structure that can be assessed.

It is through the first hand observation of family communications that the social worker learns about family dynamics. During assessment, the social worker is able to observe a cross section of the family's various behavior patterns. The social worker coaches the client family about communication patterns, including why information is transmitted, what meaning it contains, and what inferences are made. For a family to better understand its communication, it is necessary to clarify when members are clear and direct: when family members use or learn to use clear communicators they restate, clarify, or modify messages when necessary; are receptive to feedback; check their own perceptions; ask for examples; and acknowledge feelings. When unclear communication is used, family members tend to leave out connections between ideas, ignore questions, and generally respond out of context (Satir, 1972).

Satir (1972) has suggested that the practitioner can enhance family communication by keeping the following pointers in mind:

- Clarity: Is what the speaker says clear to the listener?
- Content: Does the speaker concentrate on the same verbal content as the person to whom he or she is talking?
- Agreement: Does the speaker agree or disagree with the other person's message?
- Commitment: Does the speaker take a stand on the main point or issue when appropriate?

- Congruency: Are the verbal or tonal and nonverbal aspects of the speaker's message consistent?
- Intensity: How forceful or empathetic is the speaker?
- Relationship: What does the message reflect about the relationship? Is the message attacking or accepting of the other person?

In addition, therapists need to recognize that clients use nonverbal language. For example, they may use body language to get a point across for which they lack words, to emphasize what they are saying, or to contradict what they are saying. Thus, nonverbal language can be very revealing. For example,

> An older uncle reports to the therapist that his new life is unpleasant since he joined the family of his niece. She thought that he was "getting on in years" and should not live alone. Now he is constantly told to "do this; don't do that; wash up before dinner; hang up your clothes, etc., etc., etc."

This report was given in a calm, flat, and measured voice. However, the therapist noticed that as the uncle talked, he tapped his fingers on his knees and started jerking his head nervously. Even though the voice of the client seemed unemotional, the words chosen seemed to reflect some degree of anger, while his body language communicated another meaning. Rather than assume what is involved, the social worker needs to explore the meaning of this communication with the client family.

The Family as a Developmental Unit

As discussed in chapter 4, individual development centers around a person's ability to adapt within his or her social context. While a picture of an individual's development provides insight into that person's psychological age, theorists increasingly espouse the idea that individual development must be understood within a family context (Carter & McGoldrick, 1999). This section of the chapter focuses on family development. It discusses the various life tasks the family meets as it enters the later stages of the life course, particularly those affecting intergenerational relationships.

Family Development

While individual development unfolds in the context of the family, family development is concerned with more than the concurrent development of individual family members. The family itself is a developmental unit with phase-specific and culturally shaped family tasks. As conceptualized by Rhodes (1980/1977), the study of family development is concerned with the shifting memberships and the changing status of family members as they approach each developmental stage:

> Each stage in the life cycle of the family is characterized by an average expectable family crisis brought about by the convergence of biopsychosocial processes which create phase-specific family tasks to be confronted, undertaken, and completed. These family tasks reflect the assumption that developmental tasks of individual family members have an overriding influence or effect on the nature of family life at a given time and represent family themes that apply to family members as individuals as well as a group. (p. 31)

Family Development and Stress

Carter and McGoldrick (1999) have developed a schema representing the vertical and horizontal flow of stress in the family life cycle that represents a reflection of the multi-systemic, current complex nature of family development (figure 7.2). They suggested that stressors are a natural part of life, take various forms, and have the propensity to induce distress that can occur across the life cycle. As seen in their visual representa-

Figure 7.2
Flow of stress through the Family.

Flow of Stress through the Family

Vertical Stressors
Racism, sexism, classism
ageism, homophobia,
consumerism, poverty
Disappearance of community
more work, less leisure
inflexibility of workplace
time for friends
Family emotional pattern
myths, triangles, secrets
legacies, losses
Violence, addictions, ignorance
depression, lack of spiritual
expression or dreams
Genetic makeup, abilities and
disabilities   T

Systems Levels
Sociocultural, political, economic
Community: neighborhood, work
friends, religious, organizations
Extended family
immediate family
Individual

Larger Society

Community

Extended Family

Immediate family

Individual

Horizontal Stressors
Developmental
a. Life cycle transitions
b. Migration
Unpredictable
a. Untimely death
b. Chronic illness
c. Accident
d. Unemployment
Historic Events
a. War
b. Economic depression
c. Political climate
d. Natural disasters

Carter, B., & McGoldrick, M. (1999). The expanded family life cycle: *Individual, family, and social expectives.* Boston:Allyn & Bacon

tion, stress occurs along several dimensions. Nested concentric circles represent the idea that stress comes about at any system level, from the individual level to the sociocultural, political, and economic levels.

The vertical axis represents the various types of stressors that may transpire at each systems level, such as racism or homophobia at the larger societal level or disappearance of community at the community level. The horizontal axis represents development over the life span within a specific historical context. Such developmental stressors may include life cycle transitions and migration; unpredictable events may include untimely death, chronic illness, accidents, or unemployment; and historical events may encompass economic depression, war, or political oppression, and natural disasters.

Family Developmental Tasks

Traditionally, family developmental tasks have centered around the nuclear family, child raising, and economic functions. The tasks have included establishing a household, accommodating the birth of a child, dealing with teenagers, and so forth. However, as Froma Walsh (2003) has pointed out, an approach to family development "must be relevant to our times and viewed in sociohistorical context" (p. 10). She suggested that emerging trends are

- varied family forms
- changing gender roles
- cultural diversity and socioeconomic disparity
- varying and expanded family-cycle course.

A family's developmental tasks in later life often involve the integration of loss (the process of grieving and investing in future functioning) and the development of a mutual aid system. Establishing a mutually accommodating parent-child relationship in later life involves the issue of dependency. Interdependence should be viewed as a normal family process, and an expected and important aspect of intergenerational relations. Walsh (2003) indicated that dependence

> requires a realistic acceptance of strengths and limitations of the older adult, and the ability to allow oneself to be dependent when appropriate. It also requires the adult child's ability to accept a filial role, taking responsibility for what he or she can appropriately do for aging parents, as well as recognition of what he or she cannot or should not do. This capacity may be constrained by the child's own physical, emotional, and social situation. (p. 206)

The development of a mutual aid system in late life requires adult children to meet what appears to be a universal sense of an adult child's duty to meet the needs of his or her aging parents (Boszormenyi-Nagy & Spark, 1973). While this sense of duty/loyalty may be universal, adult children confront what gerontologists have termed a *filial crisis* (Blenkner, 1965). The crisis involves an adult child acknowledging that he or she is no longer a dependent child but a mature adult who may now have to care for his or her parent. When adult children experience their parents' declining health or functional status, they often feel a sense of loss. Simultaneously, they must confront their own mortality (King, Bonacci & Wynne, 1990). The successful achievement of this task, *filial maturity*, involves the renegotiation of the parent-child relationship to one of adult-adult. The development of a mutual aid system also requires what Carter and McGoldrick (1999) described as a "self [that] connects and empathizes with others and can engage in caring and being cared for by others" (pp. 27).

Clearly, while most families deal positively with an elder's dependence, interdependence–the attainment of filial maturity–is relative and may require intervention (chapter 9). Brody (1985, 1990) argued that, although parent care can be considered a normative family event at the same time, it can be the major source of stress and guilt in adult children. The truth, said Brody (1985),

> is that adult children cannot and do not provide the same total care to their elderly parents that those parents gave to them in the good old days of their infancy and childhood. The roles of parent and child cannot be reversed in that sense. The good old days, then, may be…an earlier period in the individual's and family's history to which there can be no return. (p. 26)

The resolution of these feelings, then, is difficult and may be the focus of family treatment.

Culture, Diversity, and Developmental Tasks

Family life has tended to be described for contemporary Western, intact nuclear families (Tseng & Hsu, 1991, 1999). Changing standards for role behavior and what constitutes universal developmental tasks challenge practitioners to examine their theoretical stance and their own belief systems. The varied configurations of the family over the life course necessitate "a broader view of both development and normalcy" (Carter & McGoldrick, 1999, p. 1). For example, the popular life cycle approaches are based on a mainstream heterosexual model (see Johnson & Colucci, 1999, for a full discussion). Such models suggest that the purpose of marriage is having children, have a narrow definition of what is a family, provide little guidance about how homosexual families transmit and celebrate rituals, and use language that generally applies to heterosexual families (Slater, 1995).

Tseng and Hsu (1991) suggested factors that may vary when working with client families of different cultural backgrounds:

- In addition to marriage and the bearing of children, there are many other milestone factors relating to family system and structure. These factors may include the pattern of getting married, ways to bear and adopt children, and cohabiting members in the household, all of which affect the total configurational pattern of the family life cycle.
- Due to numerous variations (such as differences in premarital experience, patterns of childbearing, the life span of parents, and the structure of the household), the rhythm of family development may vary, the transition between phases may be clear-cut or blurred, and each stage may be short, long, or absent.
- Associated with the different cultural implications of critical issues concerning developmental milestones (such as the formal marital union, dissolution of marital relations, launching of children from the home, and widowhood), the impact of such milestones of family development on the family members has different meaning and effects. Therefore, it is necessary to examine the meaning of family development in the context of cultural background. (p. 46)

Social History

Finally, assessment of the current relationships within the family system requires an understanding of how that family has developed historically. Family therapy is based on the premise that helping a family understand how past relationships influence current difficulties provides the optimum opportunity for meaning to be established and problem-solving to take place. The following is an example:

The C. family first came to the attention of a private family service agency in 1975, when the resident manager of the building in which they lived called about their imminent eviction. The resident manager reported that "the mother and son fought every evening and that other residents were complaining."

The household consisted of Mrs. C., who was 76 years old, and her son Ralph, who was 50. Two daughters, ages 52 and 56, lived in the same community but were "not on speaking terms" with either their mother or their brother. Mr. C. had died the previous year, at which time Mrs. C. sold the family home, "wanting to move to a smaller place that would be easier to keep clean."

The developmental history revealed that Ralph was very attached to his father, who had walked him to and from school every day as a child. He "had no other friends."

He "was not allowed to go away to college" despite his outstanding academic abilities, and was encouraged to get a job as a clerk nearby upon graduation from high school. Ralph remained at home, and Mr. C. walked with him to and from the bus that he rode to work.

When Mr. C. died, Ralph expected that his mother would now accompany him to the bus; however, her worsening arthritis precluded this. Due to her physical condition, Mrs. C. was able to do less and less around the house, and Ralph "was not about to do woman's work." Arguments and a pattern of family violence escalated when the family agency was finally called.

The issues illustrated here reflect the manner in which individual and family development is intimately connected. Ralph, who was not prepared by the family to assume an adult role, was not ready to take filial responsibility for his mother when she became frail in her old age. Five years later, despite the efforts of the social worker to provide home care, the mother was admitted to a nursing home. Ralph visited daily at the dinner hour, insisting that "he wanted to eat dinner with his mother."

Note

1.   Thanks to Dr. Jirina Polivka for her original contributions to this chapter.

References

Blenkner, M. (1965). Social work and family relationships in later life with some thoughts on filial maturity. In E. Shana & G. Streib (Eds.), *Social structure and the family*. Englewood Cliffs, NJ: Prentice-Hall.

Bloom, M. (1984). *Configurations of human behavior*. New York: Macmillan.

Brody, E. M. (1985). Parent care as normative family stress. *The Gerontologist, 25*, 19-29.

Brody, E. M. (1990). *Women in the middle: Their parent-care years*. New York: Springer.

Boszormenyi-Nagy, I., & Spark, G. (1973). *Invisible loyalties*. New York: Harper & Row.

Burnette, D. (1997). Grandparents raising grandchildren in the inner city. *Families in Society, 78*(5) 489-499.

Carter, E. A., & McGoldrick, M. (1980). The family life cycle and family therapy. In E. Carter & M. McGoldrick (Eds.), *The family life cycle: A framework for family therapy*. New York: Gardner Press.

Carter, E. A., & McGoldrick, M. (1999). *The expanded family life cycle: Individual, family, and social perspectives*. Boston: Allyn & Bacon.

Johnson, T. W., & Colucci, P. (1999). Lesbians, gay men, and the family life cycle. In E. A. Carter & M. McGoldrick (Eds.), *The expanded family life cycle: Individual, family, and social perspectives* (pp. 346-361). Boston: Allyn & Bacon.

King, D. A., Bonacci, D. D., & Wynne, L. C. (1990). Families of cognitively impaired elders: Helping adult children confront the filial crisis. *Clinical Gerontologist, 10*, 3-15.

Marcus, L. (1974). Communication concepts and principles. In F. J. Turner (Ed.), *Social work treatment* (pp. 372-399). New York: The Free Press.

Parsons, T, (1951). *The social system*. New York: Free Press.

Parsons, T. (1954). *Essays in sociological theory*. New York: Free Press.

Pearlin, L. I., Aneshensel, C. S., & Leblanc, A. J. (1997). The forms and mechanisms of stress proliferation: The case of AIDS caregivers. *Journal of Health and Social Behavior 38*(3), 223–236.

Queiro-Tajalli, I., & Smith, L. A. (1998). Provision of services to older adults within an ecological perspective. In R. R. Greene & M. Watkins (Eds.), *Serving diverse constituencies: Applying the ecological perspective* (pp. 199-220). New York: Aldine de Gruyter.

Queralt, M. (1996). *The social environment and human behavior.* Boston: Allyn & Bacon.

Rhodes, S. L. (1980). A developmental approach to the life cycle of the family. In M. Bloom (Ed.), *Life span development.* New York: Macmillan. [Originally (1977) in *Social Casework, 58*, 301-311.]

Satir, V. (1972). *People making.* Palo Alto, CA: Science and Behavior Books.

Shibutani, T. (1961). *Society and personality.* Englewood Cliffs, NJ: Prentice-Hall.

Slater, S. (1995). *The lesbian family life cycle.* New York: Free Press.

Spiegel, J. P. (1968). The resolution of role conflict within the family. In N. W. Bell & E. F. Vogel (Eds.) (rev. ed.), *Modern introduction to the family.* New York: Free Press.

Strean, H. S. (1971). The application of role theory to social casework. In H. S. Strean (Ed.), *Social casework theories in action.* Metuchen, NJ: Scarecrow Press.

Thompson, K. H. & Greene, R. R. (1994). Role theory and social work practice. In R. R. Greene (Ed.), *Human behavior theory: A diversity framework* (pp. 93-114). New York: Aldine de Gruyter.

Tseng, W. S., & Hsu, J. (1991). *Culture and family problems and therapy.* New York: Haworth.

White, M., & Epson, D. (1992). *Narrative means to therapeutic ends.* New York: W. W. Norton.

Walsh, F. (2003). Normal family processes (3rd ed.). New York: Guilford Press.

8

The Functional-Age Model and Individual and Family Intervention

Chapters 1 through 7 of this text explored assessment of the older adult within a family and societal context. The assessment requires social workers to consider alternative explanations for behavior and to engage in a mutual information-gathering process. Chapters 8 and 9 describe how the practitioner uses the client's story to give direction to social work interventions and to explore where in the client system or in the client's life space it is appropriate to intervene.

Social Work Intervention and Treatment

There is no clear-cut demarcation of the assessment and treatment phases. Clients often feel helped when a social worker "merely" listens to their concerns. However, usually a time does come when the social worker and client recognize that they have reached an agreement about mutually acceptable goals (Northen, 1995). This consensus about working together provides the mandate for social work interventions or treatment (the terms *intervention* and *treatment* are used interchangeably in this text).

Social work treatment, which differs according to its specific purpose(s) and client challenges, capacities, and life situations, has been variously defined. Broadly speaking, treatment begins with the first interview, enabling clients to improve their social functioning and to cope with life situations and conditions better. Social work treatment encompasses a wide spectrum of activities ranging from interventions to make social institutions more responsive to people's needs to therapies to develop individual insight. Helping people increase their problem-solving and coping capacities, obtaining resources and services, facilitating interaction among individuals and their environment, improving interpersonal relationships, and influencing social institutions and organizations, all come under the rubric of social work treatment (Lowy, 1991).

According to Northen (1995), social workers may use various skills in the intervention process including *support*, sustaining the client; *attending*, paying purposeful attention to the client; *acceptance of feelings*, providing encouragement for clients to express their thoughts; *structuring*, keeping the client focused on achieving mutually decided treatment goals; *exploration*, obtaining sufficient information from the client about the person-group-situation configuration; *psychosocial education*, providing the client with new knowledge and skills to improve their functioning; *advice*, influencing the client with recommendations; *confrontation*, facing clients with the practitioner's view of their reality; *clarification*, engaging the client in reflection; and *interpretation*, creating meaning about behaviors with the client (pp. 138-162).

Person-Environment Focus

What makes social work treatment unique is the use of interventions that may be directed at any aspects of a client's social processes with the intention of changing them (Bartlett, 1970). Definitions of social work intervention share common elements congruent with the purpose of social work. The major concern of social work intervention is to identify, resolve, or minimize difficulties arising from an imbalance between (a) individuals, families, groups, or communities and (b) their environment. Such interventions are transactional and emphasize reducing people's stress and enhancing their coping strategies (Compton, Gallaway, & Cournoyer, 2004).

Germain (1981) was among the first theorists who suggested that social workers focus their interventions on "transactions between people and environments that, on the one hand promote or inhibit growth, development, and the release of human potential and, on the other hand, promote or inhibit the capacity of environment to support the diversity of human potential" (p. 325). In short, just as social work assessment examines the quality of person-environment fit, social work interventions are aimed at improving goodness of fit (Greene, 1999/2008).

Difficulties in goodness of fit requiring social work intervention can occur at any level, from the personal to the larger scale political. Greene and Barnes (1998) outline principles for conducting a multilevel assessment:

- Interventions may be directed at any aspect of the ecosystem.
- Interventions at the personal level need to be congruent with the client's environmental and cultural context.
- Family interventions need to be congruent with a family's form, including cultural and normative traditions.
- Group interventions rely on the expertise of group members.
- Ecological interventions combine informal and formal helping (84-89).

Theoretical Orientations

Theoretical orientation shapes the intervention process (table 8. 1). For example, social constructionists have suggested that therapeutic goals are "to help clients become more open to new ideas, new meaning, and new ways of understanding their dilemmas" (Dean 1993, p. 64). Social workers who use a social constructionist approach emphasize the need for practitioners to give heightened attention to clients who may have faced oppressive social and economic conditions. Whereas cognitive-behavioral treatment is based on the idea that treatment should follow stated, specific goals and tasks developed by client and therapist. The purpose of therapy, often used to relieve depression, is to improve a client's negative self-ideation. Clients often complete homework assignments such as a log of negative and positive life events with the intent of achieving a more positive self-concept (Gallagher-Thompson & Thompson, 1996).

Using Life Review

Because life review is frequently used in social work with older adults, it is important to discuss it as a specialized technique. In a hallmark 1963 article, Robert Butler, a major pioneer in the field of geriatric psychiatry, conceptualized the process of life review. Butler noted that the repetitive nature of storytelling among older adults is not always an indication of psychological dysfunction. Rather, it is the naturally occurring progressive return to consciousness of past experiences in an attempt to resolve and integrate them. He based his work on the work of Erik Erikson (see chapter 4) and termed this process of assessing one's life *life review*. Butler suggested that because the life review process has adaptive value for clients, practitioners should actively encourage clients to recall the past. He was optimistic that autobiographic processes could help people maintain self-identity and overcome life's difficulties, thus foreshadowing a resilience approach:

> Psychotherapeutic work with older people involves the management of small deaths and intimations of mortality. Put succinctly, the psychotherapy of old age is the

Table 8.1
Themes in Family Treatment with Families of Later Years

A Systems Perspective   A Postmodern Perspective

The practitioner:	The practitioner:
promotes the adaptive capacity of the older adult and his or her family	allows for the particular client story rather than rely on universal truths or norms
helps members adapt to changes (usually diminution) in an older adults biopsycho-social functioning	understands that a particular client story rests in his or her local, culturally-specific (and personal) experience
counteracts the effects of depletion and loss (Silverstone & Burack-Weiss, 1983)	generates meaning within therapy through participants' interaction
mobilizes the family system on behalf of the older adult	works in collaboration with a client to define the situation
deals with the stress and strain in caregiving	makes every effort to be aware of his or her own preconceived ideas
seeks means to enable the older adult to remain as autonomous as possible	avoids problem-saturated descriptions of the client
promotes positive interdependence among generations	uses an interactive process to generate and resolve negative stories
deals with the dynamics of dependency, loyalty, loss, and anger	challenges a client's "truths" that limit his or her life
uses resources from an ecological perspective	provides opportunities for the client to share, understand, and use alternative meanings
	uses a method of inquiry or curiosity, rather than one of assessment generated by family roles (Thompson & Greene, 1994)
	equalizes power difficulties within therapy and within the family

Greene, R. R., & Blundo, R. (1999). A postmodern critique of family systems theory in social work with the aged and their families. *Journal of Gerontological Social Work, 31*, 87-100.

psychotherapy of grief and of accommodation, restitution, and resolution. 'Coming to terms with', 'bearing witness', reconciliation, atonement construction and reconstruction, integration, transcendence, creativity, realistic insight with modifications and substitutions, the introduction of meaning and of meaningful, useful, and contributory efforts: these are the terms that are pertinent to therapy with older people. (Butler, 1968, p. 237)

The following case study illustrates how an older person can evaluate the meaning of his or her life and come to terms with past conflicts and relationships.

> Miss R. was referred by a senior center employee to a social worker because "she constantly argued with others at lunch." The senior center employee described Miss R. as a "small, disfigured woman with a hump." She continued to say that the other participants were complaining that Miss. R. was becoming more and more belligerent during media discussion groups. Miss R. insisted that she was the only one who knew the facts.
>
> The social worker learned that Miss R., age 85, who suffered from severe scoliosis of the spine, was one of four children. According to Miss R.'s description, her "first sibling was a brother everyone wanted; the second was a beautiful girl whom everyone admired; I was the third, whom nobody needed, and the fourth was a baby girl whom everyone loved and cuddled." Miss R.'s mother was described as tall and beautiful and her father as strict and reserved. Her father insisted that Miss. R. study diligently so that she would be able to go to college and get a good job, implying that no one would ever want to marry her. Miss R. said she had shown them all, and had become a librarian at a nationally known library. She was able to spend hours a day reading, becoming an expert on many subjects. She denied that her badly hunched back was ever a concern.
>
> One day, when the social worker was called to Miss R.'s home because of "an emergency," she found Miss R. rocking and crying before the mirror. She had fallen the day before and severe bruises now appeared on her face. She stood there looking at herself, saying "how ugly, how dumb." When the social worker first spoke to her, she said "don't look at me, don't look at me." The social worker said that no matter how ugly Miss R. thought she looked, she had savored their special time together. This brought a flood of reminiscences. Miss R. was able to say that "her disfigurement" brought back many painful memories, such as being taunted by children in school. Months of therapy and the positive regard of the social worker eventually led to reports from the senior center director that Miss R. was now a more pleasant, contributing member of the group.

Life review is more than simple recalling of the past. As seen in the example of Miss R., it involves a "restructuring" of past events and is conducive to the individual's adaptation to the aging process. Life review can be enhanced through the use of structured interviews, photographs, music, art, poetry, and dance therapy (Greene, 1977; Weisman & Shusterman, 1977). Since it was first advanced, life review therapy has become a well-accepted and widely used clinical technique for working with the aged. Mental health practitioners have found that the technique can be used in a number of different treatment approaches and settings. It is used in social work with individuals and families (Greene, 1977, 1982b) and has been effective with groups in nursing homes, senior citizen residences, and community centers (Pratt, 1981; Weisman & Shusterman, 1977). On the other hand, not all clients require intensive psychotherapy. By building on client strengths and adaptive capacities, people can be helped to age successfully (Rowe & Kahn, 1995).

Cross-Cultural Social Work Practice

Social workers aspire to culturally competent practice. However, progress in meeting the social services needs of minority and ethnic clients within a cross-cultural perspective has been slow at best, because of a number of factors. Most often gerontological research has focused on limited samples of white middle-class participants. As a result, there is insufficient information about the differing cultural patterns and life styles of the minority and ethnic aged, leaving the practitioner to base her or his assessment and intervention on broad generalizations about that group.

According to NASW (2001), cultural diversity in social work has primarily been associated with race and ethnicity, but diversity is taking on a broader meaning to include the sociocultural experiences of people of different genders, social classes, religious and spiritual beliefs, sexual orientations, ages, and physical and mental abilities (p. 2). Cross-cultural social work practice is based on the assumption that U.S. society is culturally diverse and efforts must be made to individualize the client. Acquiring accurate knowledge about how clients perceive their life situations and problem(s) within their individual cultural context is essential. Minority groups should be understood not only in relation to their minority status but also for the richness of their heritage and the benefits they can offer society (Greene, Taylor, Evans & Smith, 2002). In this way, the practitioner needs to understand the meaning of the spoken and nonspoken language of the minority elderly.

> Dr. Rodriguez was talking to Ms. Prieto, the social worker of the intensive care unit of a hospital in a large urban area, about concerns she had about her mother, Mrs. Ruiz. Mrs. Ruiz came to this country to assist Dr. Rodriguez with her new born baby several years ago, and just a year ago she received her immigration papers legalizing her status as a resident. During the first five years, Mrs. Ruiz kept herself quite busy taking care of the baby and the household with little time to socialize on her own. Now, that the child is in school, and Dr. Rodriguez can afford domestic services, Mrs. Ruiz does not have much to do in the house, yet she refuses to attend the Senior Citizen Center a few blocks from the apartment. Dr. Rodriguez is afraid she is suffering from mild depression but whenever she raises the issue with her mother, she would say, "Hija, do not worry. I am comfortable at home." Ms. Prieto said that she would like to visit

the mother, and from that day on she visited Mrs. Ruiz once a week. During the visits, Mrs. Ruiz served tea and home-made cookies, and they talked about the homeland and the way Mrs. Ruiz lived her adult life there. In this way, Ms. Prieto learned that Mrs. Ruiz came from a rather affluent family and a community with clear divisions between social classes. Ms. Prieto understood that Mrs. Ruiz was quite uncomfortable going to the Senior Citizen Center where in her mind most of the people were from a lower social economic class and of different racial and ethnic backgrounds. When Ms. Prieto shared her assessment, Mrs. Ruiz agreed and added that she knew her behavior was not right, that she would like to spend time with people of her same age group, but that she did not know how to relate to them.

Another issue of concern in cross-cultural social work is the sensitivity with which services are delivered. The process of planning, implementing, and evaluating social services for diverse groups requires the willingness on the part of the practitioner to understand their culture and incorporate dimensions of the culture into the services. From this point of view, social work with minority and ethnic group clients requires adequate preparation for and alertness to those aspects of the client's cultural background that affect social service encounters. This is a complex process involving self-awareness and a willingness to carry out one's professional activities in a manner that recognizes the client's cultural integrity.

As a powerful influence on behavior, culture encompasses the values, knowledge, and material technology that people learn to see as appropriate and desirable. *Culture* "establishes the parameters that guide, structure, and often limit thinking and behavior" (Berger & Federico, 1982, p. 10). Because cultural norms and values are group specific, the social worker engaged in cross-cultural communication must be cognizant of social boundaries and be prepared to move beyond the limits of his or her own personal experiences. The social worker must make a conscious effort to help the client in a manner that is congruent with the client's cultural values and attitudes (Greene, 1985; Greene & Watkins, 1998).

As mentioned earlier, ethnicity becomes most apparent when individuals meet others who are culturally different from themselves. In fact, it is the interaction across group boundaries that is ethnicity's defining characteristic. Practitioners need to understand the importance of this interaction, "the persons who mediate boundaries are critical social actors in the communication of information and the regulation of resources as they affect those groups" (Greene, 1982a, p. 13). According to Green (1999), "cultural competence means only that the worker has a systematically learned and tested awareness of the prescribed and proscribed values and behavior of a specific community, and an ability to carry out professional activities consistent with that awareness" (p. 87).

H. N. Weaver (1998) pointed out three major principles of cultural competence: (a) acquisition of knowledge about the specific group; (b) continuous self-reflection to detect biases within oneself and the profession; and (c) ability to integrate knowledge and self-reflection with the appropriate practice skills. Because cross-cultural social work involves interacting with clients who are ethnically distinct and serving communities that are culturally unfamiliar, the practitioner must be willing to learn about the culture from the client and how to respond appropriately in such encounters. The acquisition of cross-cultural knowledge is at the heart of ethnically sensitive practice methods.

Learning about diverse groups is a complex task. Clearly, practitioners are bombarded with negative media images about ethnic and minority groups the same way as the general population is. As a result, they need to analyze what is said about these groups critically and develop the habit of conducting reality checks about their own feelings and biases regarding the group in question. Cross-cultural practice skills develop through a process of taking the role of the learner, gaining understanding of the culture, building on generic skills of the profession, and giving oneself the opportunity to assess with the client what skills are appropriate within that group. Problem-solving skills of the practitioner and the older minority person may differ. Confrontational skills may not be appropriate when working with certain ethnic clients. Sometimes, certain words may not exist in the language of the client. In sum, on the basis of Weaver's (1998) principles, the practitioner needs to be able to gather data about the client's group, understanding that it is not always an easy undertaking because of stereotypes, generalizations, and misinformation found in the literature and the popular media. Skills in connecting clients with culturally competent services require an inquisitive and critical mind to detect discriminatory and "color blind" service policies. Finally, cross-cultural social work with older adults needs to be conceptualized as multidimensional. That is, it recognizes ethnic differences; it builds on the client reality, which often means a lifetime of discrimination and poverty; it focuses on client strengths derived from her or his culture and individual resilience; and it advocates for culturally competent services.

Functional-Age Model: Meeting Specified Needs

The person-environment orientation involves "the technical flexibility of selecting interventions on the basis of a specific client/problem/situation configuration" (Fischer, 1978, p. 237). Its basic purpose is to assist people to achieve a better match between their needs and situational, environmental conditions. Therefore, in the functional age model, the social worker selects interventions based on the assessment to address identified needs in each area of individual biopsychosocial and spiritual functioning:

- By assessing *biological age*, the social worker has obtained information about the client's physiological age-related changes, nutritional habits, ease of mobility, availability and use of health care and medication, and other health needs. This should provide an indication of how well a client is functioning in his or her home. Can he or she carry out Activities of Daily Living (ADLs)? What in-house supports do they need? Biologically interventions often include team work and consultation with other professionals. Services might include such things as locating an inexpensive wheelchair or portable commode, or transportation to chemotherapy or kidney dialysis.
- By assessing *psychological age*, the social worker has gathered information about the individual's adaptive capacities. How is the older client adapting to change, stress, and loss? The social worker's assessment focuses on a client's self-reports and life story. Can she determine whether the older adult show signs of depression? Does the client need ongoing counseling or medication? Does the older client exhibit signs of dementia? Should the client seek medical consultation?
- By assessing *social age*, the social workers learns about an individual's roles and social habits. What is the nature of his or her social support? Is the older person socially isolated? Is he or she still carrying out important family roles such as advice-giving? The practitioner's goal might be to work with the client to find alternative roles such as participating in a Retired Senior Volunteer Program (RSVP), thereby lessening the effect of role loss.
- By assessing *spirituality*, the social worker learns about a client's belief systems and sources of spiritual support. Does he or she attend religious services? Does religion play a role in crisis resolution? If so, how?

Functional-Age: The Individual

In carrying out the helping process with an individual, the practitioner generally follows general individual phases: (1) engaging the client in treatment; (2) conducting an assessment; (3) formulating a collaborative evaluation; (4) formulating a mutual treatment plan; (5) implementing the treatment plan; and (6) terminating treatment.

1. As discussed in chapter 2, the social worker's first treatment goal is to engage the client in a problem-solving relationship. Critical to maintaining that relationship is the social worker's acceptance, reassurance, encouragement, concern, understanding, and empathy.

2.   As described in chapter 3, a second goal is to conduct an assessment that serves as the bases of a treatment plan. This does not occur in distinct phases. Rather, in social work treatment "the problem-solving means contain the ends; the process and the goal become fused. Treatment, then, can be said to begin with the request for service.

3.   When formulating a collaborative evaluation, social worker and client use what Perlman (1974) called a *teaching intervention strategy* (p. 65). By asking questions, making comments, and reframing issues, the social worker not only obtains assessment information, but offers clients a different view of themselves, their situation, and events. This new meaning can set in motion the client's adaptive capacities (Hartman & Laird, 1983; Perlman, 1957; White & Epson, 1992). Critical aspects of the assessment process involve the social worker encouraging the client's self-evaluation and helping him or her to reach treatment decisions.

4.   Formulating a mutual treatment plan, the next objective, is another ongoing social work process that does not occur at a fixed time. From the first client-social worker contact, whether by phone or in person, the social worker begins listening for a client's description of his or her concerns. As this occurs, the social worker may form tentative hypotheses or "hunches" as to the client's difficulties. These concerns become more refined as the assessment progresses and there is ongoing feedback from the client. Even when assessment has led to the formulation of a treatment plan, further information and reactions from the client invariably bring about changes. From this viewpoint, intervention encompasses a wide array of factors that can lead to a sustaining or strengthening of client functioning.

      The treatment plan is formulated by using the understanding gained during assessment. Because the functional-age model provides a systematic way to explore client concerns and integrate information about the person-environment configuration, it can serve as a blueprint for formulating the treatment plan. Throughout the assessment, the social worker is examining the complex interaction among biological, psychological, social and spiritual that influence the older adult's functional capacity. As seen above the individual's treatment plan is comprised of interventions to enhance adaptational capacities and functional skills that are necessary for or instrumental in meeting environmental demands.

5.   When implementing the treatment plan the social worker and client carry out intervention strategies together. The content of treatment plans contains both a counseling component and strategies for specific health and social services. However, an artificial distinction should not be made between concrete and therapeutic services. The skillful and sensitive practitioner is able (a) to understand the complex interaction between "direct counseling" and "indirect action" (Richmond, 1922), and (b) to help the older adult in ways that are conducive to supporting optimum functioning.

6. Termination of treatment should include an evaluation of the helping process, the degree to which it has met care plan objectives. Because of ongoing frailty or diminished capacity, some older adults may need ongoing services. There are some special issues in terminating treatment with elderly clients, many of whom may be chronically ill or frail. Many older persons come to view the practitioner as surrogate family, making it difficult to terminate when treatment goals have been achieved. On the other hand, social workers may be reluctant to end services, feeling they are "abandoning" a lonely, needy person. There are cases that remain active indefinitely, sometimes terminating only at the time of the client's death. But the decision about termination with elderly clients, as with clients of any age, should be made as part of an ongoing mutual review of the client's treatment plans.

Family Therapy: Historical Background

For those older individuals with family, the next aspect of the functional age model involves the exploration of how an older adult's functional capacity is linked to the family's assessment and the subsequent enactment of a family-focused intervention plan. This section first outlines the history of the family therapy movement and discusses its influence on the conceptualization of the functional-age model. It also suggests how the model can be used in treatment of older adults and their families. The family therapy movement began in the 1950s due to the perceived growth in the number of family-related problems and to new information available about human behavior. Since the inception of family-centered treatment, family therapists have used a variety of treatment techniques, depending on their theoretical orientation (Proctor, Davis, & Vosler, 1995). However, the various approaches to family therapy have several elements in common. Generally speaking, family-centered social work is based on a person-environment perspective that suggests that the family be understood within the context of culture and larger social systems. Family therapy is indicated when the family's ability to perform its basic functions becomes strained. In attempting to understand and alleviate this stress, the practitioner attempts to modify those elements of the family relationship system that are interfering with family and individual life tasks.

Family therapists are concerned with how the family changes, and they focus their attention on the influence of one family member's behavior on another. Most family therapists share the view that if an individual changes, the family context also will change. In that sense, the ultimate goal of family therapy is no different from the goal of all therapies. It is a helping process to enhance social functioning, restore the equilibrium, and strengthen adaptation, of individual persons (Sherman, 1977, p. 485).

The family therapy movement involved a different orientation or a reconceptualization of therapy. At the end of World War II, mental health treatment centered around individual psychological functioning; however, family therapists began to realize that it was counterproductive, if not impossible, to work toward individual change without considering the family system. Family-centered practitioners also contended that, although it was usually the problems of one family member that brought the family to seek treatment, the family group needed to be the unit of attention (Hartman, 1995). By the end of the 1950s, it became clear that family therapy was a different concept of change, not just another method of treatment. The focus of treatment therefore shifted from changing the individual to altering relationship patterns within the family.

There is no consensus among practitioners about how and in what ways family functioning can be enhanced. There are a number philosophical schools of family therapy and practice techniques, leaving the social worker the choice of modes of intervention best suited to his or her philosophical bent and the needs of the family (Proctor, Davis, & Vosler, 1995). Some practitioners emphasize the exploration of family emotional issues, and others stress understanding of family behavioral patterns. Some therapists prefer to see the whole family group together on a regular basis; while others may work with a single family member to bring about change in the entire system.

For purposes of discussion, these various methods of family treatment can be viewed as forming a treatment continuum, as depicted in table 8.2. The two extremes of the continuum, which have been labeled Type A and Type Z, represent two idealized polarities. The concept that the family comprises individuals who are emotionally related to one another is central to Treatment Type A. In Treatment Type A, the family unit is believed to share a "circular interchange of emotion" (Ackerman, 1972/1981). From this perspective, family therapy is defined as a method for treating individual emotional disorders. Family interventions, such as developing insight, are psychodynamically oriented. Insight into problems is gained through interpretations of the psychodynamics of family functioning and of the therapist-client transference. As the family develops insight and gains positive emotional therapeutic experience, distress is alleviated and health and growth are promoted (Ackerman, 1972/1981).

Therapists adopting Treatment Type Z promote the idea that the family is a number of individuals who constitute a system. Family therapists

Table 8. 2
Polarities of Family Treatment Forms

Type A	Type Z
Borrows from the psychoanalytic approach and the medical model	Borrows from small group and systems theory
Emphasizes emotional/affective relationships within the family	Emphasizes structural or behavioral relationships
Suggests that family relationships are influenced by emotional tension/anxiety	Suggests that relationships are influenced by the structural and communication patterns of the family group
Adheres to the idea that transference and interpretations are therapeutic	Provides for the therapist to remain detached from the family system except for interventive inputs
Encourages the development of insight in family members through interpretation of unconscious processes	Rejects the idea of transference
Attempts to alleviate "interlocking emotional disorders" of the family group	Encourages the understanding of behavioral interactive patterns
Promotes health and growth by contributing to insight and relieving pathogenic conflict and anxiety	Attempts to alleviate dysfunctional family patterns
	Promotes functional behaviors by educating members and altering structural arrangements of the family

Note. Family treatment may be thought of as a continuum. The many differing treatment forms actually fall somewhere between the polarities A to Z and have been further modified by postmodern therapists.

who engage in this approach define family treatment as an interactional process of planned interventions in an area of family dysfunction. The goal is to alter individual behavior that results in a changed family structure. That is, family therapy is seen as a means of changing the family relationship structure by modifying the role performance. The practitioners' interventions are designed to help family members understand their communication and interactive style to alleviate dysfunctional family patterns. Minuchin (1974) and Bowen (1971), leading proponents of the systems school, distinguish individual treatment orientations from family therapy by its focus on therapeutic interventions that address the structure of the family group and the functions of individuals within the group. Needless to say, Type A and Type Z represent artificial conceptions of family therapy. In reality, family therapy most often is eclectic, with various treatment forms falling somewhere between the two extremes. Treatment takes many forms, styles, and techniques; and it varies with the setting, the specific client group, and the therapist's personality, training, and theory base.

With the advent of postmodern theories, such as feminist and social construction theory, there has been a greater emphasis on prevailing societal and political values. As a result of this change in epistemology (see Greene, 1999; Greene & Blundo, 1999), many practitioners are giving increased attention to the political, ideological, and institutional implications of family treatment (Hartman, 1995). Major themes include the need for a social worker to understand that each client is unique and must be understood within his or her sociocultural, political, economic, and historical context.

The wide variation in treatment strategies that can be derived from the various schools of family therapy allows the practitioner to establish his or her own focus of treatment. The selected interventions can be based on assessment and treatment goals. In this way, the emphasis may be placed on such seemingly diverse goals as achieving greater insight, altering disturbing behavior patterns, or generating new meanings or possibilities.

The history of family social work parallels that of family therapy, which also has no universally accepted methodological approach. Family-centered social workers have elected a school of therapy or selected particular techniques and interventions as their practice has indicated. The *Encyclopedia of Social Work* offers guidance in defining this practice domain:

> Most family therapy theorists agree that behavior is contextual, that is the outcome of complex patterns of interaction between people and their environments. This perspective, which is, of course, congruent with social work's person-in-situation perspective, led many social workers to feel comfortable in the developing movement. (Proctor, Davis, & Vosler, 1995, p. 984)

Family Therapy and Older Adults

While the family therapy movement has had a strong effect on social work practice, its influence on geriatric social work has not been a more recent phenomenon. Throughout the 1960s and 1970s, in an effort to broaden geriatric services, social workers in the field of aging were encouraged to adopt a family-centered approach (Blenkner, 1965; Freed, 1975; Greene, 1977; Spark, 1984). Over the last decades, some geriatric social workers have creatively adapted family therapy techniques to fit their practice. However, comprehensive intergenerational family therapy models are still in demand (Eyde & Rich, 1983; Greene, 1995, 1999/2008; Silverstone & Burack-Weiss, 1983).

Because family-centered practice involves such a wide range of interventions and treatment possibilities, it is ideally suited for working with older adults and their families. According to Walsh (1999), geriatric practitioners should give highest priority to four family interventions: (1) stress reduction; (2) information about medical condition, functional ability, limitations and prognosis; (3) concrete guidelines for sustaining care, problem solving, and optimal functioning; and (4) linkage to supplemental services to support family efforts (p. 314). Family counseling, day care, homemaker services, and Meals-on-Wheels–all of which are designed to strengthen and supplement family life–are among the variety of interventions that come under the umbrella of family-centered social work.

The functional-age model of intergenerational treatment is in this eclectic social work tradition. It suggests treatment strategies that range from offering life review therapy to the older adult to providing three-generational family therapy. Specific interventions may include completing a genogram, transporting an older adult to a nutrition site, obtaining day-care services for an Alzheimer's patient, or working with the staff of a nursing home–all with the basic goal to enhance or restore family functioning on behalf of the older adult.

The Functional Age Model: Prevention

Social workers may work in settings where prevention is possible, recognizing that a state of "precrisis" exists. For example, a social worker may observe that an older adult attending the senior center may suddenly seem confused. Unfortunately, the field of prevention has not been as popular in the Western Hemisphere as it has been elsewhere, particularly in Europe. However, the philosophy is changing, and practitioners are beginning to recognize the value of timely intervention.

The social work practitioner can help the family effect meaningful changes in its system whether the members find themselves in a state of crisis or whether they are beginning to plan for the future. Being aware of the usefulness of prevention is particularly important in the field of aging. A wide array of services is often accessible to enhance the quality of life and the physical rearrangements of an older individual. The social worker is ideally suited to offer the family the right kind of anchor in its search for help, being well informed about services and community resources that the client family may need. Social workers are educated to make quick and competent assessments about which resources could be tapped. Finally, they are trained to assess and give nonintrusive direction to the family.

Despite the family's need for assistance in selecting appropriate help, they may also have fear of the unknown. A chronic problem has the redeeming value of familiarity. The promise of improvement is suspect because of uncertainty about its outcome, and family members may feel threatened by change. The process is a paradox. Change is often painful, and personal discoveries necessitate much work and effort on the part of family members. For this reason, it may be easier to delay seeking help.

When practitioners have assessed and plan to intervene to ameliorate a family's stress, they should keep in mind the following five principles:

1. The family system is adaptive, [often] becoming more complex and organized over time. This means the family will have their own coping strategies on which to call.
2. Family therapy is indicated when the family's ability to perform its basic functions becomes inadequate. This is particularly true when communication is poor and organizational patterns do not suffice to carry out family tasks.
3. Therapy is designed to modify those elements of the family relationship system that are interfering with the life tasks of the family and its members.
4. Family treatment focuses on the impact of one family member's behavior on another.
5. The objective of family therapy is to alleviate the difficulty/problem through modifying the family structure and patterns of communication and by mobilizing the family as a resource (Greene, 1989, pp. 60-61).

Functional Age Model Goals: Restoring Family Equilibrium

Family therapists have a variety of treatment goals. Helping the family to establish a better system of relationships, improving communication, enhancing autonomy and individuation, strengthening role performance, and alleviating (individual) symptoms are only a few. The functional-age model suggests that a major treatment goal at the time of crisis is to assist the family in reestablishing its equilibrium so that stress can be lessened and the older member assisted. A family that is experiencing excessive stress, whether induced by a developmental or biopsychosocial/spiritual crisis, cannot adequately attend to the needs of its members. As a result, the older adult who is experiencing a problem is less likely to receive the support of the family unit. Once the family has overcome its crisis, it is better prepared to deal with the tasks that enhance the functioning of all its members.

To establish an atmosphere in which the immediate crisis can be resolved, the empathetic social worker lets the family know that he or she understands the difficulties that they face. At the same time, the practitioner should use a strengths perspective and give family members confidence that they have the capacity for change. How a family handles a crisis may often depend on how they have met previous challenges.

While first responding to the initial request, exploring the family's developmental history can give the social worker additional insight into the family's past competencies and present potential for dealing with a crisis (see chapter 7). The practitioner also should realize that problems affecting older persons often involve the need for specific services and require fast, practical decisions. In a systems approach to therapy, social workers concentrate their problem-solving energies and activities on the present, rather than spending them on an exhaustive examination of the past.

In clarifying the immediate crisis, the social worker needs to consider what influences outside the family boundaries may be affecting the functional capacity of the group. Difficulties with the housing authority, the nursing home staff, or muggers on the streets may result in dramatic changes for a family. Just as events outside the family may engender a crisis, so, too, can outside resources assist in alleviating it. In summary, the therapist who wishes to assist the family to reestablish its equilibrium must be prepared to deal with the major concerns that have brought the members to seek help. Often the family expects a quick solution. Consequently, gathering a family history, understanding family dynamics, and assessing the group's functional capacities must all be done quickly in the interest of clarifying and resolving the crisis at hand.

The Functional-Age Model: Family-Focused Treatment

This section describes Herr and Weakland's (1979) family-focused treatment approach including six overlapping phases for counseling older adults and their families: (1) connecting with the client system; (2) determining the problems or issues; (3) reframing the problem; (4) setting mutual goals with the family; (5) mobilizing the family system; and (6) evaluating, providing feedback and terminating.

Connecting

As discussed in chapter 2, the first contacts that initiate the therapeutic process establish the parameters of treatment. At that time, the social worker's theoretical view of treatment is put into action. Social workers establish a mutual helper-client relationship. The practitioner considers whom to involve in treatment. Connecting with significant members of the client system requires that the social worker be attentive to the information given at intake so that the older (pivotal) client's concerned relatives or other informal helpers can be included. This treatment focus is based on the knowledge that change in the older person's functioning influences the family group. Connecting with the client system means that the practitioner must view them as such.

Defining the family as the client does not mean that social workers impose their views; nor does it mean that they think of the family as "inadequate" or "pathological." Rather, the social worker is aware that the biopsychosocial changes in the older pivotal client may overwhelm some families, making them less able to cope without support. Questions related to the functional capacity of the family structure can be clarified during the process of discussing family concerns. However, family members usually need to be engaged early in the social work process. The practitioner who identifies who constitutes the family system is better able to understand the precipitating issue or problem from a family perspective and more likely to maintain a family focus in treatment. This approach has the potential to strengthen the family as a support network and caregiving unit.

Connecting with the family system requires that social workers have specific knowledge and skills. Understanding systems properties, for example, is essential. The clinician must also be able to quickly gain a family perspective of the problem and the solutions that have been tried or disallowed. The practitioner is then able to empathize with all family members. For example, the married daughter who calls for Meals-on-Wheels for her frail eighty-nine-year-old father and indicates that she is torn between her father, her husband, and her new job is as much the client as her father. To engage the daughter in the helping process, her needs have to be acknowledged. The social worker can make a therapeutic intervention by asking the daughter to participate (with her father and the social worker) in planning for the future. In summary, connecting with the client system means that social workers identify the people that constitute the client system and acquire family information about precipitating events and presenting problems.

Defining the Problem

As described earlier, families seek help when they have a problem, are under stress, or are in a crisis. In the situation of intergenerational families, they often request social work services after a prolonged period of struggle to provide emotional and instrumental support to a functionally impaired older member. Determining the problem, sometimes called assessment, is in simplest terms a matter of describing and understanding these family events. This enables the family to learn what family patterns are not working for them. During this phase of treatment the family begins to acquire a self-picture, an understanding of their goal, and ways family members may want to change. Many families simply need additional community resources to cope more effectively. If treatment is "successful," the family can learn to become experts in their own family, independently capable of recognizing, commenting on, and thus interrupting dysfunctional patterns (Hartman & Laird, 1983).

This learning, which is an outgrowth of assessment, is a joint endeavor of the family and social worker. Learning begins as the family clarifies why they sought help. The better the need for help is understood, the more easily solutions may be sought. Therefore, the social worker should not be reluctant to ask all family members why they came to the agency: "Could each of you give me some idea of why you have come today?" or "What concerns do each of you have?"

Problems in intergenerational therapy are usually first defined as "belonging" to the old family member. Understanding how the presenting problem is viewed enables the social worker to begin to reframe the definition of the problem from one affecting only the life of the pivotal client to one affecting the lives of each member of the family (Herr & Weakland, 1979). Hearing each family member's point of view can also provide information about what is interfering with the family's problem-solving process. Systems theory suggests that when a family experiences a crisis, members try to reestablish the family's equilibrium. Therefore, inquiring about already-tried, possible solutions is an important aspect of this phase of treatment. The social worker also wants to inquire about what resources have been used and about what other supports the family thinks are needed.

The social worker usually needs to help a family determine the problem in a relatively short time. The family often views their situation as an emergency, and the level of stress may be high. Questions about family roles and how these have changed over time are particularly useful in gathering information quickly. A family in which a mother, who used to cook a Thanksgiving dinner for her three children and their families and now lets the pots burn on the stove, may think their older mother is "losing her mind" or "incompetent." What turns out to be a slight memory loss may have a ripple effect throughout the family system. Although White and Epson (1992) cautioned that practitioners need to avoid problem-saturated family descriptions, they explained that a practitioner's questions can help a family map the influences of the problem. They pointed out that questions can assist the family in understanding a problem's sphere of influence in related behavioral, emotional, physical, interactional, and attitudinal domains (p. 62). The social worker is then better prepared to offer interventive strategies.

Reframing

Reframing the problem in family terms is one of the most critical components of family treatment. Reframing the problem means that the social worker interprets, organizes, and discusses assessment information to arrive at a family-focused, mutually acceptable description of the problem. Reframing begins at intake and is a means of helping the family learn how the "older person's problems" affect the lives of each family member. The social worker can accomplish this by expanding the focus of exploration from the pivotal client to aspects of family organization. Learning how each family member operates in relation to the perceived problem is the goal. "Reframing the problem may also take place through expanding its meaning, that is, by setting the problematic behavior in the context of the total family or in a historical context" (Hartman & Laird, 1983, p. 308).

When observing the situation of families who are caring for an older member with Alzheimer's disease, the process of reframing the problem becomes clear. Family caregiving for a person with Alzheimer's disease is usually a progressively more demanding, all-consuming activity. Because of the stressful nature of caregiving, many family members encounter difficulties of their own. Clearly, the client is the family system, and treatment interventions should be aimed at minimizing the negative effects of the older person's disease and at increasing the skills and confidence of family members. By providing knowledge about care demands and service needs the social worker may be able to decrease the anxiety and stress surrounding caretaking (Eyde & Rich, 1983, chapter 7).

Setting Mutual Goals with the Family

When setting goals with the family, there is a mutual agreement about the direction of therapy. That agreement is an outcome of discussions about goals, alternative uses of community resources, and general family responsibilities. It is also important for the social worker to clearly outline what the agency has to provide. In this way, families have a more realistic view of what treatment can achieve, as well as appropriate means of gauging their progress. In short, establishing mutual goals clarifies the reasons for treatment.

In establishing treatment goals, one of the first things that needs to be clarified is the social worker's role. Without a clear understanding, the family may have false expectations about what they can gain from treatment. At the same time, practitioners need to adopt realistic goals for themselves so they do not lose sight of treatment possibilities. Just as social workers need to narrow down a problem, they must also take care to keep their goal(s) realistic. Herr and Weakland (1979) have suggested that the practitioner can avoid being overambitious if he or she determines with the family the smallest amount of change that could give them a sense of progress in solving their problem. This process may prevent a sense of failure on everyone's part and a recognition that they may not anticipate sweeping changes.

In addition, the social worker needs to consider how responsive the family is to outside services. A relatively open family system is more likely to accept social work intervention and other community resources. The relatively closed family may be less favorably disposed to treatment interventions. In the latter situation, it is not uncommon for the social worker to seemingly think agreement about treatment goals has been reached, and later discover that plans are not carried out. For this reason, it is important to arrive at realistic, mutual goals that can be modified by the client and social worker as treatment progresses.

Mobilizing the Family System

Mobilizing the family system is akin to implementing the treatment goals. Whether the plan is to work with one member or the whole extended family network, the aim is to support family strengths so that they can best meet the needs of its members. To mobilize family strengths, it is important to understand the way families have met various tasks at earlier times in the life course. Ideally, those families that have been able to meet the developmental tasks of earlier years relatively success-fully can draw on those strengths to face these later tasks. It is, however, important for social workers to consider that family patterns that may have been successful for many years may become less so under stress. That is, the family's ability to cope (namely, to adjust to new demands and losses) depends on the system it has created over the years, as well as the nature of the biopsychosocial crises it is currently facing. Events such as a stroke or the death of a family member may overload one fam-ily system and not another.

There are several techniques a social worker can use to tap a family's therapeutic potential. For example, through the use of life review, fami-lies can reconstruct their history, major events, memories, themes, and relationships. Genograms are another valuable tool in gathering client system information. As seen in chapter 7, by using various symbols to represent family connections, the genogram provides a visual represen-tation of the family group and makes the family members collaborators in history-taking and assessment (Hartman & Laird, 1983). As most older people respond positively to sharing, a genogram also helps make history-taking a pleasant and therapeutic experience, as seen in the fol-lowing example:

> Mr. L., age 89, was brought to a family service agency for counseling by his daughter, Mrs. F. Mrs. F., a woman in her early 60s, explained that her father became depressed following the lingering death of a woman with whom he had a close relationship for 13 years (Sara). Mr. L.'s wife had died under similar circumstances 2 years before he met Sara.
>
> At the first interview, Mr. L. expressed a strong reluctance to enter individual therapy "with a stranger." His daughter insisted it would be helpful. The social worker suggested that both father and daughter attend the counseling sessions together for purposes of gaining a family history.
>
> Mr. L. needed little encouragement to talk about his life growing up in Russia. He spoke of the family's financial difficulties and their struggle to make ends meet. To earn a living, each family member sewed large aprons, which his mother sold at the market. Mr. L. recalled with sadness his mother's daily trips to the market, especially those in the cold of winter. He remembered waiting alone for her, sometimes late into the evening. On her return, he would have some hot tea waiting. Mrs. F. said she was not aware of these experiences and appeared touched as he spoke. She said she would imagine that he would have felt scared and lonely waiting for his mother to return.
>
> The exchange of feelings in this first interview established a climate for a family life review. Mrs. F. volunteered to bring in a family photo album, which facilitated the expression of feelings and exchange of ideas. For example, both Mr. L. and Mrs. F.

selected their favorite picture of Mrs. L. They remembered her as a creative and caring person and brought in a book of her poems, which was published posthumously. Mr. L. and his daughter re-experienced and spoke about their initial grief over her death.

By the sixth session, photographs of Mr. L.'s companion, Sara, also elicited feelings of loss. Mr. L. explained how he had nursed Sara through her illness despite great difficulties; Mrs. F. expressed her understanding of her father's loss and concern over his present needs for companionship. Mr. L. was visibly less depressed.

The last sessions of therapy focused on Mr. L.'s need for continued companionship and on his relationship with his daughter. Mr. L. said that he would not be comfortable seeking social relationships by joining social groups at the community center. Rather, he wanted his daughter to go out to lunch once a week, as they were doing while attending each therapy session. While Mrs. F. expressed her concern over her father's circumscribed social life, she acknowledged Mr. L.'s right to make his own decisions. They also discussed plans for shopping trips, meal preparation, etc. (Greene, 1977, 1982).

Mobilizing the family as a treatment unit is an ongoing therapeutic process. An evaluation of the family's strengths is made possible by observing them in action. The family's style for problem solving and handling stress often becomes apparent as members enact their respective roles in the here-and-now. For example,

> The social worker notices that Anna, one daughter in a family of four, is always expected to do her mother's housework and chores. Anna says she is tired and worn out because of problems with her teenage son. At a family meeting, when everyone says, "Anna will do it," the social worker decides to ask everyone how Anna came to have that role.

As the family learns about its own behavior patterns, members can decide if they want to approach things differently. To facilitate the change process, some family therapists assign tasks to be done at home between sessions (homework). In the example of Anna, if all family members agree that they will share household responsibilities with her, a specific week's plan may be drawn up. In this way, the "tasks can be used to dramatize family transactions and suggest changes" (Minuchin, 1974, p. 150). This can be empowering, as it helps to restore a family's sense of control over its difficulties.

Another way in which the family therapist works in the here-and-now is to identify roadblocks to effective family communication. As social workers listen to client meanings and flow of communication, they simultaneously learn about family structure and communication processes (Minuchin, 1974). To help family members communicate more effectively, social workers can ask them to clarify to whom they are speaking, to repeat what is heard, to request that others respond, and to ask for clarification of messages (Goldstein, 1973).

Evaluating, Providing Feedback, and Terminating

The last phase of treatment, when mutually agreed on goals have been achieved or service is concluded, is, in many respects, the most difficult. The last phase of treatment often marks the end of the client-social worker relationship and a recognition that all that can be done for the present has been done. Sometimes the family may return to the agency when a new crisis flares up. At other times, cases seem to remain in service indefinitely, without any clear reason. On the other hand, the reality of some older clients' difficulties may mean that there is a real need for indefinite service. In any of these situations, the continuation of treatment should be based on the assessment of the needs of the client and an evaluation of the progress in meeting treatment goals.

For termination to be a meaningful process, it should provide feedback and an evaluation component. Discussing with the family about the progress they feel they have made and the services rendered provides feedback for them and the social worker. It also is useful, particularly when a frail elderly individual is involved, to gain an understanding of the ongoing need for community services. The family's ability to continue to manage such resources should candidly be addressed. In summary, the purpose of termination is to help the family clarify the ways in which they are going to continue to meet their needs and those of their elderly members.

Finally, while the functional-age model of intergenerational therapy emphasizes a family-centered approach, it also provides principles and techniques with which to address the realistic need for individual social work services. Older adults who have no family, have outlived them, or reside in a geographic location other than their kin are obvious candidates. Assessment may also lead to a decision to modify family therapy techniques, such as supplementing family sessions with separate interviews for either older adults or their adult children or counseling older adults without their family members.

References

Ackerman, N. (1972/1981). Family psychotherapy: Theory and practice. In G. D. Erikson & T. P. Hogan (Eds.), *Family therapy: An introduction to theory and technique.* Monterey, CA: Brooks/Cole Publishing.

Bartlett, H. M. (1970). *The common base of social work practice.* New York: National Association of Social Workers.

Beaver, M. L., & Miller, D. (1985). *Clinical social work practice with the elderly.* Homewood, IL: The Dorsey Press.

Blenkner, M. (1965). Social work and family relationships in later life with some thoughts on filial maturity. In E. Shanas & G. E. Streib (Eds.), *Social structure and the family.* Englewood Cliffs, NJ: Prentice-Hall.

Bowen, M. (1971). Aging: A symposium. *The Georgetown Medical Bulletin, 30,* 4-27.

Butler, R. N. (1969). Directions in psychiatric treatment of the elderly: Role of perspectives of the life cycle. *The Gerontologist, 9,* 134-138.

Butler, R. N. (1968). Toward a psychiatry of the life-cycle: Implications of sociopsychologic studies of the aging process for the psychotherapeutic situation. In A. Simon & L. Epstein (Eds.), *Aging in modem society.* Washington, DC: The American Psychiatric Association.

Compton, B., & Galaway, B. (1994). *Social work process.* Pacific Grove, CA: Brooks/ Cole.

Dean, R. G. (1993). Teaching a constructivist approach to clinical practice. In J. Laird (Ed.), *Revisioning social work education: A social constructionist approach* (pp. 55-76). New York: Haworth Press.

Eyde, D. R., & Rich, J. (1983). *Psychological distress in aging: A family management Model.* Rockville, MD: Aspen Publications.

Fischer, J. (1978). *Effective casework practice: An eclectic approach.* New York: Mc-Graw-Hill.

Freed, A. O. (1975). The family agency and the kinship system of the elderly. *Social Casework, 56,* 579-586.

Gallagher-Thompson, D., & Thompson, L. (1996). Applying cognitive-behavioral therapy to the psychosocial problems of later life. In S. Zarit & B. Knight (Eds.), *A guide to psychotherapy and aging* (pp. 61-82). Washington, DC: American Psychological Association.

Germain, C. B. (1981). The ecological approach to people--environment transactions. *Social Casework, 62,* 323-331.

Goldstein, H. (1973). *Social work practice: A unitary approach.* Columbia, SC: University of South Carolina Press.

Greene, R. R. (1977). *Life review and the use of photographs in family therapy.* Paper presented at National Association of Social Workers Professional Symposium, San Diego, CA.

Greene, R. R. (1982b). Life review: A technique for clarifying family roles in adulthood. *The Clinical Gerontologist, 2,* 59-67.

Hartman, A., & Laird, J. (1983). *Family-centered social work practice.* New York: The Free Press.

Hartman, A. (1995). Family therapy. In R. L. Edwards (Ed.-in-Chief), *Encyclopedia of Social Work* (Vol. 2, pp. 983-991).

Herr, J., & Weakland, J. (1979). *Counseling elders and their families.* New York: Springer.

Lowy, L. (1991). *Social work with the aging.* New York: Longman.

Minuchin, S. (1974). *Families and family therapy.* Cambridge, MA: Harvard University Press.

Perlman, H. H. (1974). *Persona.* Chicago: The University of Chicago Press.

Pratt, H. (1981). *I Remember. . . .* Alexandria, VA: Mental Health Association.

Richmond, M. (1922). *What is social casework? An introductory description.* New York: Russell Sage Foundation.

Silverstone, B., & Burack-Weiss, A. (1983). *Social work practice with the frail elderly and their families.* Springfield, IL: Charles C Thomas.

Spark, G. (1984). Grandparents and intergenerational family therapy. *Family Process, 13,* 225-237.

Walsh, F. (1999). Families in later life: Challenges and opportunities. In B. Carter & M. McGolrick (Eds.), *The expanded life cycle: Individual, family, and social perspectives* (pp. 307-324). Boston: Allyn & Bacon.

Weisman, S., & Shusterman, R. (1977). Remembering, reminiscing and life reviewing in an activity program for the elderly. *Concern,* 22-26.

White, M., & Epson, D. (1992). *Narrative means to therapeutic ends* New York: W. W. Norton.

9

The Functional-Age Model of Intergenerational Treatment: Group and Community-Based Approaches

with Harriet L. Cohen

Social Work with Groups

There has been a growing interest in group services for the elderly over the last several decades. Social group work with the aged is varied and is offered in many different settings. There are numerous group approaches encompassing recreational, vocational, and psychoeducational groups. In addition, there has been increased attention to support groups for family caregivers (LaBarge & Trtanji, 1995; Toseland, Rossiter, Peak, & Smith, 1990). Although the approaches to working with the elderly in groups have a common social work philosophy and use social work techniques, each has its own historical roots and unique methods. However, most social work groups aim to enhance individual functioning; improve interpersonal relationships; solve problems through collective action; produce changes in the participants' environments; design action steps for institutional or organizational change; and create attitudinal or social policy change. According to Lowy (1992), however, the major purpose of social group work with elders is to provide linkages to others their own age and to enhance intergenerational relationships.

Social group work emphasizes group development. The social work group has been characterized as a unique social form and a mutual aid system that promotes individual autonomy. The group process provides collective support and is the vehicle by which individuals can improve their interpersonal relationships and their environmental conditions (Lowy, 1992). Lang (1981) suggested that the social work group promotes social work professional norms of client acceptance, respect, open communication, tolerance of differences, and democratic group functioning (see table 9.1).

Table 9.1
Special Components Contributing to the Formation of the Social Work Group[a]

Component	Specialized requirement related to worker	Specialized requirement related to group
Purpose	Differentiated helping purpose for worker	Differentiated group purpose under professional auspice
Relationships	Professional norm for acceptance in worker-member relationships	Norm for open relationships system–norm for acceptance, tolerance of difference in member-member relationships
Structure	Professional norm for respect in worker-group relationship	Norm for mutual aid
	Professional norm for activation of group autonomy	Norm for open communication system
Operation	Professional norm for constraining worker power	Norm for open, flexible role system
	Professional norm for activation of democratic group processes	Norm for democratic group functioning ·
Content	Professional norm for worker mediation in group interaction	Norm for effective participation
		Norm for participating together
		Norm for development of technical competence of members for agenda-processing
	Professional norm for worker mediation in interaction among content, group process, and individual members	Norm for productive work
		Norm for open flexible program content, forms, and range

[a] N. Lang, (1981). Some defining characteristics of the social work group: Unique social form. In S. L. Abels & P. Abels (Eds.), *Social work with groups proceedings 1979 symposium* (pp. 18–50). Louisville, KY: Committee for the Advancement of Social Work with Groups.

The use of group methods for work with the aged has many potential benefits. Groups can facilitate a person's continued social growth, provide support through crises, offer opportunities for rehabilitation, and positively affect mental health. Burnside (1990) suggested that there are some important differences between group work with the elderly and work with other age groups. She proposed that group work with older people is more directive, less confrontational, and more supportive. She also stated that group work with older adults should attempt to alleviate general anxieties; provide the opportunity for teaching and listening to others; and deal with loss, death, and physical challenges.

To achieve such treatment goals, the practitioner needs to be well grounded in effective theoretical frameworks for working with older adults. The following sections present information on the formation of five specific types of groups selected for their suitability for use with older persons and their families: (a) reminiscing groups; (b) group psychotherapy; (c) reality orientation groups; (d) support for caregivers of the elderly; and (e) mutual aid groups.

Types of Groups

Reminiscing Groups

Reminiscing was once considered nonproductive and attributed to an older person's living in the past (Creanza & McWhirter, 1994). Since Butler's hallmark article on life review in 1963, gerontologists have come to understand that reminiscing plays an important role in maintaining psychological health throughout the life cycle. Reminiscing has been used to help older persons clarify family roles, cope with stress and grief, experience pleasant images, maintain a sense of adequacy, and give renewed opportunity for ventilation about loss (Greene, 1982; Merriam, 1993; see Burnside, 1990, for a distinction between reminiscing and life review). In the course of remembering life out loud, an elder and a listener create a psychosocial legacy (Kivnick, 1996, p. 49).

In old age, introspection becomes a key factor in resolving (a) life issues or (b) as Erikson (1950) proposed the crisis of integrity versus despair. In addition, Ebersole (1978) maintained that "the major reason to encourage reminiscing among a group of aged people is to produce or enhance a cohort effect" (p. 237). A *cohort effect* allows individuals to realize their historical connections. By sharing reminiscences, individuals can identify their accomplishments, tribulations, and shared viewpoints.

They may also have increased opportunities for socialization and multiple interactional possibilities.

Reminiscing groups can be short term (ten weeks or less) or long term (more than a year). The group should be kept small (five or six, but no more than ten), and each person should be approached individually when given the opportunity to join. The group should meet regularly. Content can be structured (a) with visual devices such as "the time line." (Ingersoll & Goodman, 1980; Jewish Family and Children's Service of Baltimore, 1978) or (b) with plays, dramas, or videotapes (Hargrave, 1994). The group process should be well planned and should include beginning, working, and termination phases.

The practitioner also should plan, depending on his or her theoretical orientation, whether the group's main purpose would be, among other things, to support social functioning, uncover unconscious conflicts, or ascribe new meaning to past events (Burnside, 1989, 1990; Greene, 1982; Hargrave, 1994). For example, Comana, Brown, and Thomas (1998) described research results that underscored the use of reminiscence therapy to increase family coping strategies. Ott (1993) discussed the implementation of sensory reminiscence, including seeing, hearing, touching, tasting, and feeling, to stimulate memory recall and communication among older nursing home residents with cognitive challenges. Zuniga (1989) explained the ways that reminiscence can transmit cultural values. He stated that many older adults experience reminiscence through *storytelling*, a medium for reliving ethnic community oral history or tribal lore (Andrada & Korte, 1993; Crimmens, 1998).

Group Psychotherapy

Group psychotherapy, a more formal type of group treatment, involves regularly scheduled voluntary meetings of acknowledged clients with an accepted, trained leader. The purpose is expressing, eliciting, accepting, and working through various aspects of the clients' concerns and developing healthier and more satisfying modes of behavior. Before the group begins, the group leader usually determines what role he or she will play. There is some debate about what that role should be. Should the leader be passive, function as listener, and let clients ventilate their feelings; or should the leader be active and assume the role of teacher, facilitator, questioner, comforter, and moderator (Zarit & Knight, 1996)?

Group therapy, which can be conducted by psychiatrists, nurses, psychologists, or social workers, often examines the relationship between the therapist and client or between group members. The theoretical background of the practitioner, which provides the rationale for treatment, defines the nature of that relationship and the goals of the group. Among the approaches the practitioner may use are those based on Freudian psychodynamic theory or social systems theory. Group leaders with a Freudian orientation help group members to recall, reconstruct, and gain insight into past events and emotions that may have been hurtful. The practitioner's role is to interpret how group members relate to other group members and the therapist. The treatment goal is to improve a client's social relationships (Zarit & Knight, 1996).

Group leaders with a systems orientation view the group as an entity, and they focus on its process and structure. Their role is to assist participants in understanding the group culture, norms, and values. The educational role of the social worker is central to changing group structure, improving its stability, and increasing its ability to achieve common goals or tasks (Anderson, Carter, & Lowe 1999). Group psychotherapy is a difficult technique to use with a cohort of older people who are not accustomed to expressing personal problems in a group. Therefore, it is not uncommon for members to drop out. Careful preplanning about the purposes, goals, composition, and leadership of the group may help overcome these difficulties.

Reality Orientation Groups

Reality orientation groups are for confused, disoriented elderly persons and are often conducted in nursing homes and other institutions. However, reality orientation programs can be modified to fit a variety of settings, such as day-care and multiservice centers. Reality orientation is concerned with the maintenance and relearning of current information, including time, place, names of other people, and current events. Verbal repetition, the use of visual aids like weather boards, and stimulation of the senses are the main methods of teaching this information. While nonprofessionals can learn many of the techniques of conducting a reality orientation group, factors that distinguish social work groups include proper assessment of the client, appropriate selection of group members, suitable programming based on cognitive level(s), and timely evaluation of the progress of group members.

One benefit of social group work with cognitively challenged older adults is that they can empathize with others who have similar difficulties. By participating in a well-programmed group, participants may hear the "successes" and "failures" of others and experience their own accomplishments. This is particularly helpful for people who have become increasingly unable to interact positively with others. Reality orientation groups have some limitations. They are most useful with adults in the early stages of dementia who have mild cognitive impairments and want to be oriented to the present (McInnis-Dittrich, 2005), and less appropriate for people in later stages of dementia who can not remember the meaning of the environmental clues.

Group Work with Diverse Older Adults

Working with older adults from diverse ethnic, cultural and racial groups requires that workers be knowledgeable about the cultural values and beliefs of diverse populations and be willing to explore their own ethnic membership and past experiences in dealing with other cultures (Green, 1999). As the population not only ages, but becomes more ethnically diverse, it becomes more critical that social workers develop culturally competence in group settings.

Strengths Perspective and Groups

Social group work with older adults share four common principles with the strengths perspective: the individual has the potential and capacity to change; people have the capacity to transform illness, disappointment, and regret into life lessons that serve as a source for growth and change; all environments have resources for the group members; and people's strengths and resiliency can be enhanced. The group can provide an environment for problem solving, decision making, resolution of shared themes, and relationship building that leads to the development of resiliency factors in older adults.

Support Groups for Caregivers of the Elderly

It is well documented that families, not the formal system, provide 80-90 percent of medically related and personal care. There is an ever growing body of literature that continues to document the difficulties and strain experienced by the adult children of dependent elderly (Bourgeois, Schulz, & Burgio, 1996). What can be a physically and emotionally difficult task was poignantly described by Brody (1986):

> Study after study has identified the most pervasive and most severe consequences [of caregiving] as being in the realm of emotional strains. A long litany of mental health symptoms such as depression, anxiety, frustration, helplessness, sleeplessness, lowered morale, and emotional exhaustion are related to restrictions on time and freedom, isolation, conflict from the competing demands of various responsibilities, difficulties in setting priorities, and interference with life style and social and recreational activities. (p. 22)

A growing number of groups have become available to the families of frail or cognitively challenged older adults (Haight & Gibson, 2005; Toseland, 1990). Such groups provide support, enhance understanding of the older relative's problems and behaviors, suggest plans that can be made for inevitable changes in the older adult, provide insight into the feelings of both the older person and the caregiving relative, and improve coping strategies. Some common themes in caregivers groups are (a) relocating a person who becomes too frail or dependent to remain in the original residence; (b) engaging other relatives or secondary caregivers; (c) making decisions and taking responsibility when an older relative cannot do so alone; (d) dealing with feelings of impatience, frustration, entrapment, and guilt; (e) improving communications; (f) reducing conflict; and (g) understanding the biopsychosocial changes of aging (Cohen, 1983; Hartford & Parsons, 1982).

Other examples of caregiver support groups may include those families who work together to share responsibilities and tasks and recognize the rewards of caregiving; or community members, sometimes referred to as a circle of caring, who meet to negotiate caregiver's tasks for a community member or friend, who needs assistance in remaining in the community. The strengths perspective can assist caregivers to view the illness as a resource for change and growth and help practitioners to focus on client competence rather than on problems, leading to client and caregiver resiliency and well-being (Saleebey, 2006). The support group then becomes a place where family members talk about their successes as caregivers and about how they made meaning of the experience, recognized their strengths and took charge of the caregiving situation (Allen, Kwak, Lokken, & Haley, 2003; Boerner, Schulz, & Horowitz, 2004; Hepburn et al., 2002; Kramer, 1997; Paun, 2003; Roff et al., 2004).

As with the other groups discussed, practitioners should consider in the planning phase the group's goals, format, membership, time and size, content and focus, and termination and evaluation procedures. Because caregiver groups often struggle with difficult issues of loss, death and dying, and grief, they require that the social workers use great skill and give of themselves emotionally.

Social and Recreational Groups

These groups offer opportunities for socialization and for members to learn something new, to share interests with others and to find companionship. Social and recreational groups may include topics as diverse as travel, cooking, dancing, crafts, lifelong learning, gardening, movies, community politics, intergenerational activities, or investment clubs. These groups may occur in a variety of formats, such as face to face meetings, online chats, meeting for dinner or attending a cultural or religious event together.

Tasks Groups: Learning Circles and Community Collaborative Partnerships

Learning circles are another format for group work related to older adults. Learning circles bring health and social service professionals together to explore issues and to promote lifelong learning. Examples of learning circles include staff in nursing homes who meet regularly to discuss organizational culture changes or social workers who choose to continue to meet after a continuing education program to explore a topic in more depth.

Mutual Aid Groups

Mutual aid groups center around people's need for self-fulfillment and their desire to share ideas and concerns (Lee & Swenson, 1986). Because people in mutual aid groups see each other as a resource to work on common problems, participating in the group can be empowering (Cox & Parsons, 1994). The social worker uses nine processes in conducting a mutual aid group: (a) sharing data, or obtaining information; (b) using dialectical discussions, or advancing and countering an idea; (c) discussing taboo topics, or exploring forbidden ideas; (d) experiencing the "all in the same boat" phenomenon, or feeling that one is not alone; (e) offering mutual support, or providing empathetic remarks; (f) making mutual demands, or asking for help from group members; (g) rehearsing possible solutions, or anticipating a conversation; (h) attempting to solve individual problems, or mobilizing feedback and advice; and (i) creating a sense of strength-in-numbers phenomenon, or dealing with societal issues together. Because mutual aid groups do not necessitate a professional leader, are often naturally occurring, and are community based, they may be seen more frequently in the twenty-first century.

Community-Based Services

Social work with the aged and their families reflects the profession's traditionally person-environment philosophy in which a middle ground is struck between interventions that address client's psychological development and those that address a client's social and environmental situation. The majority of elderly clients come to the attention of health or social services agencies when they are in need of some kind of supportive service. Most services involve environmental interventions that center around the matching of client needs to necessary resources. Northen (1995) termed this role *resource consultant*, and she considered it as important as the counseling component in reducing anxiety and stress and in strengthening and supporting the client system.

The Long-Term Care Continuum of Services

Community resources may be thought of as forming a long-term care service continuum. Long-term care refers to and includes a range of services that address the health, psychosocial, and personal care needs of individuals who are lacking some capacity for self-care. It encompasses resident facilities as well as social service and health programs, and it is designed to provide supportive care for an individual over a prolonged period of time at home or in a variety of protective and semi-protective settings. Services to older adults usual are a combination of (a) formal services, those services that are delivered by health and social service agencies and (b) informal services, those that are derived from significant others and people in a person's social support network (see chapter 5). Informal helping is dependent on people's natural tendency to care for others (Greene, 2007). When working with older adults who may not be as well connected to their informal networks of care, the social worker may want to consider recreating informal supports.

The focus of a long-term care system is the person (and his or her family) who is frail or has lessened functional capacity and needs assistance with activities of daily living, such as housekeeping, finances, transportation, preparing meals, or administering medication. With advanced age, people may experience increased frailty and vulnerability to chronic disabling diseases. The delivery of appropriate long-term care services involves an appreciation of the biopsychosocial aspects of functional capacity and an understanding of the specific conditions that can interfere with autonomous functioning.

In addition to understanding the effect and consequences of functional changes, social workers who provide long-term care services need to appreciate the cultural implications of behavior (National Association of Social Workers, 1984). In a pluralistic society such as the United States, people of diverse cultural backgrounds may perceive and report their experiences differently. These differences can encompass help-seeking behavior(s) as well as methods of problem resolution (Barresi & Stull, 1992; Green 1999). For social workers to become more effective in working with different cultural groups, they must develop cross-cultural communication skills. These skills and knowledge of human behavior allow social workers to plan and arrange for services most suitable to the client's level of functioning.

A well-developed, long-term care system should provide options to meet the needs for services along a continuum of care. Such a care system needs to have linkages among services so that the client can receive resources that include home- and community-based options as well as residential facilities (Vourlekis & Greene, 1992). Basic to the provision of care along the continuum is a clear need.

> Old age in itself is not a need. Needs are determined by the complex interaction of biological, psychological, and social variables....The sum total of the biological, psychological, and social person with an individual history defines the need and subsequently the level of care along the continuum (Eyde & Rich, 1983, pp. 34-38).

Whereas long-term care was previously associated with the institutional care of adults, the current belief is that care encompasses a whole range of community services. The continuum of community-based, long-term care services is graphically presented in figure 9.2 and generally includes

- Outreach and case findings or screening services: locates the ill but untreated and the still-functioning elderly who may be at risk.
- Comprehensive assessment services: evaluates the older individual in order to determine the need for service.
- Primary medical, dental, and nursing services: provides the core health maintenance in response to acute illness.
- Home support services: supplies necessary in-home management and personal care of older persons.
- Home health care services: assists the chronically ill with nursing and related personal health care, including social work services.
- Day health care or day-care services: provides daytime care to frail or impaired individuals to improve or maintain levels of social, emotional, and health functioning, and to give respite to families.
- Day hospital (rehabilitation) services: aims to rehabilitate the older person stricken with physical illness and/or impairments that are amenable to rehabilitation and retraining.
- Home hospice service: serves the terminally ill with pain management, counseling, and home supports. (Iowa Gerontology Model Project, 1982)

Social Work Case Management

The role of the social worker in coordinating and linking the components of the long-term care services is referred to as *case management*.

Table 9.2
Long-Term Continuum of Care[a]

Access to services	Array of services	Setting
	Least Restrictive	
• Outreach	Monitoring Services	
	Homemaker	In Home
	Home Health Care	
• Information/Referral	Nutrition Programs	
	Legal/Protective Services	
	Senior Centers	
• Assessment	Community Mental Services	Community
	Dental Services	
• Case Management	Community Mental Health	
	Adult Day Care	
• Linkages	Respite Care	
	Hospice Care	
	Retirement Villages	
	• life care	
	• services	
• Evaluation/Quality	Domiciliary Care	
	Foster home	
	Personal Care Home	
Special	Group Home	Institutional
Housing	Congregate Care	
	• meals	
	• social services	
	• medical services	
	• housekeeping	
FAMILY		
	Intermediate Care	
	Skilled Nursing Care	
	Mental Hospitals	
	Acuate Care Hospitals	
	Most Restrictive	

[a]Adapted from Brody et al., *Planning for the Long-Term Support/Care System: The Array of Services to be Considered.* Region III Center for Health Planning, 7 Benjamin Franklin Parkway, Philadelphia, Pennsylvania (1979 June).

Case management may be thought of as an intensive type of intake to match the elderly person with appropriate services along a continuum of care. Case managers help their clients by doing a comprehensive needs assessment, drawing up a case plan, facilitating access to services, coordinating the work of a number of professionals, and advocating on behalf of the client. These activities are intended to improve or maintain the older person in the least restrictive and safest environment possible.

Like all aspects of social work practice, case management rests on a foundation of professional values, knowledge, and skills. Case management may be considered both a direct and indirect social work method. Direct practice includes such activities as client and family assessment and counseling, whereas indirect practice involves program financing and planning.

Social work case management is

an *interpersonal process* based upon a relationship between case manager and client (system). Mutually developed care plans are intended to enhance/maximize the *functional capacity* of those in need of long-term assistance and their support networks and facilitate and ensure the effective delivery of a range of services along a continuum of care. Interventions reflect social work *values* and are aimed at improving the match between the client's capacity and the demands of the environment. This includes ameliorating problems accompanying loss of function or illness, building support networks, effective *client level* service coordination, and processing *systems level* effectiveness (Greene, 1992, p. 29)

Weil and Karls (1985) outlined eight case management functions: (a) client identification and outreach, determining the target population and eligibility; (b) client assessment and diagnosis, evaluating a client's level of functioning and service needs; (c) service planning and resource identification with clients and members of service networks, describing the steps and issues in service delivery, monitoring, and evaluation; (d) linking clients to needed services, connecting or securing client services; (e) service implementation and coordination, service assessment and trouble shooting, getting the work done or putting all the plan's pieces in place; (f) monitoring service delivery, overseeing and supervising client services; (g) advocacy for and with client in service network, pressing for client needs; and (h) evaluation of service delivery and case management, determining the progress of the service plan that may result in continued service with same or revised service plan, termination, or basic follow up.

In addition to practice functions, social work case managers need to keep in mind the values suggested in the literature on strengths-based case management (Kisthardt & Rapp, 1992; Rothman, 1994). Such literature, which addresses the principles of social work practice with vulnerable populations, is particularly useful here. For example, although the principles were originally designed for practice with people with severe and persistent mental illness, Kisthardt and Rapp (1992) suggested that a positive intervention process should be guided by six principles: (a) persons posses an inherent capacity to learn, grow, and change; (b) the focus is on individual strengths, not deficits or pathology; (c) the helping process is guided by a rigorous standard of consumer self-determination; (d) the consumer-case manager relationship is primary and essential; (e) the community is viewed as an oasis of resources, not as an obstacle or target for blame; and (f) community integration is fostered by assertive outreach (pp. 112-113).

To summarize, the concept of continuum of care has emerged in response to the need for a model that would integrate different levels of client functioning with the provision of services. The major social work case management function is to assess the individual and match the type of services rendered to the level and type of need. This case management process is a mechanism to ensure a comprehensive program of care by coordinating and linking components of a service delivery system (National Association of Social Workers, 1984). Finally, it should be emphasized that the majority of the impaired elderly continue to live outside institutions, receiving primary support and care from family members. It is important, therefore, that social workers be sensitive to the needs of family members and that they engage families in case management (table 9.3). Because families have the history and continuity of interest in their older relative, they may serve as "facilitator, protector, advocate, buffer against bureaucracy, and source of information about housing, pensions, medical care, and other service options...and as case manager" (Seltzer, Ivry, & Litchfield, 1987, pp. 722-728).

Asset-Based Community Development for Older Adults

Community practice with older adults should not overlook an assessment of community assets and resources, rather than problems and unmet needs (Greene & Cohen, 2005). Older adults should be recognized as contributing members of the community who make it a better place for all to live and work. These elder friendly communities are beginning to explore new opportunities to build community capacity and to create a client-friendly, long-term care system that offers a range of services to an increasingly culturally diverse aging population. Groups of older adults and their families, health and social service professionals, business and

Table 9.3
Key Features of Family-Focused Social Work Case Management

Family-focused social work requires that the case manager
- identify the family as the unit of attention
- access the frail or impaired person's biopsychosocial functioning and needs within a culturally sound family context
- write a mutually agreed on family care plan
- refer client systems to services and entitlements not available within the natural support system
- implement and coordinate the work that is done with the family
- determine what services need to be coordinated on behalf of the family
- intervene clinically to ameliorate family emotional problems and stress accompanying illness or loss of functioning
- determine how the impaired person and family will interact with formal care providers
- integrate formal and informal services provided by the family and other primary groups
- offer or advocate for particular services that the informal support network is not able to offer
- contact client networks and service providers to determine the quality of service provision
- mediate conflicts between the family and service providers to empower the family when they are not successful
- collect information and data to augment the advocacy and evaluation efforts to ensure quality of care

From Vourlekis, B., & Greene, R. R. (1992). *Social work case management*. New York: Aldine de Gruyter.

community members are meeting to determine how their community can become more elder friendly, that is, a place where older adults will be recognized, respected, vitally involved and empowered (Austin, Camp, Flux, McClelland, & Sieppert, 2005; Bolda, Lowe, Maddox, & Patnaik, 2005).

This approach to community development is asset and strengths based, internally focused on individual and group capacities, and is relationship driven (Saleebey, 2006). Community partnerships, which engage older adults and their families in planning, implementing and evaluating services in order to develop a vision and a plan for addressing the fragmented and disjointed long-term care system, are emerging; however, these relationships—linking public, private and voluntary sectors and older adults and their families—require time to develop and to build trust. Older adults bring economic potential; culture, history and tradition; knowledge gained from a variety of personal and professional experiences; time; and connections with other older adults through civic and social engagements (Greene & Cohen, 2005). Elder-friendly communities promote social and civic engagement, maximize independence for frail and disabled, optimize physical and mental health, and address basic needs (Feldman & Oberlink, 2003).

According to the AARP, the following factors define an elder friendly or livable community: dependable transportation, well designed sidewalks, roads designed for safe driving, transportation options, security and safety, affordable housing options and home design that allows for maximum activities of daily living if mobility is limited, well-run community centers, recreation centers, parks, and other places where older people can socialize, and ample opportunities to become a volunteer (AARP, 2005).

Community Services for Successful Aging

Perhaps, the greatest challenge in social work with the aged and their families is designing services for successful aging (Rowe & Kahn, 1998). During the 1990s, an increasing number of theorists have addressed this policy-practice issue (Greene & Knee, 1996; Saltz, 1997). For example, Rothman (1994) proposed that although most professionals gauge success by continued client improvement, prevention of downward movement or maintenance of stability also should be criteria. Greene, Kropf, and Pugh (1994) contended that the continuum of care should include health education programs based on a wellness model. Collopy (1988) suggested that practitioners not consider autonomy as absolute, rather, they should make a distinction between autonomy of execution versus autonomy of choice.

Social workers in program planning have also considered what activities can contribute to successful aging. They have suggested that as longevity increases, older adults will be healthier, use more assistive technology to remain in their own homes, and need more avenues to remain productive (Kiyak & Hooyman, 1999). There will be more interest in volunteer programs, possibly enhancing informal support services. The demand for an *age-integrated society*–in which education, work, and leisure opportunities are open to people of all ages–is also likely to be a reality (Rowe & Kahn, 1998).

References

AARP. (2005). *Livable communities and successful aging: AARP offers check list to grade your hometown*. Retrieved June 24, 2006, from *www.aarp.org/research/press-center/presscurrentnews/beyond50_05_quiz.html*

Anderson, R. E., Carter, I., & Lowe, G. (1999). *Human behavior in the social environment: A Social systems approach*. Hawthorne, NY: Aldine De Gruyter.

Allen, R., Kwak, J., Lokken, K., & Haley, W. (2003). End-of-life issues on the context of Alzheimer's disease. *Alzheimer's Care Quarterly, 4*, 312-330.

Austin, C. D., Camp, E. D., Flux, D., McClelland, R. W., & Sieppert, J. (2005). Community development with older adults in their neighborhoods: The elder friendly communities program. *Families in Society, 86*(3), 401-409.

Boerner, K., Schulz, R., & Horowitz, A. (2004). Positive aspects of caregiving and adaptation to bereavement. *Psychology and Aging, 19*(4), 668-675.

Bolda, E. J., Lowe, J. I., Maddox, G. L., & Patnaik, B. S. (2005). Community partnerships for older adults: A case study. *Families in Society, 86*(3), 411-418.

Bourgeois, M., Schulz, R., & Burgio, L. (1996). Interventions for caregivers of patients with Alzheimer's disease: A review and analysis of content, process, and outcomes. *International Journal of Aging-Human Behavior, 43*(1), 35–92.

Brody, E. (1986). Parent care as a normative family stress. *The Gerontologist, 25*, 19-29.

Burnside, I. (1990). Reminiscing: An independent nursing intervention for the elderly. *Issues in Mental Health Nursing, 11*, 33-48.

Butler, R. N. (1963). The life review: An interpretation of reminiscence in the aged. *Psychiatry, 26*, 65-76.

Cohen, P. M. A group approach for working with families of the elderly. *The Gerontologist, 28*, 10-17.

Collopy, B. J. (1988). Autonomy in long-term care: Some crucial distinctions. *The Gerontologist, 23*, 248-250.

Comana, M. T., Brown, V. M., & Thomas, J. (1998). The effects of reminiscence therapy on family coping. *Journal of Family Nursing, 4*, 182-198.

Cox, E. O., & Parsons, R. J. (1994). *Empowerment-oriented social work practice with the elderly*. Pacific Grove, CA: Brooks/Cole.

Crimmens, P. (1998). *Storymaking and creative groupwork with older people*. London: Jessica Kingsley.

Daatland, S. O. (1983). Care systems. *Aging and Society, 3*, 1-21.

Ebersole, P. E. (1978). Establishing reminiscing groups. In I. M. Burnside (ed.), *Working with the elderly: Group process and techniques* (p. 233). North Scituate, MA: Duxbury Press.

Erikson, E. (1950). *Childhood and society*, 2nd ed. New York: W. W. Norton, 1950.

Eyde, D. R., & Rich, R. (1983). *Psychological distress in aging: A Family management model*. Rockville, MD: Aspen.

Feldman, P. H., & Oberlink, M. (2003). The advantage initiative: Developing community indicators to promote the health and well-being of older people. *Family Community Health, 26*(4), 268-274.

Green, J. (1999). *Cultural awareness in the human services*. Englewood Cliff, NJ: Prentice-Hall.

Greene, R. R., & Cohen, H. L. (2005). Social work with older adults and their families: Changing practice paradigms. *Families in Society, 86*(3), 367-373.

Greene, R. R. (1997). Emerging issues for social workers in the field of aging. In C. C. Saltz (Ed.) *Social work response to the White House Conference on aging* (pp. 79-95). New York: Haworth.

Greene, R. R. (1982). Families and the nursing home social worker. *Social Work in Health Care, 7,* 57-67.

Greene, R. R., Kropf, N., & Pugh, K. L. (1994). Planning health education for older adults: The use of a health model and interview data. *Gerontology and Geriatric Education, 15,* 3-18.

Haight, B., & Gibson, F. (2005). *Working with older adults: Group process and techniques.* Sudbury, MA: Jones & Bartlett.

Hargrave, T. D. (1994). Using video life reviews with older adults. *Journal of Family Therapy, 16,* 259-268.

Hartford, M., & Parsons, R. (1982). Groups with relatives of dependent older adults. *The Gerontologist, 22,* 394-398.

Hepburn, K., Lewis, M., Narayan, S., Tornatore, J., Bremer, K., & Sherman, C. (2002). Discourse-derived perspective: Differentiating among spouses' experience of caregiving. *American Journal of Alzheimer's Disease and Other Dementias, 17*(4), 213-226.

Hooyman, N. (1983). Social support networks in services to the elderly. In J. Whittaker & J. Garbarino (Eds.), *Social support networks: Informal helping in the human services* (pp. 134-166). New York: Aldine Gruyter.

Ingersoll, B., & Goodman, L. (1980). History comes alive: Facilitating reminiscence in a group of institutionalized elderly. *Journal of Gerontological Social Work, 2,* 305-320.

Iowa Gerontology Model Project. (1982). A training manual on the components of a community-based long-term care system for the elderly. Davenport: The University of Iowa.

Jewish Family and Children's Service of Baltimore. (1978). *Getting the best from the rest: An experiential handbook for senior adult groups.* Baltimore, MD: Author.

Kisthardt, W. E., & Rapp, C. A, (1992). Bridging the gap between principles and practice: Implementing a strengths perspective in case management. In S. M. Rose (Ed.), *Case management and social work practice* (pp. 112-125). New York: Longman.

Kivnick, H. Q. (1996). Remembering and being remembered: The reciprocity of psychosocial legacy. *Generations, 20,* 49-54.

Kiyak, H. A., & Hooyman, N. R. (1999). Aging in the twenty-first century. *Hallym International Journal of Aging, 1,* 56-66.

Kramer, B. (1997). Gain in the caregiving experience: Where are we? What's next? *The Gerontologist, 37*(2), 218-232.

LaBarge, E., & Trtanji, F. (1995). A support group for people in the early stages of dementia of the Alzheimer type. *Journal of Applied Gerontology, 14,* 289-302.

Lang, N. (1981). Some defining characteristics of the social work group: Unique social form. In S. L. Abels & P. Abels, (Eds.), *Social work with groups proceedings 1979 symposium* (pp.18-50). Louisville, KY: Committee for the Advancement of Social Work with Groups.

Lee, J., & Swenson, C. (1986). The concept of mutual aid. In A. Gitterman & L. Shulman (Eds.) *Mutual aid groups and the life cycle* (pp. 361-380). Itasca, IL: F. E. Peacock.

Lowy, L. (1992). Social group work with elders: Linkages and intergenerational relationships. *Social Work With Groups, 15,* 109-127.

McInnis-Dittrich, K. (2005). *Social work with elders: A biopsychosocial approach to assessment and intervention* (2nd ed.). Boston: Person Education.

Merriam, S. B. (1993). The uses of reminiscence in older adulthood. *Educational Gerontology, 19,* 441-450.

National Association of Social Workers. (1984). *NASW standards and guidelines for social work case management for the functionally impaired.* Silver Springs, MD: Author.

Northen, H. (1995). *Clinical social work*. New York: Columbia University Press.

Ott, R. L. (1993). Enhancing validation through milestoning with sensory reminiscence. *Journal of Gerontological Social Work, 20*, 147-159.

Paun, O. (2003). Older women caring for spouses with Alzheimer's disease at home: Making sense of the situation. *Health Care for Women International, 24*(4), 292-312.

Roff, L., Burgio, L., Gitlin, L., Nichols, L., Chaplin, W., & Hardin, M. (2004). Positive aspects of Alzheimer's caregiving: The role of race. *Journal of Gerontology: Psychological sciences, 59B*(4), 185-190.

Rothman, J. (1994). *Practice with highly vulnerable clients*. Englewood Cliffs, NJ: Prentice-Hall.

Rowe, J. W., & Kahn, R. L. (1998). *Successful aging*. New York: Pantheon Books.

Saleebey, D. (2006). Community development, neighborhood empowerment and resilience. In D. Saleebey (Ed.), *The strengths perspective in social work practice* (pp. 241-260). Boston: Allyn & Bacon.

Saltz, C. (1997). *Social work response to the White House Conference on aging: From Issues to Action*. New York: Haworth Press.

Taulbee, L. R. (1978). Reality orientation: A therapeutic group activity for elderly persons. In I. M. Burnside (Ed.), *Working with the elderly: Group process and techniques*. North Scituate, MA: Duxbury Press.

Toseland, R. W. (1990). *Group work with older adults*. New York: New York University Press.

Toseland, R. W., Rossiter, C. M., Peak, T., & Smith, G. C. (1990). Comparative effectiveness of individual and group interventions to support family caregivers. *Social Work, 37*, 209-216.

Voulekis, B. & Greene, R. R. (1992). *Social work case management*. New York: Aldine de Gruyter.

Weil, M., & Karls, J. (1985). *Case management in human service practice*. San Francisco, CA: Jossey-Bass.

Zarit, S. H., & Knight, B. B. (1996). *A guide to psychotherapy and aging*. Washington, DC: American Psychological Association.

Zuniga, M. (1989). Mexican-American elderly and reminiscence: Interventions. *Journal of Gerontological Social Work, 14*, 63-73.

Index